WITHDRAWN

The Liberalism of Thomas Arnold

EUGENE L. WILLIAMSON, JR.

The
Liberalism
of
Thomas Arnold

A STUDY OF HIS
RELIGIOUS AND POLITICAL WRITINGS

UNIVERSITY OF ALABAMA PRESS

University, Alabama

Grateful acknowledgment is made to the following for permission to quote material: To Appleton, Century, Crofts, for quotations from Thomas Arnold's *Miscellaneous Works, History of Rome*, and *History of the Later Roman Commonwealth*; to Cambridge University Press for quotations from Duncan Forbes, *The Liberal Anglican Idea of History* and *Political Tracts of Wordsworth, Coleridge and Shelley*, ed. R. J. White; to Clarendon Press for a quotation from *The Works of Richard Hooker*; to Columbia University Press for quotations from Bernard Schilling, *Human Dignity and the Great Victorians* and Basil Willey, *Nineteenth Century Studies* and *More Nineteenth Century Studies*; to Cornell University Press for quotations from Giambattista Vico, *New Science*, translated by T. G. Bergin, and M. H. Fisch; to Harper and Brothers for quotations from W. W. Bartley, III, "I Call Myself a Protestant" in *Harper's Magazine*; to Harvard University Press for quotations from John H. Finley, *Thucydides*; to Holt, Rinehart and Winston, and to Constable and Company, Ltd. for quotations from Arnold Whitridge, *Dr. Arnold of Rugby*; to Houghton, Mifflin for quotations from John Henry Newman, *Apologia Pro Vita Sua*, ed. A. Dwight Culler; to Longmans, Green and Co. Ltd. for quotations from G. P. Gooch, *History and Historians in the Nineteenth Century*, from V. F. Storr, *The Development of English Theology in the Nineteenth Century*, and from G. M. Trevelyan, *British History in the Nineteenth Century and After*; to John Murray, Ltd. for quotations from Benjamin Jowett, *Epistles of St. Paul to the Thessalonians, Galatians and Romans*, ed. Lewis Campbell; to Oxford University Press for quotations from F. J. Woodward, *The Doctor's Disciples*; to Charles Scribner's Sons for quotations from Sir Joshua Fitch, *Thomas and Matthew Arnold and Their Influence on English Education*; and to Yale University Press for quotations from Walter E. Houghton, *The Victorian Frame of Mind*.

FOR
August H. Mason

Acknowledgments

I AM GRATEFUL to many persons for the help which they have given me in writing this book. Professors Frank O. Copley, Karl Litzenberg, Warner G. Rice, and Bennett Weaver, all of the University of Michigan, are to be thanked for their comments on an earlier version. Mr. Arnold Whitridge, of New York City, graciously responded to inquiries about his illustrious great-grandfather and allowed me to study unpublished materials in his care. Mr. Whitridge's own excellent biography of Dr. Arnold has provided general guidance no less useful to me than to other scholars since its appearance in 1928. Thanks are also due Professor Arthur Kyle Davis, of the University of Virginia, whose great knowledge of Matthew Arnold's correspondence has more than once been placed at my disposal. To these and to colleagues and other friends at the Universities of Michigan, Kentucky, and Alabama, I wish to express gratitude for strictures as well as for encouragement.

It is a pleasure to specify other assistance which has forwarded my work. Grants from the Southern Fellowships Fund and the Research Committee of the University of Alabama enabled me to carry my study through to completion. I also wish to thank reference librarians at the universities mentioned, and especially Miss Marjorie Wynne, Librarian of the Rare Book Room, Yale University Library. The editors of *PMLA, Modern Language Notes,* and *Modern Language Quarterly* have permitted me to incorporate materials from articles of mine in their publications. For permission to quote I am indebted to the following publishers: Appleton, Century, Crofts; Cambridge University Press; Clarendon Press; Columbia University Press; Constable and Company Ltd.; Cornell University Press; Harper and Brothers; Harvard University Press; Holt, Rinehart and Winston; Houghton Mifflin; Longmans, Green and Co. Ltd.; John Murray, Ltd.; Oxford University Press; Charles Scribner's Sons; The Johns Hopkins Press; and Yale University Press. Finally, I wish to thank the director and staff of the University of Alabama Press for their guidance on many particulars.

EUGENE L. WILLIAMSON, JR.
University, Alabama

Contents

Acknowledgments   7

Chronology   11

Abbreviations Used in References   14

Introduction   17

ONE: *The Shaping of Arnold's Mind*   25
Winchester and Oxford
Arnold and the Lake Poets
Arnold's Historical Researches
Arnold's Friendship with Christian Bunsen

TWO: *Arnold and the Bible*   67
The Crisis of Belief
Arnold's Biblical Criticism
Arnoldism and the Later Nineteenth Century

THREE: *Arnold and the Church*   112
Dangers to the Church
A Reform Program
Aftermath: Broad Church Liberalism

FOUR: *Arnold and the State* 158
The Need for the Spiritual Critique
Christian Politics
Critics, Christian Socialists, and Educators

Rugby Curriculum under Arnold 223

Notes 228

Selected Bibliography 251

Index 254

Chronology

1795   Thomas Arnold born 13 June, third son of William and Martha Delafield Arnold at West Cowes, Isle of Wight, where his father was Collector of Customs

1801   Death of father

1803   Began formal education at Warminster Grammar School, Wiltshire

1807–11   Attended Winchester where he pursued already well-developed interests in ancient and modern history

1811–14   Scholar of Corpus Christi College, Oxford. His fellow students included John Taylor Coleridge and John Keble. First Class, *Litterae Humaniores*, 1814

1815–18   At Oriel College where elected Fellow on recommendation of Richard Whately. Engaged in a program of independent reading enriched by common room discussion with Whately and other Oriel Noetics. Chancellor's Prize Essays, 1815, 1817. Ordained Deacon by Bishop of Oxford, 1818

1819   Settled at Laleham on the Thames, near Staines, Middlesex, where for the next eight years took private pupils in preparation for the Universities

1820   Married Mary Penrose, daughter of the Rector of Fledborough, Nottinghamshire. Matthew, the first of nine surviving children, born two years later

1821–27   Articles on early Roman history in *Encyclopaedia Metropolitana*. Studied German in order to read Barthold Niebuhr's *History of Rome* and other historical and theological works by continental writers. During a trip to Rome in 1827 became acquainted with Christian Bunsen, Prussian statesman, historian, and liberal theologian, who became his life-long friend

1828   Elected Headmaster of Rugby on recommendation of Edward Hawkins, Provost of Oriel. Took B.D., D.D. degrees

1829   Death of mother. *The Christian Duty of Conceding the Roman Catholic Claims. Sermons* (first of six volumes)

1830   Edition of Thucydides, I

1831   Founded *The Englishman's Register*, a short-lived periodical, in which he addressed himself to contemporary religious and social questions. Later his journalistic work appeared chiefly in the Sheffield *Courant* and Hertford *Reformer*

1832   *Sermons*, II. The volume also contains an essay, "On the Right Interpretation and Understanding of the Scriptures"

1833   *Principles of Church Reform*, a widely attacked pamphlet advocating comprehension of dissenters in the Establishment. Thucydides, II

1834   *Sermons*, III. With Wordsworth's assistance established residence at Fox How, Ambleside, in Westmoreland near Rydal Mount. Thereafter the Arnold family spent most school vacations here

1835   Thucydides, III. Articles on Rugby and on school discipline in *Quarterly Journal of Education*

1836   "The Oxford Malignants and Dr. Hampden," *Edinburgh Review*, a scathing denunciation of writings by Newman and other Tractarians who opposed the

appointment of Renn Dickson Hampden as Oxford
Regius Professor of Divinity

1838   *History of Rome*, I

1839   *Two Sermons on the Interpretation of Prophecy*

1840   *History of Rome*, II

1841   Appointed Regius Professor of Modern History. His
        lectures widely and enthusiastically attended. Mat-
        thew Arnold, Arthur Stanley, Arthur Hugh Clough,
        and other Old Rugbeians in residence at Oxford.
        Balliol had become an "Arnoldian college." *Chris-
        tian Life, Its Course, Its Hindrances, and Its Helps*,
        which contained a polemical introduction on the
        Oxford Movement

1842   *Introductory Lectures on Modern History*. Slight
        illness from which he apparently recovered only to
        succumb 12 June to an attack of *angina pectoris*.
        *Christian Life, Its Hopes, Its Fears and Its Close.
        Sermons*, V (posthumous). *History of Rome*, III
        (unfinished)

1844   Arthur Penrhyn Stanley, *The Life and Correspon-
        dence of Thomas Arnold, D.D.* The work reached
        twelve English editions by 1881 and was translated
        into several languages

1845   *Sermons Chiefly on the Interpretation of Scripture.
        Miscellaneous Works. History of the Later Roman
        Commonwealth* (collection of articles written for
        the *Encyclopaedia Metropolitana*)

1857   Thomas Hughes, *Tom Brown's Schooldays*

1867   Matthew Arnold, "Rugby Chapel"

Abbreviations Used in References

CLC   *Christian Life, Its Hopes, Its Fears, and Its Close. Sermons Preached Mostly in the Chapel of Rugby School.* 5th ed. London: B. Fellowes, 1849.

CLH   *Christian Life, Its Course, Its Hindrances, and Its Helps. Sermons Preached Mostly in the Chapel of Rugby School.* 5th ed. London: B. Fellowes, 1849.

ER   *Englishman's Register.* 7 May 1831-2 July 1831.

FC   *Fragment on the Church.* London: B. Fellowes, 1844.

HLR   *History of the Later Roman Commonwealth*, ed. Bonamy Price. 2 vols. New York: D. Appleton, 1846.

HR   *History of Rome.* 3 vols. in one. New York: D. Appleton, 1868.

IS   *Sermons Chiefly on the Interpretation of Scripture.* 3rd ed. London: B. Fellowes, 1851.

LMH   *Introductory Lectures on Modern History.* Oxford: John Henry Parker, 1842.

MW   *Miscellaneous Works,* ed. Arthur Penrhyn Stanley. London: Longmans, Green and Co. Ltd., 1874.

MWA   *Miscellaneous Works: With Nine Additional Essays Not Included in the English Collection.* New York: D. Appleton, 1845.

PE   "The Effects of Distant Colonization on the Parent State," *Oxford English Prize Essays*, III, 119-45. Oxford: D. A. Talboys, 1830.

Sermons, I
>*Sermons. To Which Is Added, A New Edition of Two Sermons on the Interpretation of Prophecy.* 5th ed. London: B. Fellowes, 1845.

Sermons, II
>*Sermons, With an Essay on the Right Interpretation and Understanding of the Scriptures.* 4th ed. London: B. Fellowes, 1845.

Sermons, III
>*Sermons.* 3rd ed. London: B. Fellowes, 1845.

Introduction

IT IS LIKELY that no one of the "eminent Victorians" lampooned by Lytton Strachey in 1918 has remained a topic of more persistent interest to twentieth century readers than Thomas Arnold of Rugby. Indeed, to the considerable quantity of writing about Dr. Arnold in his own nineteenth century, recent years have added a stream of articles, chapters, and books which shows no signs of diminishing well over a century after his death in 1842. That he became a "tidal force" in British opinion, no modern writer seems likely to deny;[1] nor is there any very extensive disagreement about the principal causes of his influence. Clearly these were his wholehearted commitment to moral ideals, his forceful personality, and his ability to make his views widely known. Arnold's personality and moral idealism may perhaps be traced to his inheritance and childhood training; his opportunity to be heard he made for himself, becoming in the course of his short life well-known in the diverse fields of educational administration, liberal theology, social criticism and historiography. Because he was a great teacher and a compelling spokesman as well, he was extraordinarily successful in impressing his ideas on the minds and hearts of his students, students who were the potential leaders of England and who later made those ideas prevail in national life.

Perhaps it is the combination of such traits and achievements (together with the fact that he was the father of Matthew Arnold) which has been chiefly responsible for the continued interest in Dr. Arnold. In the last decade alone, there have been no fewer than two biographies, an annotated edition of one of his pamphlets, and numerous extended discussions of his influence on other Victorians.[2] The present work is therefore not intended to serve as a general introduction to Dr. Arnold's life and work since that need has already been amply met elsewhere.[3] On the other hand, despite the lively critical interest in the elder Arnold's views, and despite frequent references by critics to those views, no detailed study of his religious and political criticism is now available, a hiatus which has seemed to me to bring in question the validity of summary accounts of his thought, as well as various claims made for his influence on well-known literary figures and Churchmen.[4] I have therefore undertaken here what seemed to be lacking, a full-length analysis and historical evaluation of Dr. Arnold's work.

Because such an evaluation depends in some measure on whether his ideas were influential, and if so, on whom, I have also described the ways in which Dr. Arnold's ideas were maintained, developed, and carried into practice by certain well-known nineteenth century liberals. Since it seemed desirable to have something approaching a cross section of his many continuators, I have also included brief accounts of the work of several lesser known followers of the elder Arnold. In addition, I have sampled reactions to Arnold's work by his contemporaries to make clear how his ideas were received in his own time, and have further noted specific instances in which his recommendations anticipated legislation or were given other historically significant forms.

It is to be hoped that the present work will enable the reader to settle for himself points of controversy which, in contrast to the unanimity of opinion about Dr. Arnold's character, have always arisen about his published works. From the time that John Henry Newman was put in doubt by certain of Arnold's views about the Bible as to whether his liberal antagonist was a Christian,* opinions have been divided as to the precise nature and effects of the elder Arnold's Biblical criticism.[5] Correspondingly, his writings about Church reform have been variously pronounced an unprincipled attack on the Church of England and an attempt to adapt the Church to current needs in order to prevent its destruction.[6] Again, the logical result of his political theory has been seen on the one hand as the secularizing of religion, and on the other as the evangelizing of

---

* Aside from all questions of theological animus, the judgment as to whether Arnold was a Christian will of course depend upon the definition of " Christian " held. According to Basil Willey, a change has taken place in the common usage of the word in the present century. Instead of denoting moral virtues (especially self-lessness) as it chiefly did in the nineteenth century, it is now more often employed to mean adherence to particular doctrines (*Christianity, Past and Present*, pp. 3-4 cited by Francis J. Woodward, *The Doctor's Disciples*, p. 17. Cf. William Warren Bartley, III, " I Call Myself a Protestant," *Harper's Magazine*, CCXVIII (May, 1959), 49-63. Mr. Bartley notes that modern Protestant theology is largely a reaction against nineteenth and early twentieth century liberalism, particularly as seen in its two prevailing attitudes: "(1) [that] Christianity should be concerned primarily with building the Kingdom of God as quickly as possible on earth; (2) [that] doctrinal differences were comparatively unimportant. What was vital was a tolerant sharing of the religious experience " (p. 53). If belief in the divinity of Christ be taken as the criterion of Christianity, Arnold was a Christian. See the discussion of his arguments for the truth of the Resurrection, Chapter Two.

politics.[7] Finally, it is intended that the reader should be
in possession of such facts as will enable him better to
judge of the nature and extent of Dr. Arnold's effect upon
the minds of those who sat in Rugby Chapel, who anx-
iously followed the fortunes of their teacher's writings in
the contemporary press, and who in later years were apt to
find themselves thinking in Arnoldian terms.

It is perhaps as well to state at the outset the conclusions
which I have reached. Though they need not prevent
others from different interpretations of the evidence, to
some they may prove a useful guide. Arnold's religious and
political criticism is best understood as a coherent and pur-
poseful response to a complex of specific historical problems. Aside from occasional inconsistencies, his views are
those of a "concessive" religious liberal faced with the
possibility of the imminent collapse of Christian belief and
the disappearance of Christian morals as the ruling force in
the lives of his contemporaries. Thinking the cause of religion to be seriously jeopardized by the unwillingness of
Churchmen to recognize existing social and intellectual changes, he undertook to know and to use the Spirit of
the Age, to see the meaning of the present and the future,
in order to perpetuate the vital elements of the past. With
a definite practical goal in mind, the preservation of Christian belief and conduct, he risked giving up what he took
to be the indefensible and unessential religious outworks of
technically expressed doctrine and authoritative claims for
the Bible and the Church, and sought to shift the main line
of apologetics from metaphysics to history, sociology, and
ethics. He attempted to ground his liberalism in distinctions (e.g., that between the truth of the Resurrection of
Christ and the possible falsity of other Biblical miracles)
which liberals who followed him could not always observe.

His views on the Bible were the basis of his religious and political thought, for it was to the Bible rather than to ecclesiastical tradition that he looked for guidance as to what the Church should be. Similarly, his Christian politics were an attempt to apply the moral teachings of the Scriptures to public life.

Dr. Arnold's views, though not widely effectual in his own day, were profoundly influential on Victorian liberals of later generations. Matthew Arnold, Arthur Hugh Clough, Thomas Hughes, Arthur Penrhyn Stanley, Benjamin Jowett, Archibald Campbell Tait, Frederick Temple, W. E. Forster, J. P. Gell, and William Delafield Arnold— all, in varying degrees, received inspiration and impetus from the man whom extravagant young Rugbeians of even a later day were likely to think of as " the greatest Englishman of the nineteenth century." [8]

The Liberalism of Thomas Arnold

. . . when the general feeling becomes divided, and the cause of Christianity has lost many of its artificial supports, nothing will support our faith effectually, but a real and earnest love of its principles, and a lively hatred of everything that is evil. When unbelief, instead of being received with general abhorrence, becomes generally fashionable,—when our profession of faith loses that confidence which is given by seeing the majority are on its side,—then a man must begin in earnest to examine his own foundations,—to look for a stay within him, when outward aids begin to fall away.

Thomas Arnold, *Sermons*, II (1832)

The [Liberal] party grew, all the time that I was in Oxford, even in numbers, certainly in breadth and definiteness of doctrine, and in power. And, what was a far higher consideration, by the accession of Dr. Arnold's pupils, it was invested with an elevation of character which claimed the respect even of its opponents.

. . . but is *he* a Christian?

John Henry Newman, *Apologia* (1864)

No [great] religious reformer for the present age has yet shown himself. Till he appears, the true religious teacher is he who, not yet reconciling all things, at least esteems things in their due order, and makes his hearers so esteem them; who, shutting his mind against no ideas brought by the spirit of his time, . . . still puts that first which is first; who, under the pressure of new thoughts, keeps the centre of the religious life where it should be.

Matthew Arnold, " Dr. Stanley's Lectures
on the Jewish Church " (1863)

The Shaping of Arnold's Mind

IT WAS TRUE of Thomas Arnold, as doubtless it is true of all men, that his understanding of the problems of his time was affected by the nature of his intellectual tempering. Indeed, perhaps it can even be said that his perception of what *were* problems was to a considerable degree dependent on the cultivation which he brought to his work as a religious and political critic. Certainly some attention to his rich intellectual background is likely to enhance any analysis of his religious and political ideas. For this reason, this chapter will be devoted to the bearing of each of the following on Dr. Arnold's religious and political thought: (1) education, (2) Lake Country associations, (3) historical researches, and (4) friendship with Christian Bunsen.

WINCHESTER AND OXFORD

Arthur Penrhyn Stanley suggested that many of Arnold's interests in later life had their beginnings during his schooldays.[1] Certainly this might be said justly of many of Arnold's religious and political ideas for, almost from its outset, his education was such as to influence his thinking on the great religious and political issues of his time.

Between the ages of eight and eleven, he was under instruction at Warminster Grammar School, which, judging from Arnold's account of it in later life, must have been primarily distinguished by a good library and teachers who were astute enough to give precocious students some time to themselves. Certainly Arnold lost no time in making the most of the happy conditions which he found at Warminster. The record of his reading during this period shows that he was freely pursuing interests which were to remain with him throughout life. True, he read novels by Smollett and Cervantes, but these he discounted as merely " ludicrous." Of more solid merit were Priestly's *Lectures on History*, Caesar's *Commentaries* [2] and the enormous and erudite work, *The Old and the New Testaments Connected in the History of the Jews and Neighboring Nations*, by the seventeenth century liberal clergyman, Humphrey Prideaux.[3] Arnold's interest in the latter may well have been aroused by Prideaux' attempt to show how the prophecies of the Book of Daniel were fulfilled by the decay of the Roman Empire.[4] If so, we can trace his interest in the nature of prophecy, one subject of his Biblical criticism, to the Warminster period.

At the age of twelve Arnold enrolled in the ancient public school of Winchester, then in its " greatest era " under the tutelage of William Stanley Goddard.[5] Goddard, a veteran who had been at the job for eleven years,[6] set high standards for his scholars. On one occasion Arnold wrote of having to arise at 3:00 A.M. every day for a week in order to prepare himself to " say without book " 3000 (sic) lines of Homer.[7] Far from killing his interest in the classical authors, however, arduous study seemed only to draw Arnold closer to the ideas and temper of the ancients. He was especially fond of the Greek historians and read

Herodotus, Xenophon, and Thucydides for pleasure at the same time that he had Demosthenes, Sophocles, Homer, Cicero, Horace, and Virgil for his "regular school business."[8] Before he had reached the age of fifteen Arnold had laid the foundation of the classical scholarship which was to culminate in his edition of Thucydides and his habit of bringing ancient wisdom to bear on modern problems.

Arnold's avid interest in history and politics also led him to the close study of the English historians. In a letter written while he was at Winchester, Arnold gravely advised his old tutor at Warminster to read Adolphus' *History of the Reign of George III* which he said he had found rewarding.[9] He was also a careful student of Russell's *Modern Europe* and had read Gibbon's *Decline and Fall of the Roman Empire* and Mitford's *History of Greece* twice before he left Winchester at the age of sixteen.[10] Arnold undertook these studies from the point of view of one who has an awakened conscience. It may be amusing to read his boyish statement that he will need all his orthodoxy to combat the irony of Hume and Gibbon,[11] but there can be little doubt of the reality of his religion to him at this early date. His censure of the same two writers shows that his orthodoxy was sufficient. They are taken to task for "wilfully confounding, as is often done, the Purity of Religion, with the Vices and Follies of its Ministers."[12] It was an error which Arnold found it necessary to controvert throughout his life. The end effect of his reading and his reflection on it is to be seen in his decision at about this time to become a minister in order to help bring about a revival of religion and a reform of the Church.[13]

Not all of a Winchester education was to be obtained from books, however. The mingled formality and rough and tumble of English public school life was probably

invaluable to Arnold in adding to a nature inclined to indi-
viduality a sense of the importance of the community. In
addition, there was the influence of the masters. For one of
these, Henry Dison Gabell, Arnold had much admiration.
From Arnold's point of view, Gabell was a more interest-
ing teacher than the better known Goddard primarily because he was the better scholar. In fact, Arnold was so
impressed with the master that he ventured to suggest that
Gabell supplement the regular curriculum with courses in
English and Greek composition, a suggestion doubtless
more complimentary to the teacher than welcome to
Arnold's classmates.[14] The most important thing which the
young scholar learned from his teacher, however, may well
have been the duty of the teacher not to remain aloof from
public life, for Gabell fearlessly entered into politics as a
pamphleteer on the Corn Law question (*DNB*, VII, 784).

After Winchester the next step in Arnold's education
was to be taken at Oxford. In 1811 he entered the small
but distinguished college of Corpus Christi where he became a part of the lively circle of young men then enrolled,
many of whom afterwards became well known in the public
life of the nation. Among these were John Taylor Coleridge, later Chief Justice, and John Keble, later to become
one of the founders of the Oxford Movement.[15] Both men
may be considered leaders in the circle of " Tories in
Church and State " in which Arnold found himself placed.
There he had the broadening experience of having to defend his religious and political views against those who held
views diametrically opposed to them. From friendly arguments in the Corpus common room, it is probable that
Arnold gained a deepened awareness of the potentiality
for good in established institutions. At any rate, we are
told that during this period he was brought to opinions

more moderate than those which he had previously held (*Life*, I, 12-13).

During the same period in which Arnold was debating the great questions of his day with Coleridge and Keble, he was also making his first acquaintance with developments in the natural sciences. Again Arnold was fortunate in the choice of his school, for the small faculty at Corpus included two professors who became well known in the field of science. Arnold studied with both. From George Leigh Cooke, Sedleian Professor of Natural Philosophy and later the editor of selections from Newton's *Principia* with an " Introduction on the Atomic constitution of matter and the Laws of Motion,"[16] Arnold received his first instruction in the natural sciences. Later, he was an enthusiastic pupil of William Buckland, Professor of Mineralogy and Geology, who later published a Bridgewater Treatise on those subjects.[17] When this work appeared, it was felt by some Churchmen to be too dangerous in its implications properly to accomplish its avowed purpose as apologetic literature.[18] By means of his study with Cooke and Buckland, Arnold was able to supplement the traditional classical curriculum of his day and thus to become aware of the degree to which scientific advances appeared to threaten Christian belief. Probably it was at this time that he first considered the problem of the relation between religion and science, a problem which was a major topic discussed in his essay on scriptural interpretation published in later life.

Since Arnold attained a First Class, *Litterae Humaniores* in 1814, we know that he was also busy with humanistic and theological studies while he was at Corpus (*Life*, I, 7). Edward Copleston, a Corpus man who later became Oxford Professor of Poetry and Provost of Oriel, has left a good account of the curriculum which led to the B.A.

degree in this period. According to Copleston, the object
of the educational program was the laying of "a foundation of liberal literature, ancient and modern, before any
particular pursuit absorbs the mind." [19] The University
authorities sought to attain this end through a program of
guided reading on which candidates for the degree were
examined. First, the candidates were required to pass a
preliminary examination in which they construed one Latin
book (commonly a work by Virgil, Horace, Sallust, Livy,
or Cicero) and one Greek work (usually by Xenophon,
Homer, Herodotus, Sophocles, Euripides, or Demosthenes).
Then, one or two years later, the students were given the
examination for honors. This examination might include
questions on the works of Homer, the Greek tragedians,
Thucydides, Pindar, and Quintilian, but was inevitably
heavily weighted in favor of Aristotle's *Organon, Rhetoric,
Ethics,* and *Politics.* These Aristotelian works Copleston
thought the best fitted of all for "bringing into play all
the energies of the intellect, and for trying not merely the
diligence of the scholar, but the habit of discrimination
which he has formed, the general accuracy of his thoughts,
and the force and vigour of his mind. . . ." [20]

From such a course of study Arnold was destined to
obtain much. By means of his close study of Aristotle's
works he was able to make "familiar even fond" use of
the philosopher's words and during his school days, at
least, often pointed his own remarks with quotations from
Aristotle (*Life,* I, 17). Nothing could have been more
acceptable to one of Arnold's mind than Aristotle's conception of political science and ethics as inextricably bound
together. Later Arnold developed a philosophy of history
which allowed him to bring forward the practical political
wisdom of Aristotle and other ancient writers in support of

recommendations for religious and political reform. In his first approaches to the theory of the Christian State in after life, one can see evidence that he had thought deeply and long about Aristotle's discussions of the good for man, in the First Book of the *Nicomachean Ethics*, and of the nature of the state, in the Third Book of the *Politics*.[21]

As for the theological studies then required for the degree, these were inconsiderable, being limited, as Copleston tells us, to some study of the Greek New Testament, the "evidences" of Christianity (probably in some such work as William Paley's *Evidences of Christianity* [1794]), and the Thirty-Nine Articles of Religion together with some commentary on them (Copleston, p. 140). In view of Arnold's later opinions, it would appear that his study of the Articles of Religion, at any rate, was not such as to lead him to subscribe them wholeheartedly. Because he "doubted the proof and the interpretation of the textual authority" for one of the Articles, he demurred until advised otherwise by the Bishop of Oxford.[22] A later subscription to the Articles only upon assurance that they were "Articles of Peace" as well as his view that they should be reduced to that status by legislation,[23] further suggests that his theological studies at Corpus were in Arnold's case relatively unsuccessful as a means of fostering orthodoxy.

Fortunately for Arnold's intellectual development, however, his theological readings at Corpus were not restricted to those then required for the B.A. According to J. T. Coleridge, Arnold was also a diligent reader of some of the English theologians, including Richard Hooker (*Life*, I, 20). In Hooker's *Of the Laws of Ecclesiastical Polity* (1593-97) Arnold doubtless found almost the equivalent of a religious and political education in itself. In this weighty and learned apology for the Church of England, Hooker brought the best fruits of humanistic learning to the consideration of the proper relations between Church and State.   Aristotle, St. Thomas, and a multitude of other authorities were marshalled in support of a theory of a National Church coextensive with the State and no less than the State subordinate to the King.

That Arnold approved of this position may be seen both by his own political theory (see Chapter Four) and by his specific exclusion of Hooker from the ranks of those English theologians who did not seem to attend to the truth or falsity of what they believed (*Life*, II, 66-67). Certainly there can be little doubt that Hooker's noble ideal of a Christian monarch whose purpose was to lead his subjects to God was such as to appeal to Arnold and to foster in him the religious and political idealism which was already a part of his nature:

> A gross error it is, to think that regal power ought to serve for the good of the body, and not of the soul; for men's temporal peace, and not for their eternal safety: as if God had ordained kings for no other end and purpose but only to fat up men like hogs, and see that they have their mast.[24]

Also during his stay at Oxford, Arnold probably formed his lasting admiration for the works of Bishop Joseph Butler (1692-1752), the author of the *Analogy of Religion* and *Sermons* preached at the Rolls Chapel.[25] In Arnold's judgment (expressed in later life), Butler, along with Hooker, did not suffer from the general " want " among British theologians " of believing or disbelieving anything because it [was] true or false " (*Life*, II, 66). Arnold found Butler to be a " far more cautious and wiser writer " on religious subjects than many, and expressed his feeling that he was " never to be named without respect. . . ." [26]

In his *Analogy* Butler had chiefly concerned himself with refuting the arguments of English deists who in the first quarter of the eighteenth century had put in doubt the authority of the Christian revelation by work in Biblical criticism and the comparative study of religions. Although the deistic attack was unsystematic, it was greatly disturbing to the religious orthodoxy of the time.[27] The effectiveness of Butler's reply which has been evaluated as " crushing," was attributable to his learned representation of the experience of this life as " only a fragment of . . . a larger scheme of things." [28] Arguing that such a limited creature as man cannot hope to have certainty in religious matters and must therefore be satisfied with probabilities, and further, that in talking about religion, he must move from the known to the unknown, Butler sought to demonstrate to those who accepted natural religion that they had no valid reason to reject the Christian revelation.[29] His demonstration hinged on a method of argumentation in which the attributes of the Creator's moral government of the unseen world were inferred from what could be directly known from the ordered universe (p. 50). He then proceeded to show that the course of nature was in no sense inconsonant with the Christian revelation. As he found the two to be analogous, he defied the deists to make Christianity the " subject of ridicule unless that of Nature be so too." [30]

Arnold adapted this tenuous mode of argumentation to his own uses in the following passage for which he specifically acknowledged his indebtedness to Butler:

> . . . the resemblance . . . between the course of things earthly and that of things spiritual, is one which we should never fail to notice. We can discern the type . . . of the highest truth of our Lord's sayings in the experience of our common life in worldly things. When he tells us,

speaking of things spiritual, that " many are called, but few
are chosen " . . . although the highest truth contained in
these words be yet in part a matter of faith, for we have
not yet seen the end of God's dealings with us: yet what
we do see, the evident truth of the words . . . in respect
to God's dealings with us in the course of his earthly
providence, may reasonably assure us of their truth no
less in respect to those dealings of God which yet are
future.[31]

Butler also made some use of " evidences " in attesting
the truth of Biblical miracles. He conceded that the
Apostles may possibly have been deceived in their accounts,
but he pointed out that men commonly believe the testimony of others on ordinary matters and hence have no
reason to reject testimony on a matter so important as
practically to insure great obligation to veracity. Moreover, since " *great numbers* of earnest men gave testimony
to what they saw and heard " in a time when " education,
prejudice and authority were all against Christianity,"
Butler concluded that the Gospel miracles were well at-
tested.[32] Arnold apparently found this form of argumentation convincing, for on the few occasions when he found
it necessary to consider the question of miracles, he adapted
it to his particular uses.[33]

Though Arnold was of the opinion that Butler had effectively answered the deist criticism, he did see that the
arguments of the *Analogy* had no force against those who
acknowledged no God at all (*Sermons*, II, 165). Despite
his recognition of this limitation of Butler's apologetic,
however, Arnold was in perfect agreement with his great
theological opponent and fellow Oxonian J. H. Newman,
who in *The Idea of a University* described Butler as a
" great Protestant writer." [34]

In 1815 Arnold began the final phase of his formal education by being elected fellow of Oriel College, then the most intellectually alive of all the Oxford colleges. The historian of the college described it at this era as " a Society dedicated to dialectic, to the destruction of abuses, to the clarification and purification of thought." [35] It had become so by the institution there around the turn of the century of public examinations for the B.A. degree. These so raised scholarly standards that Oriel, retaining some of its better graduates, had by Arnold's time become distinctive for the quality of its fellows. By the date of Arnold's entry, these men had come to be known as " Noetics " (i. e., " intellectuals ").[36] This name was evidently well chosen, for the Oriel group were celebrated for their practice of " subjecting to the criticism of reason and history the conventionalities and dogmas of traditional religious orthodoxy." [37] In short, the intellectual atmosphere at Oriel during the first two decades of the nineteenth century was diametrically opposed to what it was in the thirties when it became the scene of another Oriel movement, Tractarianism.

The principal Noetics at Oriel in Arnold's time were Edward Copleston (1776-1849), John Davison (1777-1834), Richard Whately (1787-1863), Edward Hawkins (1789-1882), and Renn Dickson Hampden (1793-1868). These men, though not really organized as a specific party or interested in proselytizing, nevertheless had certain common beliefs. The more important of these were their fundamental agreement on the need for free Biblical scholarship, a strongly Protestant Church, and a state sensitive to the changing social needs of the nation.[38] These views in differing degrees and shades of opinion were asserted in pamphlets and from the University pulpit so vigorously that, as one conservative Churchman has said, many of the older University men " felt the ground shaking under them." [39] Such at any rate must have been the reaction to the works by Hampden which occasioned some of the bitterest controversies arising out of the Oxford Movement. These were chiefly a product of the 1830's, however, and will be discussed in the account of Arnold's defense of Hampden against the party of Newman (see pages 140-42). During Arnold's stay at Oriel, the theological scene was considerably quieter than it became a few years later. Copleston, then Provost of the college, was doubtless relatively absorbed in administrative duties. Hawkins, somewhat atypically for a Noetic, was then concerning himself with a defense of ecclesiastical tradition.[40] Only Davison and Whately were active at the work of liberal Churchmanship. In 1840, looking back on his Oriel days, Arnold could list only these two Noetics as influential on his own intellectual development (*Life*, II, 197).

Certainly in John Davison, Arnold was brought into association with one of the most astute religious liberals of the day. Three excellent judges of religious intelligence, S. T. Coleridge, John Henry Newman, and Matthew Arnold, have noticed Davison's intellectual gifts.[41] Like Whately, Davison was known as a great reasoner and, within Oriel at least, as a vigorous leader of the discussion of religious topics of the day.[42] In fact, his statement as to the benefits of such discussion might well be taken to illustrate the prevailing attitude of the Noetics toward religious inquiry:

Controversy, when it is carried on in the sound and manly spirit of investigation, is so favourable to the advancement or the more firm establishment of our knowledge, that we shall never presume to check or decry it. While it is so conducted, Religion is only more securely rooted by its friendly violence. Indolent and implicit knowledge is aroused by it to a more honest discipline; and error flies before it.[43]

Davison's Warburtonian lectures on prophecy (1819) were important in "freeing man from the older mechanical idea of prophecy."[44] In this work he took the position that prediction was only one element in prophecy, others being moral and religious teachings. Davison carefully distinguished between the historical and, as he called it, the "Evangelical" elements of prophecy. According to his findings, the political and social conditions surrounding each prophet "coloured his pictures of the future." Although modern Biblical criticism would find Davison's theories still too insistent on prediction and literal fulfillment of prophecy as the test of its inspiration, his work marked a considerable advance over then current treatments of the subject.[45] His teachings were taken to heart by Arnold in his *Sermons on the Interpretation of Prophecy* (1839).

He also admired the "moderation and piety" exhibited in Davison's *Inquiry into the Origin of Sacrifice* (1824), which Arnold defended against Tractarian attack during a discussion of the shackles on free Biblical inquiry in England in the early 1830's.[46] He observed that with the appearance of Tractarianism at Oxford, Davison was in the condition of a man caught in an "aguish district" and, living in the "fens," obliged to get his water from afar.[47] The rise of the same movement doubtless greatly limited Davison's effect on the religious thought of the day. Unlike Arnold, he did not have a forceful personality and was incapable of opposing the Tractarians in any effective way. Tuckwell tells us that he was so reluctant publicly to avow his opinions that Newman's party even took him for an ally at one point (p. 18). His practice outside the Oriel common room was therefore not in accordance with his theories of free discussion, and his influence lived only with those who, like Arnold, recognized the ability shown in his books.

Almost exactly the reverse was true of Richard Whately, another of Arnold's Oriel colleagues, who from 1831 to 1863 served as Archbishop of Dublin. It was he who had recommended Arnold for his Oriel fellowship in 1815, on the grounds of the capacity for " growth " shown by his trial essays. In later years he saw his judgment vindicated in Arnold's development (*Life*, I, 27). Whately's voluminous writings scarcely reflect the penetration and mental force which he seems to have possessed in conversation and private correspondence.[48] Despite fundamental differences with Arnold about the proper relations of Church and State and despite somewhat defective learning which kept him out of touch with intellectual developments abroad,[49] Whately nevertheless appears to have been a great stimulus to Arnold's thinking. He had a keenly logical mind and a large fund of common sense which made him especially gifted in clarifying thought. It was evidently this gift which put him in the debt of thinkers as dissimilar as Arnold and Newman.[50] Thomas Arnold, Jr., wrote of him as the principal figure in the circle of his father's friends and recalled Whately's " habit of continual reflection and constant search for exact and logical expressions," his " incurable rationality," and his customary efforts " to judge of events and probabilities without bias." [51] Another writer has noted Whately's tendency to play down the importance of metaphysics and systematic theology. On the other hand, he strongly emphasized the need for a careful attempt to ascertain the exact meanings of the language of Scriptures (*DNB*, XX, 1338-39).

According to Arnold's own statements, conversations with Whately in 1822 were helpful in clarifying the younger man's understanding of the nature of the Christian priesthood. Both men fundamentally disapproved of most of the claims which the Tractarians made for sacerdotal authority, although Whately did not publish his major anti-Tractarian work, *Cautions for the Times*, until 1853, long after Arnold's death.[52]

Probably Whately was also instrumental to some degree in bringing about Arnold's deepening suspicions of the way in which Evangelical theologians had been employing certain Pauline words and phrases. Whately's method in his *Essays on Some of the Difficulties in the Writings of St. Paul* (1828) was that of expositing St. Paul's literary expressions apart from " the metaphysical sophistications which encumber them." He undertook to distinguish between the meaning of such terms as " election," " imputed righteousness," and " grace " in their Biblical contexts and as employed by theologians.[53] Certain of Arnold's sermons of 1827 and later have a similar aim (IS, pp. 271-73, 498-99).

In publishing a volume of sermons in 1829, Arnold noted the similarity of some of his views to those expressed by Whately, but stated that he had written his work prior to becoming aware that Whately "had expressed the same sentiments more clearly and more forcibly " in his essays on St. Paul and *On the Peculiarities of Christianity* (1825). He further suggested that his own views were " confirmed and extended " by their concurrence with Whately's (*Sermons*, I, viii). On the whole it appears that Whately served Arnold as a discriminating critic during his formative years and maturity and remained his lifelong friend without dominating his thought at any time. This is borne out by Whately's statement in after years to one of Arnold's sons that the elder Arnold was not given to " copying anyone, or taking anyone's opinions as his standard." [54]

On his part, Arnold always held Whately in high regard. In 1831 he lamented that Whately's liberalizing influence at Oxford had been brought to a close by his elevation to the See of Dublin.[55] Arnold, who had left Oxford a decade before, was doubtless aware that in the absence of Whately, the most vigorous of the Noetics, religious conservatism would be likely to close over the intellectual life of the University. Such a realization would be doubly painful to one who recognized the liberal spirit of good schools as important in his own intellectual preparation.

ARNOLD AND THE LAKE POETS

A great critic of the Victorian period characterized the respective influences of William Wordsworth and S. T. Coleridge on nineteenth century English thought thus:

> . . . one of the best and deepest spiritual influences of our century. (*Works*, XV, 59.)

> . . . a stimulus to all minds capable of profiting by it; in the generation which grew up around him. (*Works*, III, 301.)

In so writing, Matthew Arnold also unwittingly described another of his father's intellectual resources. Through long residence in the English Lake Country and through friendship with members of the Wordsworth and Coleridge families, Thomas Arnold was brought in touch with the ideas and spirit of the two great Romantics.

The acquaintance began early. Through J. T. Coleridge, one of Arnold's school-fellows at Corpus and the nephew of S. T. Coleridge, Arnold in 1811 was introduced to *Lyrical Ballads* and to a separate edition of Wordsworth's poems. According to Coleridge, Arnold's response to this reading, especially of Wordsworth's poetry, was one of deep appreciation. Apparently Arnold, whose previous inclinations, Coleridge said, had been " too direct for the practical and evidently useful," found much in these poems of which his spirit had been in need. Coleridge even traced the first appearance of the " lofty and imaginative " traits of Arnold's character back to this reading (*Life*, I, 17). In this respect, Arnold's experience paralleled that of John Stuart Mill who in his *Autobiography* has recorded a similarly appreciative reading of the poetry of Wordsworth.[56]

If Arnold's early reading of the great poetry of the Lake Country made him in some sense one of the " zealous disciples of Wordsworth's philosophy," as Coleridge claimed, the events of later life could only have increased the extent of his admiration for the poet. In 1818, Arnold, while on a tour of the Lakes, became personally acquainted with Wordsworth.[57] The association was renewed on succeeding visits in 1824 and 1831 during which the friendship evidently ripened, for in the latter year Wordsworth suggested that the Arnolds lease a house in the vicinity of Rydal Mount for occupancy during summer and mid-year vacations.[58] Christmas of 1831 found the Arnolds situated in a house at the foot of Nabb's Scar, where, as Arnold wrote delightedly, he could see snow-capped mountains on one side of the house and could hear the Rotha's " perpetual music " from the other (*Life*, I, 316). The pleasant aspects of this " mountain paradise of Westmoreland and Cumberland," [59] plus the cordial friendship of the Wordsworths drew the Arnolds in successive years to Rydal, Brathay, and Allan Bank, until finally it became clear that the Lake Country was to be of continuing interest to them. Accordingly, with the poet's help in selecting a site and in supervising the construction of a home, Dr. Arnold and his family in 1834 became permanently established at Fox How, some three-quarters of a mile from Rydal Mount. There, during school vacations they were intimately associated with the Wordsworths.[60]

Probably the most valuable of these associations to Arnold were the long walks which he was accustomed to take with the poet. These, as is clear from Dr. Arnold's account of one of them, gave occasion for the testing of religious and political opinions as well as for the enjoyment of the surrounding natural beauty. During a walk up Greenhead Ghyll " to see ' the unfinished sheepfold ' recorded in ' Michael,' " Wordsworth and Arnold had " a good fight " about the Reform Bill. Arnold's comment on this occasion illuminates the nature of his intellectual relation with Wordsworth:

> But I am sure that our political disagreement did not at all interfere with our enjoyment of each other's society: for I think that in the great principles of things we agreed very entirely. . . ." (*Life*, I, 322.)

It was this fundamental agreement which caused the friendship to endure despite their disagreement on many specific religious and political issues. Although it is quite possible that Arnold profited from hearing the objections raised by a man of genius to his opinions on the Reform Bill, Catholic Emancipation, inheritance laws, Tory politics, the importance of dogma and the need for Church reform,[61] their agreement on the " great principles " is more important for the purposes of this discussion.

Among the most striking of these principles was the belief by both that man was steadily losing sight of the religiousness of everyday life. In this respect, Arnold could scarcely have encountered a better teacher than Wordsworth, who asserted the importance of the spiritual aspect of life in what one of Arnold's friends characterized as a " shallow, hard and worldly age." [62] Certainly Arnold could expect to have his religious consciousness deepened by the author of such lines as the following from Wordsworth's " Essay Supplementary to the Preface " of the 1815 edition of his poems:

> Faith was given to man that his affections, detached from the treasures of time, might be inclined to settle upon those of eternity:—the elevation of his nature which this habit produces upon earth, being to him a presumptive evidence of a future state of existence; and giving him a title to partake of its holiness. [63]

In a pamphlet of 1833 Arnold recognized this aspect of Wordsworth's teachings by taking occasion to quote the sonnet " The World Is Too Much With Us " in full, in support of his own discussion of the proper ends of the State. As an alternative to " a national society formed for no higher than physical ends;—to enable men to eat, drink, and live luxuriously," Arnold suggested that the establishment of paganism would be preferable. He then subjoined the " beautiful lines " in which " Mr. Wordsworth sympathized so entirely " with his view. [64]

A second " great principle " on which Arnold could agree with Wordsworth was that individual moral reform must precede social reform. So Wordsworth had argued in his *Convention of Cintra* (1809) in which he called for national regeneration through individual moral improvement instead of by means of "machinery." [65] Such a position is well illustrated by the following words from this tract:

> How base! how puny! how inefficient for all good purposes are the tools and implements of policy compared with these mighty implements of Nature! (i.e., "pure passions and high actions")—There is no middle course: two masters cannot be served: Justice must either be enthroned above might, and the moral law take the place of the edicts of selfish passion; or the heart of the people, which alone can sustain the efforts of the people, will languish. . . . (*Prose Works*, I, 208-209.)

Though there is no evidence of a specifically Wordsworthian influence on this point, similar thinking can be seen in Arnold's program of "Christian Reform" in his *Englishman's Register* (1831) and in his abiding suspicion that political reforms would be insufficient to "raise the moral and intellectual character of the poor" (MW, p. 188).

A third "great principle" on which Arnold could agree with his friend was that all the classes of society must be brought to work together for the improvement of English social conditions. Although he believed at one time that nothing was required "but that the Government and the higher orders of society should deal sincerely towards the middle class and the lower" (*Prose Works*, I, 249), Wordsworth later came to see that those of the lower class must be brought to realize their responsibility also. Accordingly, he sought to remind them of advantages inherent in the English social system and to deter them from responding to the agitation of political journalists:

Opulence, rank, station, privilege, distinction, intellectual culture—the notions naturally following upon these in a Country like England are protection, succour, guidance, example, dissemination of knowledge, introduction of improvements, and all the benefits and blessings that among Freemen are diffused. . . . The mass of the people are justly dealt with and tenderly cherished. (*Prose Works*, II, 325.)

[Newspapers] impress the Body of the People with a belief that neither justice can be expected, nor benevolence hoped for, unless power be transferred . . . to Demagogues and Incendiaries! (*Prose Works*, II, 327.)

Later, Arnold engaged in a program of palliative journalism and in a critique of partisanship which are sufficient indication of his acceptance of the same principle.

A final "great principle" on which Dr. Arnold and Wordsworth were united was that continuity was of vital importance in social development. Wordsworth deplored the "insurrectionary banner" of VAST GAINS WITH LITTLE PAINS under which he said "unthinking humanity" marched (*Prose Works*, II, 327). He was opposed to radical alterations in the existing social order. For example, in 1833 when many were talking of the need for educating the illiterate masses of the population, Wordsworth advocated the more conservative program of improved education for the middle and upper classes as likely to do more good. This he thought could be followed by education of the lower class.[66] A similar emphasis can be seen in Arnold's "Letters on the Education of the Middle Classes" and more generally, in his application of Wordsworth's lines "The Child is father of the Man" to the social development of a nation. He suggested that it was quite as important for nations as for individuals to experience days "bound each to each by natural piety" (LMH, p. 327). In this respect as in the others already discussed, it is apparent that Arnold had much more in common with the poet of Rydal than their differences of religious and political parties would lead one to expect. Arnold saw the value of Wordsworth's reflections on the " great principles " of life. Although in the last analysis he could scarcely be called Wordsworth's " disciple," he was at least a discriminating admirer of the poet and had felt his " healing power." [67] Wordsworth, on the other hand, although he felt Arnold to be injudicious " on the great points of secular and ecclesiastical polity," nevertheless recorded his favorable opinion of Arnold's character:

> His benevolence was so earnest, his life so industrious, his affections,—domestic and social—so intense, his faith so warm and firm, and his endeavour to regulate his life by it so constant, that his example cannot but be beneficial even in quarters where his opinions may be most disliked. How he hated sin, and loved and thirsted after holiness! Oh, that on this path, he were universally followed! [68]

Thomas Arnold's relations with Coleridge were less direct. These also began at Corpus Christi College. There in 1811 Coleridge's nephew regaled his school-fellows with anecdotes of a visit which he had recently made to his great relative. At least some of these were later collected in the edition of the poet's *Table Talk*, for Arnold, taking up that work in 1835, wrote that he found there " divers anecdotes which used to excite the open-mouthed admiration " of the Corpus common room (*Life*, I, 440). Among those undoubtedly discussed by the circle of earnest young men were S. T. Coleridge's undeveloped but suggestive remarks about the state of religion in Germany and the excesses of the rationalistic Biblical critics there. [69] In these remarks alone, Arnold could have found the basis for his longstanding belief that Coleridge was a great man who had no English peer for his "rich and vigorous and comprehensive and critical" mind (*Life*, II, 165). This opinion seems only to have become stronger during Arnold's subsequent reading of Coleridge's "Essay on Method" in the *Encyclopaedia Metropolitana*, *On the Constitution of Church and the State According to the Idea of Each*, *Table Talk*, *Aids to Reflection*, and *Literary Remains* (including "Letters on Inspiration," later *Confessions of an Inquiring Spirit*).[70]

Although Dr. Arnold was by no means an uncritical reader of these works and was quite willing to criticize Coleridge for deficiencies of style, "unsteadiness of mind and purposes," alienation from active life, and occasional historical naïveté,[71] he was nevertheless convinced of the poet's greatness as a thinker if not as a man (*Life*, II, 26). Perhaps he saw as did James Martineau in later years that in an age of growing materialism there was in Coleridge's thought the power to "effectually set man on his feet again. . . ."[72] In any case, Arnold's religious and political writings show that he profited from his readings in Coleridge's works even where he differed from the older man.[73] I shall therefore consider the bearing of Coleridge's work on Arnold's Biblical criticism, writings on the Church, and political theory and practice.

Coleridge has come to be recognized as a great pioneer in the field of Biblical criticism. His special contribution to nineteenth century thought in a time of doubt and spiritual unrest was that of showing that the Bible retained its value as a source of spiritual inspiration and guidance despite the apparently discrediting attacks of science and the continental "higher" Biblical criticism. Moreover, his own treatments of religious questions were replete with references to or translations from such monuments of religious criticism as Spinoza's *Tractatus Theologico-Politicus* (1670) and *Ethics* (1677), and G. E. Lessing's "Education of the Human Race" (1780).[74] It is probable that Coleridge's writings powerfully contributed to the great influence which these works had on liberal theology of the later nineteenth century.

Coleridge's *Confessions of an Inquiring Spirit*, his great work in the field of Biblical criticism, was only published posthumously in 1840, some eight years after the publication of Dr. Arnold's "Essay on the Right Interpretation and Understanding of the Scriptures" which also considers the key critical problem of the inspiration of the Bible. Yet after he had read Coleridge's work in manuscript in 1834 (two years after the publication of his own essay) Arnold wrote to Coleridge's nephew commenting on the importance of the work:

> Have you seen your Uncle's "Letters on Inspiration," which I believe are to be published? They are well fitted to break ground in the approaches to that momentous question which involves in it so great a shock to existing notions; the greatest probably, that has ever been given since the discovery of the falsehood of the doctrine of the Pope's infallibility. Yet it must come, and will end, in spite of the fears and clamours of the weak and bigoted, in the higher exalting and more sure establishing of Christian truth.[75]

Arnold approved the editing and publication of Coleridge's "letters" and offered his own assistance in the task.[76]

It is quite probable that Arnold benefited from the scattered hints and speculations about Biblical criticism in other works by Coleridge. One such occurs in the *Statesman's*

Manual (1816) where Coleridge suggests that facts and persons in Scripture have a twofold significance, "a particular and a universal application" (Shedd, I, 437). This idea was a key one in Arnold's *Sermons on Prophecy* (1827).[77] Also in the *Statesman's Manual*, Coleridge makes use of the distinction between the faculties of the Reason and the Understanding which Arnold later adapted to his own uses. According to Coleridge, this distinction was that while "reason is the knowledge of the laws of the whole considered as one," understanding "concerns itself exclusively with the quantities, qualities, and relations of particulars in time and space."[78] Again in his *Aids to Reflection* (1825) Coleridge made use of this idea in attempting to show that "Christianity was the crown and perfection of human intelligence, the truth in which all lesser truths found their fulfilment."[79] Finally, Coleridge's speculations as to the authenticity of some of the Biblical books may well have suggested to Arnold the need for showing that neither the fundamental historicity of the Bible nor its value as a source of moral guidance was lessened by its lack of plenary inspiration.[80]

His indebtedness to Coleridge is more obvious in his writings about the proper relations of Church and State. In his *On the Constitution of Church and State According to the Idea of Each* (1829), Coleridge undertook to expound this relation according to the *a priori* "idea" (in the Platonic sense of a perfection not necessarily ever attained in actuality) of each of the institutions. He found the "idea" of the State to be an equilibrium between "permanence and progression" (Shedd, VI, 38-44), that is, between the interests of the landed class on the one hand and the professional, manufacturing, mercantile, and distributive classes on the other. The "idea" of the Church was that of a " National Church " or " third organ of the State " which would make healthy civil life possible by providing requisite intellectual cultivation of citizens and thereby help to improve the possibility of social equilibrium. Such cultivation was to be provided by the " Clerisy " comprised of clergymen, teachers, and scholars.[81] Although Coleridge was aware that the history of the Anglican Church did not always show it to have been directed to this end (Shedd, VI, 44), he nevertheless considered the national establishment a great blessing and a great advantage in the accomplishment of the goal which he set for the " Clerisy " as a whole:

> That to every parish throughout the kingdom there is transplanted a germ of civilization; that in the remotest villages there is a *nucleus*, round which the capabilities of the place may crystallize and brighten; a model sufficiently superior to excite, yet sufficiently near to encourage and facilitate imitation; this inobtrusive, continuous agency of a Protestant Church Establishment . . . the patriot and philanthropist . . . can not estimate at too high a price. (Shedd, VI, 71.)

Some of these ideas were particularly attractive to Arnold, who incorporated them into his own writings on the Church and State. Although he considered Coleridge's work " historically very faulty " (*Life*, II, 195), Arnold could agree with Coleridge that there should be a strong *National* Church organized to bring about the intellectual and moral improvement of the people, that its head should be the King, that it should not be thought of as clergy only, and that it should not be theologically exclusive.[82]

Arnold may also have been indebted to Coleridge to some degree for the program of "Christian Reform" which Arnold expounded in newspaper editorials during the 1830's.

Coleridge undertook to follow a similar program in his *Lay Sermons, The Statesman's Manual; or the Bible the Best Guide to Political Skill and Foresight* (1816) addressed to "the higher classes of society," and *A Lay Sermon Addressed to the Higher and Middle Classes on the Existing Distresses and Discontents* (1817). In the second work he well summarized the religious basis of his political thinking:

> . . . I persist in avowing my conviction, that the inspired poets, historians, and sententiaries of the Jews are the clearest teachers of political economy: in short, that their writings are the Statesman's best manual, not only as containing the first principles and ultimate grounds of state-policy, whether in prosperous times or in those of danger and distress, but as supplying likewise the details of their application, and as being a full and spacious repository of precedents and facts in proof. (White, p. 62.)

In the same work, Coleridge, having traced most of the evils of the times to the spirit of commercialism pervading national life, made clear his belief that only moral regeneration attendant on Christian social action could effectively improve matters:

> If we are a Christian nation, we must learn to act nationally, as well as individually, as Christians. . . . Let us become a better people, and the reform of all the public (real or supposed) grievances, which we use as pegs whereon to hang our own errors and defects, will follow of itself. In short, let every man measure his efforts by his power and his sphere of action, and do all he can do! Let him contribute money where he cannot act personally; but let him act personally and in detail wherever it is practicable. Let us palliate where we cannot cure, comfort where we cannot relieve; and for the rest rely upon

the promise of the King of kings by the mouth of His
Prophet—"Blessed are ye that sow beside all waters."
(White, pp. 115-16.)

None of Arnold's political writings is more indicative of
his acceptance of this Coleridgean principle than an article
of 1841 in which he observed that no sound knowledge
about public matters could be gained without the " previous
moral improvement " of talking, writing, and acting on
political problems " in the fear of God " (MW, pp. 517-
18). In his thinking on this topic as in the others previously
discussed, he was indebted to the English Lake poet. On
the other hand, perhaps without knowing it, Coleridge had
helped forward the man for whom he was looking in 1831
when he said despairingly, " Alas! I look in vain for some
wise and good man to sound the word Duty in the ears
of this generation " (Shedd, VI, 371).

ARNOLD'S HISTORICAL RESEARCHES

Arnold's historical researches were among the important
intellectual preparations which enabled him to descry what
he took to be the " characteristic faults of the English
mind,—narrowness of view, and a want of learning and a
sound critical spirit . . ." (*Life*, II, 191). His extensive
studies in ancient and modern history were to a considerable degree the source of the breadth of view which he
brought to his consideration of English religious and political problems. As it is not the purpose of this study to deal
with Arnold's significance as a historian,[83] I shall restrict
my discussion to those aspects of his historical work which
directly bear upon his religious and political ideas. These
are three in number: (1) the principles of historical criticism which Arnold applied to the special problem of Bibli-

cal interpretation, (2) the accurate knowledge of ecclesiastical history which enabled him to counter the Tractarian
appeal to the past, and (3) the philosophy of history which
made it possible for him to apply ancient wisdom to the
treatment of contemporary social problems and which lent
the weight of "scientific" authority to his pronouncements.

Considering the range of Arnold's other interests and
duties, his productions in the historical field are surprisingly
numerous and weighty. They include an article in the
Quarterly Review (June, 1825) on Barthold Niebuhr's *History of Rome*, a critical edition of Thucydides with several
accompanying essays and extensive notes (three volumes,
1830-35), a number of articles collected as *History of the
Later Roman Commonwealth* (two volumes, 1821-27), an
uncompleted *History of Rome* (three volumes, 1838-42),
and a series of Oxford *Introductory Lectures on Modern
History* (1842).

In all of these works except the *Lectures on Modern
History*, he was by his own admission indebted to the historian and statesman Barthold Niebuhr (1776-1830) whom
Christian Bunsen succeeded as Prussian diplomatic minister
in Rome.[84] In the excepted work he stated as his ultimate
end the writing of an "internal" institutional history of
the kind produced by Niebuhr.[85]

Even prior to meeting Bunsen, Arnold in 1824 had
studied German solely in order to be able to read Niebuhr's
Römische Geschichte (1811-12). This work, later well
translated into English by Arnold's friend Julius Charles
Hare (1795-1855) and Connop Thirlwall (1797-1875) was
so far in advance of English treatments of the same subject
that Macaulay declared that it created "an epoch in the
history of European intelligence."[86] Arnold himself characterized it as a work of "extraordinary ability and learn-

ing " (*Life*, I, 45), and felt obliged to postpone any further historical work of his own until he had acquainted himself with some of the vast range of materials employed by Niebuhr.

Characteristically for a schoolmaster, his impulse was to make known what he had learned. In 1825 he reviewed Niebuhr's history in the *Quarterly Review*, becoming in the German's own words, " the scholar who introduced the first edition of this history to the English public." [87] In this review, Arnold hailed Niebuhr's great learning and penetration but indicated disapproval of incidental remarks which the German made about the Scriptures (MW, p. 397). Arnold's strictures clearly show his fear that Niebuhr might hold purely rationalistic religious views. It was therefore with considerable relief that on visiting the German at Bonn in 1830, he was able to conclude from Niebuhr's tone when speaking of religious matters that his fear was unfounded (*Life*, I, 298, 389).

The association was not destined to be resumed, however, for Niebuhr died in the same year. It has been said that his health was permanently damaged by anxiety at the outbreak of the French Revolution of 1830, which appeared to him to be a revival of the liberal revolutionary tendencies of 1789. If this is true, he was certainly far removed in his political sympathies from Arnold, his English " disciple," who rejoiced wholeheartedly at the same event.[88] In other respects, too, Arnold did not follow his continental friend. For one thing, he was able to carry on his historical researches without being led to the profound skepticism and pessimism about religious matters which overtook Niebuhr. That historian on one occasion was so convinced that his method of critical evaluation of historical sources utterly discredited the Old Testament that he gave up a projected

Biblical study, fearing to " give pain to those whom he did not wish to offend. . . ." [89] Arnold, however, did not base his estimate of the true worth of the Bible on its literal accuracy.

In certain other respects Arnold found himself fundamentally indebted to the great German historian. Particularly was this true of Niebuhr's theory (on which he proceeded as if it were fact) that " early Roman history was the prose rendering of still earlier national ballad poetry. . . ." [90] Accepting this theory in his own *History of Rome*, Arnold came to see that it might also apply to the ancient contents of the Bible as well (Campbell, p. 193). Another Niebuhrian principle he once characterized as " doubting rightly and believing rightly " (HR, p. vii). Essentially, this was the application of tests of internal consistency to narratives in order to determine their authenticity or relationship to other narratives. Arnold later employed this principle in defense of the factuality of scriptural narratives. [91]

Moreover, he also gained certain concepts from Niebuhr in the political sphere. Especially noteworthy here was the German historian's theory of institutional history. Prior to Niebuhr no historian had systematically studied Rome as a great state " the institutions of which, political, legal, and economic, must be traced to their origin and followed through their successive changes." [92] A key to the historian's method is given in his statement that he " never could have understood a number of things in the history of Rome without having observed England." [93] This remark suggests his practice of drawing analogies between civilizations ancient and modern. From this practice, which made Niebuhr " the first of the modern historians to see antiquity in the realistic light of social conflict . . . ," [94] Arnold gained a tool which he not only employed in his own histories but which added the breadth of historical perspective to his analyses of the " condition of England " in the 1830's and 1840's.

Arnold's writings on the Church also benefitted from his historical study. Because of his thorough study of history, he was brought to see that the Tractarian " appeal to the past " was in many respects misleading and grossly unhistorical.[95] Having traced " social helplessness and intellectual frivolousness " from their origin in the corruptness of later Roman society to the modern Church with its " fatal strifes of words," [96] Arnold did not hesitate to point out the dangerously reactionary tendencies of that movement which seemed likely to make needed administrative reforms of the Church difficult if not impossible. Many of his most telling strictures on the Oxford Movement are given additional authority by his historical knowledge. Among these might be mentioned his critique of some of the key terms of the Movement. " Primitive antiquity " and " authority " were not likely to overawe a scholar thoroughly in command of the political and religious history of classical and medieval times. Instead, he was able to call attention to the vagueness of such terms (CLH, pp. 470-74). After bringing his own historical learning to bear on the works of the early Christian writers about the nature of the Church, he was led to conclusions quite different from those reached by his theological opponents. Examining the Church with the same historical acumen that he would apply to any other political or social institution, Arnold was led to conclude that it had passed from its " first and perfect state," where specific forms were considered unessential, through a stage in which its continued existence depended " on the adherence to particular outward regulations," and was now in a final stage in which the forms, though upheld, were really a bar to further growth. He argued that the Tractarians were doing the Church irreparable harm by trying to maintain forms which once " protected the seed of life " but which were now the " means of stifling it." [97]

An additional result of Arnold's historical studies was the philosophy of history which he formed. By means of this he was able to apply the political wisdom of ancient writers to contemporary problems. The uneasy days of Peterloo made him think " of Thucydides, and the Corcyrean sedition, and the story of the French Revolution, and of the Cassandra-like fate of history, whose lessons are read in vain even to the very next generation " (*Life*, I, 50). It is not difficult to see that Thucydides' " tenseness . . . , absorption with political forces [and] sense that the events of his time were of a magnitude and complexity never known before " [98] also reflected Arnold's own feelings about English society in the second quarter of the nineteenth century. Thucydides' account of the downfall of a great state about 400 B.C. through the combined causes of external war and the weakness of popular democracy appeared immediately relevant. All too applicable to the 1830's and 1840's were Alcibiades' speech to the Lacedaemonians on the difficulties of practicing political moderation when " demagogues . . . led the people into evil ways . . . ," or Cleon's castigation of the Athenian magistrates as fond of using their eyes to attend to speeches and their ears to actions. [99] Such applicability led him finally to urge that Thucydides' reflections on the bloody Corcyrean dissensions gave him significance as a " modern " author. These reflections, Arnold said, clearly showed that Thucydides had gone beyond an " age of feeling . . . of ignorance and credulity " characteristic of " ancient " history to a " mod-

ern age of inquiry and scepticism." Along with other
Greek literature, therefore, Thucydides' history was an
invaluable source of political guidance for modern times
(MW, pp. 396-97).

Arnold's ability to draw upon classical wisdom in a
systematic and authoritative way was greatly enhanced by
his study of Niebuhr and the great Italian thinker of the
eighteenth century, Giovanni Vico (1668-1744). The results of this study can best be seen in Arnold's essay " The
Social Progress of States " (1830), an appendix to the first
volume of his edition of Thucydides. Arnold took as his
text a brief quotation from the Greek historian:

> As Hellas grew more powerful and the acquisition of
> wealth became more and more rapid, the revenues of her
> cities increased, and in most of them tyrannies were estab-
> lished; they had hitherto been ruled by hereditary kings,
> having fixed prerogatives.[100]

He then expounded a theory of the " progress of States "
on the analogy of the human individual:

> . . . states, like individuals, go through certain changes
> in a certain order, and are subject at different stages of
> their course to certain peculiar disorders. (MW, p. 82.)

According to this theory, nations undergo regular stages
of development: the ascendancy of nobility, the ascendancy
of wealth, and the ascendancy of numbers. This evolution
was regarded as natural and, in the absence of interfering
causes, inevitable and peaceful. As each stage of the evolution was marked by particular dangers which altered the
peaceful nature of the change, however, it was necessary
to avoid these in order to make the social change, as Arnold
said on another occasion, " as easy and imperceptible as

possible" (MW, p. 116). War was the particular danger facing an England which was, according to Arnold's theory, then on the point of passing from an ascendancy of wealth to one of numbers (MW, p. 109). Because of the cultural difference between the wealthy few and the impoverished many, there was a grave danger that the transition would take place in a great social convulsion:

> The final struggle here only takes place when the real differences between the contending parties have reached the widest point of separation; when the intermediate gradations of society are absorbed in one of the two extremes, and the state is divided only between the two irreconcilable opposites of luxury and beggary. This is no contest between men really equal, to do away with a fictitious distinction; it is a struggle between utter contraries; between parties who have absolutely no point in common, no knowledge of each other's pursuits; and who are contending for a prize which one cannot gain without a proportional loss to the other. (MW, p. 106.)

With such an explanation for the "social progress" of states Arnold was in excellent position to urge the necessity of palliative measures both to the upper and to the lower classes. His belief that such measures could avert outright revolution and his recognition of the unpredictable role of national character, geography, and race in this progress differentiated Arnold's theory from a thoroughgoing historical determinism such as that advanced by Marx in his *Das Kapital* (1867). Arnold considered the "higher causes" of national character, geography, and race as proceeding "directly from the inscrutable will of our Maker." He observed that these differences had the effect of "humbling the presumption of fancying ourselves the arbiters of our own destiny" (MW, pp. 109-10).

Despite these limitations, Arnold made good use of the implications of this philosophy of history in his social criticism. By means of the " philosophical " divisions of history Arnold could argue that since Greece in Thucydides' time was in a state of development analogous to that of nineteenth century England, much might be learned from the classical author which would be of current value. In fact, the theory allowed him to make use of an author with which he was perhaps uniquely familiar under the aegis of a " science " of history.[101] To those English intellectuals who sought for something more " scientific " than the ordinary results of humanistic education, the theory may well have added to the acceptability of Arnold's political criticism. For this and for other reasons Arnold was therefore greatly indebted to Niebuhr and Vico, the authorities on which he based his theory.[102]

In Niebuhr's *History of Rome* (1811-12) Arnold had ample precedent for the relation of history to the contemporary scene. Like Arnold, Niebuhr accepted the idea that with reservations the " lessons " of history could be useful in the guidance of modern political action. As long as one could be sure that the example from history applied to the same " phase " of a nation's development, the lesson would hold good. On the whole, however, he did not seek to work out this idea systematically or to apply it except to further his purely historiographical purpose of " resurrecting the history of Rome. . . ." His thinking on this matter was swayed by nationalism instead of by a desire to work out a theory of universal history. As a result, he was more likely to view Rome as an inspiration of " patriotism and civic virtue " than as the source of any independent principles of political wisdom (Forbes, pp. 17-18).

The same did not hold true of Giovanni Vico, the substance of whose *Principi di Scienza Nuova* (1725) Arnold found to be "so profound and striking that the little celebrity which he has obtained out of Italy was one of the most remarkable facts in literary history." [103] Comparison of Vico's division of the governments of nations into theocracies, aristocracies, and "human governments" in which "all are accounted equal under the law," [104] with Arnold's own classification of ascendancy of blood, wealth, and numbers makes it clear that Arnold did not wholly adopt the Italian thinker's theory. Nevertheless, he acknowledged his indebtedness to Vico's discussion of the "ascendancy enjoyed in the earliest states by noble birth. . ." (MW, p. 82).

Certainly Arnold approved of the ideas expressed in Vico's summary of his *New Science*:

> . . . from all that we have set forth in this work, it is to be finally concluded that this Science carries inseparably with it the study of piety and that if one be not pious he cannot really be wise. (*New Science*, p. 383.)

In the last analysis, the value of Vico to Arnold was that through him history became "not an idle inquiry about remote ages and forgotten institutions, but a living picture of things present fitted not so much for the curiosity of the scholar as for the instruction of the statesman and citizen" (MW, p. 399). By these means, history could be shown to support Arnold's religious and political teachings. It was through his historical study that he first began his stimulating friendship with a European intellectual for whom he came to have the highest respect.

ARNOLD'S FRIENDSHIP WITH CHRISTIAN BUNSEN

Arnold's intellectual preparations were not limited to a good education, association with the poets of the Lake Country, and historical researches. Another important means by which he " got himself out of the narrow medium in which . . . his English friends lived " (*Works*, XIV, 189) was his European travels. These not only sharpened his eye for the anomalous and provincial aspects of English religion and society, but brought him into contact with foreign intellectuals like Barthold Niebuhr and Christian Bunsen. Arnold was deeply indebted to the historical researches of the former. His friendship with the Prussian statesman, theologian, and historian, Christian Bunsen (1791-1860) was almost as important to his intellectual development.

The friendship began during a visit to Rome which Arnold made in 1827 partly to further his historical researches. Bunsen, then minister of the Prussian legation in that city, was able to render considerable assistance to Arnold in guiding him to many of the Roman ruins and other points of historical interest. Like Arnold, Bunsen was widely traveled, and profoundly interested in theology, politics, and history. Accordingly, it is not surprising that a deep and, as it proved, enduring friendship sprang up between the two men. After a brief association in Rome, they began a correspondence which lasted until Arnold's death in 1842.[105] In later years the relationship was deepened by Bunsen's visits to England and, on one occasion, to Rugby. This visit merely confirmed Arnold's opinion of Bunsen, in whose character he found " God's graces and gifts " to be united.[106]

Seeking in after years to account for Dr. Arnold's high admiration of Bunsen, Thomas Arnold, Jr., ascribed it largely to Bunsen's scholarly thoroughness, his successful efforts to establish a comprehensive Protestant Church in Prussia, and his association with the German historian Barthold Niebuhr.[107] He might well have added Bunsen's combination of piety and erudition. In spite of the great learning which Bunsen had amassed at Göttingen, Berlin, Paris, and elsewhere, he avoided the barren rationalism characteristic of many erudite German religious thinkers of the time.[108] It was this ability which helped him later to become "unofficial leader of continental Protestantism." [109] In the years after Arnold's death, he also exercised some liberalizing influence in England through his Biblical researches, which were the subject of one of the *Essays and Reviews* of 1860 (Storr, p. 435). Partly through his friendship with Arnold and his diplomatic work in England, Bunsen had by then become well known in English scholarly circles. It is a mark of Arnold's judgment that he recognized Bunsen's ability some years before he had written the works for which he became famous.

Bunsen rewarded the good opinions of his friend by a stimulating criticism of Arnold's religious, political, and historical writings and by calling Arnold's attention to developments in German theology and history which paralleled the Englishman's work. For example, on several occasions the two men seriously discussed Arnold's controversial theory of the Christian State which Bunsen found himself unable to accept.[110] It is noteworthy that one of several of Arnold's attempts to make the ramifications of this theory clear is addressed to Bunsen (MWA, pp. 491 ff.). Again, Bunsen read Arnold's newspaper editorials to English workers with the feeling that he himself would have taken a "different line"—perhaps addressing the Tory upper classes instead. Yet he could not believe that Arnold favored " levelling " tendencies, as he wrote in a highly colored passage which gives some idea of the man's moral intensity:

> . . . you . . . will never bend the knee before the Trinity of the Utilitarians—the idol of shallowness;—in which Washington is the Father, Franklin the Son, Steam the *Pneuma*; and, further, Lafayette the John, Robespierre the Paul, and Napoleon the Mahomet! [111]

On the subject of Church reform the two men could find much on which to agree. Bunsen hailed Arnold's writings on Church reform, believing as did the Englishman that liturgical and administrative reforms were necessary to save the Anglican Church from disestablishment.[112] Similarly, he agreed with Arnold that comprehension of dissenters was the very course of action required to save the Church in the 1830's. He himself had been active in attempts to reunite the Prussian Lutheran and Calvinistic Churches and could therefore compare notes with Arnold on a program for comprehension (Owen, pp. 28-29).

In a measure which John Henry Newman said " shattered [his] faith in the Anglican Church " (*Apologia*, p. 146), Bunsen in 1841 succeeded in negotiating between Prussia and England an agreement which made concrete the theory of comprehension in Church matters on which he and Arnold agreed. According to the plan, a Protestant Jerusalem Bishopric was established to be filled by a clergyman who should subscribe both to Anglican articles and to the Augsburg Confession of Prussian Protestantism. In such a measure, which anticipated modern ecumenical thinking, Arnold delightedly saw the fulfillment of the fundamental principle of his Church reform pamphlet:

> . . . the Protestant Church of Jerusalem will comprehend

persons using different Liturgies, and subscribing different Articles of Faith; and it will sanction these differences, and hold both parties to be equally its members. (*Life*, II, 283-84.)

Also through his friendship with Bunsen, Arnold was able to compare his own thinking on Biblical criticism with the latest intellectual developments on the continent. Along with his friend, Arnold deplored " the principle of the division of labour carried into excess " among German theologians like D. F. Strauss, whose *Leben Jesu* appeared in 1835 (*Life*, II, 61). With Bunsen also, Arnold could appreciate the efforts of other German theologians like Karl Ullman and Friedrich Umbreit, who in 1828 founded the German periodical *Theologische Studien und Kritiken* with the special intention of combating the rationalistic theology associated with the great universities of Bonn and Göttingen.[113] As early as 1835, Arnold was reading this work, which he characterized as a remarkable combination of " the spirit of love with the spirit of wisdom " (*Life*, I, 414). Again, like Bunsen, Arnold could discuss his agreements and disagreements with Friedrich Schleiermacher, whose *Critical Essay on the Gospel of St. Luke*, translated into English in 1825, was prefaced by an account of continental Biblical scholarship on the Gospels.[114] Arnold was in basic sympathy with the efforts of Bunsen, Schleiermacher, Ullman, and Umbreit to separate the spiritual principle of scripture from its temporal expression.[115]

Though it cannot be claimed that Arnold was first made aware of the work of either rationalistic or devout German theologians by Bunsen, he did profit throughout the period of his correspondence with Bunsen from the latter's critical acumen fostered by wide reading in continental theology. Together the two men planned a work on prophecy and a critical edition of the Greek New Testament.[116] Though the completion of these projects was prevented by Arnold's death, doubtless they would have reflected the "union of philological, historical, and philosophical research all to minister to divine truth," which Arnold found to be the most attractive of Bunsen's ideas (*Life*, I, 411-12). During the 1830's when Arnold was bitterly assailed for his scriptural views by the conservative party of Hurrell Froude,[117] Bunsen's sympathetic and intellectually stimulating correspondence was doubtless of great value to him. It was his friendship with Bunsen, together with his education, Lake Country associations, and historical researches which chiefly fitted him to speak on the religious and political questions of his time. His intellectual preparations enabled him to deal with problems of Biblical interpretation scarcely perceived by many of his fellow countrymen.

Arnold and the Bible

"As THINGS NOW ARE, a man cannot prosecute a critical inquiry as to the dates and authors of the books of Scripture, without the fear of having his Christian faith impeached should his conclusions in any instance be at variance with common opinion." So wrote Thomas Arnold in 1831 in his "Essay on the Right Interpretation and Understanding of the Scriptures" (*Sermons*, II, 421). He wrote with good reason, for it was precisely his own critical inquiries which evoked John Henry Newman's doubt on one occasion that Dr. Arnold was a Christian.[1] The expression of that doubt sums up as well as anything could, the short-sightedness and insularity of most of the English clergy of the time. All too often, their attitude was one of "hostility to changes whose advent nothing could prevent."[2] Unlike many of his clerical contemporaries, however, Arnold, who shared neither their abhorrence to change, their cultural limitations, nor their reliance on outmoded forms, perceived a great challenge to the Christian religion in England and set himself to meet it.

The challenge was threefold. It included a questioning of the Bible as a source of religious authority, a dissatisfaction with the Church of England because of its exclusive-

ness, inefficiency, and " priestly inutilities," [3] and an inclina-
tion to deny the relevance of religion to political affairs.
Arnold's writings on Church reform and Christian politics,
the second and third of these matters, will be considered in
subsequent chapters. Since his views on the Bible are basic
to an understanding of his religious and political thought,
they will be discussed first.

THE CRISIS OF BELIEF

As has been previously suggested, Arnold's education,
associations with the poets of the Lake Country, historical
researches, and contacts with foreign scholars were such as
to make him sensitive to intellectual trends at home and
abroad. Particularly was this true of ideas which had a
bearing on religion. It is therefore to be expected that in a
time when British theology was notably lagging behind
that of the continent in meeting the ever-growing demands
of the intellect Arnold should have used his knowledge to
meet difficulties of which many English clergymen were
only dimly aware. Especially disquieting to Arnold were
the problems raised for Christian belief by the work of continental Biblical scholars and British and foreign scientists.
By the last quarter of the eighteenth century, German
orientalists and classical scholars had begun to point out
internal inconsistencies in the Scriptures which seemed to
suggest that they were no more free from error than any
other ancient work. From about 1800, German critical historians subjected the alleged fulfillments of Biblical prophecy to tests which indicated that some " prophecies " were
probably priestly interpolations. From about 1830, advances in geological investigation and theory suggested that
natural processes followed a course incompatible with

Biblical accounts of the Creation. Finally, during the first forty years of the century, progress in the sciences of biology, medicine, and physics engendered such a respect for the idea of natural " laws " that the evidence for miraculous suspensions of these " laws " was subjected to much closer scrutiny than previously.[4] One result of all this work was a revolution in men's attitudes toward the Bible.

The way for this revolution had been paved prior to 1780 by Lessing's publication of Reimarus' *Wolfenbüttel Fragments*, an elaborate attack on religion which among other things offered proof that the Resurrection was a fable. Lessing, whose inclinations previously had not been atheistic or even fully agnostic, found it necessary to defend this publication in a series of forceful pamphlets whose ulterior effect was " to eradicate the notion of Biblical interpretation more thoroughly from men's minds in Germany than anywhere else " (Benn, I, 181). By 1801, Henry Crabb Robinson, later an intimate member of the Wordsworth-Arnold circle, was able to report from his travels in Germany that many German clergymen disbelieved in the Gospel miracles and put their trust wholly on the moral doctrines of Christianity.[5]

German research into the formation of the Biblical canon also tended to discount the idea of plenary inspiration of the Bible. Instrumental in this work was Johann Semler (1725-91), who maintained that there was a lack of evidence for any inspiration of the compilers of the canon and denied that the canonical books were preserved or selected miraculously (Storr, p. 171). Of similar effect was the work of Johann Gottfried Eichhorn (1752-1827), whom E. B. Pusey heard lecture on the Pentateuch and the Pauline Epistles in 1825. The great Tractarian was struck by Eichhorn's " total insensibility to the real religious import " of the Biblical books.[6] Eichhorn, a Göttingen professor, published a study of the New Testament which propounded the theory of a primitive Gospel source utilized by the canonical writers. His published work on the Old Testament shows a frank treatment of the Scriptures as literature and sets forth his contention that the documents of the Old Testament had undergone constant re-editing.[7] The wide acceptance of this contention helped to discredit evidence for alleged Biblical prophecy, one of the important "proofs" of the plenary inspiration of the Bible.

In 1835 the rationalist critique was brought to bear on the life of Christ. In that year appeared the first volume of David Strauss's *Leben Jesu*, a work which soon became notorious for its complete denial of supernatural influences in the biography of Christ, its reduction of much of the Gospel story to myth, and its treatment of Jesus as rather the creation of the Church than its creator. Although George Eliot was impelled to translate this work into English in 1846, she could not do so without finding its rationalistic tone repellent at some points.[8] Strauss sought to dissociate himself from all previous schools of Biblical criticism, but there can be little doubt that his argument that Christianity was rather a " ' mental ' product than a piece of history " [9] was damaging to contemporary orthodox belief. In the powerful blow which it dealt to the still widely held doctrine of the inerrancy of Scripture, Strauss's work can be regarded as a culmination of the whole critico-historical movement which then appeared to make the perpetuance of religious belief no longer possible.

The findings of investigators in the physical sciences had a similar effect. Although the " warfare between science and theology " (Andrew White so entitled his study of the relation between scientific progress and religious belief) had not in Arnold's time reached the intensity that it was later to do with the publication of Darwin's *Origin of Species* (1859), certain preliminary skirmishes had taken place. From the very beginning of the century a new idea of nature and of man had begun to develop. To a considerable degree, the change was the result of a sharp delimitation of the field of scientific inquiry to what could be experimentally verified. Frequently the resulting focus was on the minute in physics, biology, and medicine. The conclusions of Young on the character of light (1801), Dalton on the atomic constitution of matter (1802), Liebig on the importance of organic chemistry (1826), Schleiden and Schwann on the cellular structure of plants and animals (1838), and Muller on the purely materialistic composition of the human body (1842), are all exemplary of the intellectual current which was moving toward the mechanistic explanation of all phenomena by the operation of scientific " law." [10]

None of these, however, had such direct effect on religious thought as the work of a British geologist, Sir Charles Lyell. In 1830, Lyell published the first volume of a work whose title is indicative of its thesis: *Principles of Geology: being an Attempt to Explain the Former Changes of the Earth's Surface by Reference to Causes Now in Operation.* Lyell, a former pupil of William Buckland whose Oxford lectures on geology and mineralogy had also been attended by Thomas Arnold, advanced theories which undercut those long used to support the Biblical account of Creation. Until the appearance of Lyell's work, the idea of Special Creation had been widely accepted. [11] A conservative school of geologists calling themselves " catastrophists " adhered to a view of natural creation and development through a series of great " catastrophes " which could be so understood as to harmonize with the Biblical account.

Lyell rejected the catastrophist theories and offered strong arguments that the processes of nature were marked by gradual development according to a principle which he called " uniformitarianism." By so doing, he provided the intellectual climate for the acceptance of Darwin's work on evolution.[12] In addition, the uniformitarian theory not only brought the historicity of the Genesis account into question, but by suggesting that geological evolution extended through great tracts of time, also discredited the chronologies of Archbishop Ussher and others who had tried to show that Scripture was consonant with history.

The combined effects of this series of developments were such as to force English clergymen into the fortress of tradition where they " had the anguish of seeing the outworks carried one by one."[13] For a time traditional religious belief was protected by rather widespread ignorance of intellectual developments on the continent.[14] When rationalism became too obvious to be overlooked, however, most British clergymen could only assert their beliefs that the Bible was inspired either wholly or at least sufficiently to preserve the Scriptures from any but copyists' errors. The chief " proofs " of this inspiration were to be found in the Biblical record of miracles and prophecies. Miracles were thought to be the mark of Divine authorship of the revelation, and the fulfillment of prophecies the best indication of the infallibility of the scriptural records. Accordingly, since Christian belief was thought to depend on Biblical inspiration, the acceptance of the results of criticism was widely regarded as equivalent to unsound faith and hostility toward the Church.[15] So powerful was the will to believe and so profound the confusion between religious and scientific matters that attempts were made on

the part of Churchmen to explain the findings of the geologists by suggesting that God had created the fossils which
were discovered in rock formations.[16]

Only a few Englishmen were by learning and temper
capable of dealing effectively with the problems posed for
Christian belief by the work of the German critics and
the scientists. The work of S. T. Coleridge has already
been mentioned. This, however, did not come to light
until 1840. Prior to that date perhaps only Connop Thirlwall, Julius Charles Hare, and Henry Hart Milman (1791-
1868) in Arnold's time were equipped to approach the
problem of Biblical inspiration. For various reasons they
did not do so to any significant extent. All of these men
were personally known to Arnold, however, and through
their learning may well have enriched Arnold's own treatments of the problem, though I have found no evidence of
his intellectual borrowing.

Thirlwall, while still a layman, had in 1825 published
Schleiermacher's *Essay on Luke* with an important introduction in which he suggested that Scripture was inspired
only " in the continual presence and action of what is
most vital and essential in Christianity itself." [17]   This
view, though " an immense advance on current traditional
theory," was expounded in a work whose appeal was limited
to " the circle of the learned." [18]   Thirlwall's later work,
published after he became a clergyman, was more conservative in tendency as evidenced by his opposition to *Essays
and Reviews* (1860), " the revival of the liberal spirit " in
Anglican theology.[19]   Thirlwall's friend Julius Hare was an
ardent disciple of S. T. Coleridge and a profound student
of German literature. Though he had perhaps the finest
private library of German theological literature in England,[20] Hare was lacking in the power of independent

thought and memorable expression which would have enabled him to meet the religious needs of the times.[21] H. H. Milman, an abler man than Hare, was the author of a series of weighty historical works including *History of the Jews* (1829) and *History of Latin Christianity* (1854-55). The first of these was widely attacked because of its assimilation of sacred to profane history. On the whole, however, Milman endeavored to show the spiritual greatness of Christianity irrespective of the verbal inspiration of the Bible.[22] He differed from Arnold in failing to provide for the needs of those intellectually unfitted to profit from his erudite works.

To Arnold, dissatisfied alike with the Germans whose criticism showed them to be *einseitig* in their lives and philosophies and with the narrow bibliolatry of British Evangelical clergymen who interpreted St. Paul " no better than they would interpret Aristotle," it became clear that a sound approach to Biblical interpretation was a great need of the time.[23] Otherwise, when the findings of the critics and the scientists became popular knowledge, how was the edifice of belief to endure?

ARNOLD'S BIBLICAL CRITICISM

Arnold's answers to the problems confronting him are to be seen in a series of essays, exegetical works, and sermons written from 1825 to 1842. The most important of these are " Essay on the Right Interpretation and Understanding of the Scriptures " (1831), *Sermons on Prophecy* (with an Introduction and notes, 1839), and *Sermons Chiefly on the Interpretation of Scripture* (1827-40), published posthumously. These are supplemented by essays in the *Englishman's Register* (1831), a preface on the study

of theology and a note on atheism in the third volume of
Sermons (1834), and notes on rationalism and inspiration
in *Christian Life, Its Course, Its Hindrances, and Its Helps*
(1841). These works were principally devoted to the accomplishment of two main purposes: (1) the demonstration
that the Bible was not historically discredited because it
was sometimes erroneous and, in the technical sense, uninspired, and (2) the demonstration that the primary value
of the Bible was independent of critical and scientific
considerations.

Arnold's study of Niebuhr's *History of Rome* made him
forcibly aware of the need of showing the Bible's historical
validity in spite of its lack of plenary inspiration. He cen-
sured Niebuhr for his failure to approach the Scriptures in
a " teachable and humble spirit." In 1825, Arnold suggested that this shortcoming was traceable to Niebuhr's acquaintance with German latitudinarian theologians (MWA,
pp. 397-98). Though he did not name them, it is probable
that Arnold was referring to the school of rationalistic
scholars best exemplified by Eichhorn. Such men, as Arnold
afterwards wrote of Schleiermacher, were inclined to allow
" small objections to prevail over greater confirmations "
(*Life* [1901], p. 371). As a result, German theology was
marked by a " covert rationalism " particularly noticeable
in the " coldness and irreverence of tone " of Biblical
commentaries.[24]

Arnold was doubtless conscious that this rationalistic
criticism not only made belief in the plenary inspiration
of the Scriptures difficult but by its tone suggested that
the Bible was historically discredited and hence not a valid
ground for Christian belief. He therefore urged the formation of a British school of Biblical criticism to offset the
effects of the German work:

... if we would hope to restrain that wildness of criticism on theological subjects which is too prevalent in Germany, we must learn to tolerate among ourselves a sober freedom of honest and humble inquiry; our censures at present lose some of their weight as proceeding from a national school too little accustomed to question old opinions to be able fairly to judge when they are questioned without reason. (MWA, p. 398.)

His own opinion was that " freedom of honest and humble inquiry " would lead men to the recognition that the case for plenary inspiration was not defensible. In a letter of March 1827 to John Tucker, Arnold referred to an earlier conversation in which he had offended Tucker by arguing against the plenary inspiration of the Old Testament. He felt bound to point out that the Bible had once been held an infallible authority in matters of physical science. Since that claim had been exploded, why insist on its full inspiration as to historical matters (*Life*, I, 84). Such a view, which does not seem especially liberal today, was shocking in a time when a leading clergyman could write that it was impossible even to imagine material error in the Bible.[25] The significant thing was that Arnold was able to maintain this advanced attitude toward Biblical inspiration and at the same time assure Tucker of his deep reverence for the Scriptures and his desire to make them a force in his day to day life. That he could do this suggests that he was confident of the historicity of the Gospels. He explicitly stated this opinion in 1829 in a letter to Henry Hart Milman:

It is the mere want of Faith which impotently longs for the assurance of an imagined inspiration, and cannot be satisfied with the moral probability which exists in a human narrative when supported by the ordinary laws of evidence.[26]

A heightened sense of the inroads of rationalism made him doubly anxious to enforce his own beliefs on the matter of the Bible's historicity. In a sermon preached between 1829 and 1832, he warned that "the question between Christianity and unbelief is now assuming a form essentially different from that it wore in the last century. . . ." He suggested that a lingering deism, the legacy of the eighteenth century, had given way to an even more dangerous skepticism, atheism, and self-centeredness (*Sermons*, II, 164-67). In fact, he so feared the breakdown of belief in the Bible as a source of religious authority that in 1831 he even treated the subject of scriptural interpretation in newspaper articles, hoping thereby to extend the range of his influence beyond Rugby.[27] In a series of papers published in the *Englishman's Register* he undertook the difficult task of showing that even Genesis, the most nearly discredited of all Biblical books, was substantially historical in spite of its apparent moral anomalies and its darker, perhaps allegorical or parabolical, aspects (MW, pp. 130-65). Implicit in these essays is Arnold's recognition that plenary inspiration could no longer be insisted on.

About the same time, he announced his intention of publishing an "Essay on the Right Interpretation and Understanding of the Scriptures" specifically designed to meet the spiritual needs of young educated laymen who Arnold thought required "better satisfaction to the working of their minds than . . . is commonly given them." [28] These, Arnold wrote, were all too likely to be pained by the discovery of inconsistencies in a work which they had been taught to regard as necessarily flawless (*Sermons*, II, 377-

78). As a young man, Arnold had himself experienced religious doubts about another matter and had probably felt at firsthand the futility of trying to ignore or stifle them. John Keble's advice to him at that time to " put down the objections by main force " could scarcely serve as a model for the present occasion (*Life*, I, 22). Instead of proffering similar counsel Arnold proposed to make clear a set of principles which would meet the intellectual needs of the thoughtful reader. In the course of his essay, he took up the question of inspiration which he was coming to see as the central one in maintaining Christianity as a force in England.[29]

In a discussion of the alleged improbabilities of Biblical narratives, Arnold maintained that even proven errors would not " invalidate the *truth of revelation*, but merely the *inspiration of the historical record of it*." He said that most of the objections which had been brought against the various books of the Bible proved nothing about their basic truth:

> It is only the *inspiration* of the books of the Scripture, and not their general *truth*, and far less the truth of the revelations recorded in them, that is, or can be, affected by the great majority of objections, critical, scientific, historical, and chronological, which have been brought at different times against various parts of the Bible. By the eagerness with which they have been urged and repelled, one would imagine that our Christian faith depended upon their issue, whereas in fact it has been totally unconcerned in the dispute. (*Sermons*, II, 417.)

The real difficulty lay, he wrote, in making the inspiration of Scripture history synonymous with its authenticity so that the disproof of the first was thought to disprove the second. Similarly, he rejected arguments for the inspiration of Old Testament books grounded on the fact that they contained a *record* of prophecies proved to be true:

> . . . is it not as absurd to argue the inspiration of the history from the truth of the facts contained in it, as to argue the falsehood of the facts from the history not being inspired? (*Sermons*, II, 419.)

Arnold concluded that the *credibility* of the historical books did not depend on their inspiration unless we are prepared to reject all uninspired narratives as untrue.

By 1831 when he wrote his essay, Arnold could regard a book of the Bible as an authentic and credible *record* of a revelation without insisting that the book was inspired. The important problem of a book's *genuineness* Arnold considered separately. He would regard a book as genuine as long as the author was actually in the circumstances which he gave us to believe that he was. Even if a book was proven not to be written by the author to whom it was ascribed, it might still be genuine as long as the real author had done nothing to cause the mistaken ascription (*Sermons*, II, 418-20). Subsequent years brought no significant change in this opinion as can be seen by Arnold's repudiation in 1841 of the notion of an inspired work as one " to which God has communicated His own perfections " (CLH, p. 486). The consequence of such an assumption was, of course, that the work which contained imperfection could not be inspired. Further, Arnold noticed the tendency (especially common among evangelical churchmen) to make the additional unwarranted assumption that if *all* Scripture was not inspired, then Christianity could not, as he put it, " be true." Arnold's own view was that the Gospels were " divinely framed and superintended " only in the sense that " many of our words and many of our

actions are spoken and done by the inspiration of God's
Spirit. . . ." He observed further that if one were obliged
to relinquish the inspiration of the Scriptures, " their whole
credibility as a most authentic history of the most important facts would remain untouched . . ." (CLH, p. 487).
Although it is probably true that Arnold had no " accurate,
precise, and sharply defined theory of inspiration " (*Life*, I,
221), he was nonetheless able to render a service to his
generation, the demonstration that the fundamental truth
of the Gospel records was not invalidated by errors or
inconsistencies.

His treatment of Biblical miracles well illustrates the
nature of his approach. In Arnold's time, it was customary
to rest the case for the inspiration of the Scriptures largely
on its record of miracles. Consequently, when scientific
investigators began to advance hypotheses which seemed
to explain " miraculous " happenings through the operations
of nature, religious apologists were aghast:

> The further science investigated the secrets of nature's
> working the more was the presence of law or uniformity
> revealed. What room was left for the supernatural? . . . It
> seemed as if God was being excluded from His universe, as
> if secondary causes alone were operative, and no place
> could be found for the direct activity of the divine will.
> (Storr, pp. 140-41.)

Arnold by means of his Oxford studies in natural philosophy and his continuing interest in scientific progress in
medicine and other physical sciences [30] was doubtless aware
of the difficulty of defending the inspiration of the Bible
on the truth of its accounts of miracles. In any case it is
certain that he minimized their importance as a basis of
Christian belief.

In his essay on scriptural interpretation he said that no *attempt* to defend the actuality of miracles need be made against the *a priori* assumption that they were not possible. Arnold observed that against such an assumption, no proof would be acceptable. Again, once the possibility of miracles was admitted, then only one miracle need be subjected to proof. As far as religion was concerned, the Resurrection of Christ was the crucial miracle:

> If this be false, the truth of all the other miracles recorded in Scripture would not warrant our faith as Christians; if it be true, the falsehood of all the rest would be no excuse for our renouncing the Gospel. (*Sermons*, II, 407-408.)

He considered the circumstances of this central miracle in a sermon in which he adduced as evidence for its occurrence the fact that Jesus had prophesied his Resurrection, thus making it the special interest of the Jews to see not only that he was dead, but also that his body was not spirited away by disciples. There was also the Roman efficiency which by the spear thrust eliminated the possibility of a protracted swoon:

> In the first place, the centurion and soldiers appointed for that very purpose examined his body, and found that it was dead: yet, to make sure of it, so little was their inclination to make a false report in order to save Jesus, one of them pierced his side with his spear—the Roman pilum— the shaft of which was four inches wide, and which made therefore, a wound so large, that, as appears afterwards, a hand might be thrust into it. (*Sermons*, III, 135.)

He further pointed out the inevitable effect of the cerements of the time. From his examination he found the testimony of the Resurrection wholly satisfactory according to the canons of internal evidence in use among historians (*Sermons*, III, 136).

In 1842 Arnold took up the question again. In speaking of the credibility of miracles recounted in Bede's history, he had occasion to contrast the external evidence in favor of these with the evidence attesting Biblical accounts of miracles. Although he rejected most of those of which Bede wrote, Arnold found the Biblical ones more credible. He rested his case in part on his knowledge of Roman culture:

> The miracles of the Gospel and those of later history do not . . . stand on the same ground of external evidence; I cannot think that the unbelieving spirit of the Roman world in the first century was equally favourable to the origination and admission of stories of miracles, with the credulous tendencies of the middle ages. (LMH, p. 133.)

He suggested further that, considering the character of the Christian revelation, the absence of miracles accompanying it " would have been far more wonderful than their presence." His position was that they were possible and credible if well-attested, but by no means necessary for acceptance of revelation. Indeed, he pointed out that it was not that we believe in the Gospel because of its accompanying miracles, but that we accept the possibility of miracles because of our belief in the Gospel. The whole effect of his writing on the matter was therefore to divorce belief in the Gospel from belief in the necessary truth of the miracles.

For similar reasons, Arnold was dissatisfied with the efforts of contemporary British theologians to " prove " Biblical inspiration by the historical fulfillment of prophecy. By means of his own studies in history and theology he had come to realize that such attempts tended to be fanciful and, as a consequence, really weakened the Christian position. As early as 1825 he expressed this opinion in a letter to John Tucker:

> My own notion is, that people try to make out from prophecy too much of a detailed history, and thus I have never seen a single commentator who has not perverted the truth of history to make it fit the prophecy. (*Life,* I, 77.)

This attitude was also reflected in Arnold's *Sermons on Prophecy* in which he specifically maintained that the function of Biblical prophecy was not the anticipation of history. For this reason, he did not favor attempts to demonstrate the inspiration of the Bible by literal fulfillment. He suggested that prophecy was dual in nature: it was the utterance of a " preacher of righteousness to his own generation," and, at the same time, a statement of spiritual significance "not relating to particular places, persons and times, but to pure good and evil in all times and everywhere."[31] In neither instance, therefore would literal fulfillment be indicative of Biblical inspiration.[32] The result of his work on prophecy was such as to render innocuous the critical work which by exploding the historical truth of prophecy had imperiled belief in the validity of the Bible as a trustworthy account of God's revelation.

In Arnold's work on prophecy as in that on miracles and on inspiration in general, he turned to the age-old resource of educated men, the making of necessary distinctions. His special gift as an interpreter of Scripture lay in his ability to distinguish between " that Christian faith, which is the guide and comfort of our lives, and a variety of questions, historical, critical, scientific . . . connected

with the parts of that volume from which the grounds of
our faith are derived " (*Sermons*, II, 424-25). His ability
to make such a distinction in specific instances was based
on a clearly apprehended difference between the operations of faith and intellect. In a note to the fourth volume
of his *Sermons* (1841), he put this in Coleridgean terms:

> It is important to bear in mind the distinction which Cole-
> ridge enforces so earnestly between the understanding and
> the reason. . . .[33]

In his description of the proper work of the " understanding," Arnold made it clear that he was using the term in
a sense usually attached to " reason " or the " rational
faculty ":

> [The work of the understanding] is this—that it should
> inquire into the truth of the outward signs of revelation;
> which outward signs being things necessarily visible and
> sensible, fall within the province of its judgment. Thus
> understanding judges the external witnesses of a revelation;
> if miracles be alleged, it is the business of the understand-
> ing to ascertain the facts of their occurrence; if a book
> claim to be a record of a revelation, it belongs to the un-
> derstanding to make out the origins of this book, the time
> when it was written, who were its authors, and what is the
> first and grammatical meaning of its language. (CLH,
> p. 464.)

Reason, on the other hand, was a direct intuition of the
idea of God. Arnold suggested that this faculty was the
one from which *faith* comes:

> A sign of power exhibited to the senses, might through
> them, dispose the whole man to acknowledge it as divine;
> yet power in itself is not divine; it may be devilish. But
> when reason recognizes that along with this power, there

exist also wisdom and goodness, then it perceives that here
is God: and the worship which, without reason, might
have been idolatry, being now according to reason, is faith.
(CLH, pp. 462-63.)

The implication for him was that though *faith* may exist
without the action of the *understanding* (though never
without that of the *reason*), the understanding should be
employed within its proper sphere (CLH, pp. 463-64).
He defined " rationalism " as " the abuse of the understanding in subjects where the divine and human are
intermingled " (CLH, p. 465).* For Arnold, the route to
true wisdom was also the route to be taken by the Christian
apologist: " Wisdom is gained, not by renouncing or de-
spising the understanding, but by adding to its perfect work
the perfect work of reason, and of reason's perfection,
faith " (CLH, p. 467). As one of his pupils observed,
Arnold served as a fine example to those who were " aware
of the importance of harmonizing the progress of knowledge with Christianity," and, as he added, " of asserting
. . . the objective truths of Christianity and its lifegiving
power. . ." (*Life*, I, 221).

He performed the latter function in his demonstration
that the primary value of the Bible as a great storehouse of

* Cf. J. H. Newman's definition of liberalism: ". . . false liberty
of thought, or the exercise of thought upon matters, in which, from
the constitution of the human mind, thought cannot be brought to
any successful issue. . . . Liberalism then is the mistake of subjecting
to human judgment those revealed doctrines which are in their
nature beyond and independent of it, and claiming to determine on
intrinsic grounds the truth and value of propositions which rest for
their reception simply on the external authority of the Divine
Word " (*Apologia Pro Vita Sua*, ed. A. Dwight Culler [Boston:
Houghton, Mifflin, 1956], p. 271). The two are surprisingly similar,
though Arnold would certainly have wanted to know precisely
by whom the " revealed doctrines " were formulated.

moral truth was independent of critical and scientific considerations. So conceived, the Bible was impregnable against any attack except that of a world which chose to think its moral teachings were obsolete. Much of Arnold's activity was therefore directed at showing the relevance of the Gospel to everyday life. Thomas Hughes caught this in his statement that Arnold taught Rugbeians that they "could not cut [their lives] into slices." [34] Arnold himself put it in one terse sentence:

> Depend upon it, unless your common life is made a part of your religion, your religion will never sanctify your common life. (CLH, p. 329.)

On looking around him, he came to the conclusion that "never at any time since the Gospel was first preached were its peculiar qualities better fitted to the peculiar qualities of the world" (IS, p. 314). He could not imagine "by what strange error" it had happened that the doctrines of the Gospel were regarded as having such slight bearing on religious practice unless it was that "the practice of so many, who call themselves Christians has been unfit to receive them" (*Sermons*, II, 105-106). The word "doctrine" itself he defined not as "truth" but as "efficacy as a means of moral good." From his Biblical studies he concluded that the scriptural idea of doctrine involved a "mixture of direct precept with the revelation of facts or characters calculated to produce a certain moral effect" (MWA, p. 449). Significantly, his discussion of inexplicable passages of Scripture hinges on the ability of the interpreter to "know what to do with a passage, what lesson [he] ought to learn from it. . ." (IS, p. 178).

With these considerations in mind, he sought to provide a means whereby the moral teachings of Scripture could more readily be brought to bear on modern life. The result was a theory of progressive revelation of which his essay on scriptural interpretation (1831) was " probably the first and clearest statement " in nineteenth century England.[35] This theory was implicit in Arnold's writings as early as 1827 when he wrote that he had come to look on the goodness of the Old Testament patriarchs as relative rather than absolute (*Life*, I, 51). Arnold argued that if the standard of goodness rose, the implication was that God was progressively revealing his truth to men. The conduct which does not seem estimable to us did to those living in the time of the patriarchs.

He worked the idea out more fully in his essay of 1831. By means of it, he attempted to explain such difficult Biblical problems as the reason for God's command to Saul to slaughter the Amalekites. Although modern men would regard the slaughter as an atrocity, to Saul, it represented " self-denial: destruction for God instead of exploitation for Saul's own enrichment." [36]

To Arnold the problem was clearly that of God's accommodation to the moral state of mankind:

> The revelations of God to man were gradual and adapted to his state at the several periods when they were successively made. And on the same principles, commands were given at one time which were not given at another. . . . (*Sermons*, II, 383.)

In keeping with this doctrine, imperfect individuals were treated as good and just " if up to the extent of their knowledge they endeavoured to do what was right " (*Sermons*, II, 387).

The acceptance of this principle led to certain further developments in Arnold's theory of Biblical interpretation.

For one thing, it meant that one could not learn how God's will should be interpreted in the nineteenth century directly from what God had allowed in Biblical times. Arnold pointed out on one occasion that the Bible contained not truths but lessons, "medicines fitted for our particular want" (*Sermons*, III, 356).* The problem was to discover what the lesson was in each case. Arnold sought to help his readers do this by giving them a rule which would distinguish the eternal principles in Scripture from their temporal settings. The principles could then serve as a guide to the modern believer:

> . . . a command given to one man, or to one generation of men, is, and can be, binding upon other men and other generations, only so far forth as the circumstances in which both are placed are similar. (*Sermons*, II, 380.)

Those commandments which carried an eternal and universal obligation related to the points in which men of any time were alike. Arnold used the second commandment of the Decalogue as an illustration of this principle, pointing out that any were violators of it who " image . . . an object of worship without the warrant of God." In other words, Arnold maintained that this universally binding commandment was broken by any who thought of God as less severe in His condemnation of sin, or more tolerant of disobedience than He had revealed Himself to be (*Sermons*, II, 392).

---

* Arnold was strongly opposed to the literal reading of isolated passages as a guide to conduct. He pointed out that it was necessary to consider both the particular circumstances of those to whom a passage was addressed and other, apparently contradictory passages whose teachings might well be supplementary to it. Cf. CLH, pp. 374-75; CLC, p. 359 cited by John O. Waller, " The Arnolds and Particular Truth," pp. 163-64. See also IS, pp. 449, 464.

On the other hand, commandments transitory in nature and hence not directly binding on modern Englishmen nevertheless might be of universal application indirectly; that is, knowing God's will in a particular circumstance, they might employ " parity of reasoning " to know what it would be in other circumstances:

> Namely, the same when the circumstances are the same; analogous when the circumstances are analogous; and absolutely contrary, when they also are contrary. (*Sermons*, II, 380-81.)

The modern significance of the Abraham-Isaac story would therefore be that fathers may be " called upon—to sacrifice their children's fairest earthly prospects in order to obey the will of God " (*Sermons*, II, 397).

Arnold thought that the application of these rules would enable the student to use the Old Testament to his own moral advantage. Through their use, he would not only be able to apply the principles implicit in God's dealings with other men, to his own case, but would also be able to avoid applications to his own situation of rules which he was " never intended to obey " (*Sermons*, II, 381).

He was well aware of the weight of responsibility put on the individual by such an interpretation of the Bible:

> . . . there is a serious responsibility for everyone to determine how far what he reads in the Bible concerns himself; and no doubt . . . if a man chooses to cheat his conscience in such a matter, he might do it easily; but the responsibility is one which we cannot get rid of. . . . (*Life*, I, 365.)

He recognized three important aids to the Christian believer in making use of the Scriptures as a guide to con-

duct: a ministry with sufficient humanistic learning to dis-
engage the Bible's eternal teachings from their transient
historical expression, a conscientious testing of religious
views by the teachings and spirit of Christ, and "an experimental knowledge of the power and living truth of the
Gospel" (*Sermons*, II, 379). The first of these was assumed
by his exegetical theory of progressive revelation, for he
who would make clear the teachings of the Bible must
necessarily possess the historical tact required to distinguish
the essential from the accidental in Scripture. As he wrote
in an essay of 1834, however, Arnold found few British
clergymen with the necessary culture properly to perform
their function as interpreters of the Bible. He suggested
that the difficulty originated in the mistaken emphasis in
clerical education. Too much time was given to controversial theology at the expense of exegesis:

> It is not enough considered, that the great matter of
> Christianity, the way of saving souls, must be learnt from
> the Scriptures alone; and that by getting at a full under-
> standing of them we are getting at the only means of dis-
> covering Christian truth. (*Sermons*, III, xxii.)

As a result, energies which might better be expended in
making Christianity a vital force in England were being
dissipated in clerical squabbles.

Arnold's own advice to theologians was that they should
study not only the Scriptures and the philological and anti-
quarian works required to interpret them, but also the
master productions of secular literature:

> . . . the Scriptures, to remind us without ceasing that
> Christianity in itself is wholly free from the foolishness
> thrown around it by some of its professors; the great
> works of human genius, to save us from viewing the

Scriptures themselves through the medium of ignorance and prejudice, and lowering them through our perverse interpretations, in order to make them countenance our errors. (*Sermons*, III, xv.)

In addition to the Scriptures which furnished the clergy-man with his " principles of teaching and acting," Thucy-dides, Tacitus, Plato, Cicero, and the *Ethics* and *Politics* of Aristotle were to be studied as a " means of keeping the mind fresh and comprehensive." Finally, he recommended a thorough knowledge of history as a source of political wisdom and as another means " to arrive at the truth as it is in Christ." Arnold maintained that such an education would be far more valuable to the interpreter of Scripture than studies which laid great stress upon " points of contro-versy between Christians and Christians " (IS, p. 86).

Arnold's own exegetical practice is illustrative of his endeavor to make clear the moral relevance of the Scrip-tures to his time. Through use of the principle of progres-sive revelation he was able to derive moral lessons from passages in the Old Testament which would have been ex-tremely troublesome when approached in any other way. For example, in a sermon on Jael, Arnold found a lesson of sincere, though unenlightened obedience:

. . . for ourselves, how great is the lesson here given us of the necessity of a sincere obedience. For if the single-minded man be accepted, even amid much moral ignor-ance, what becomes of those who are double-minded amidst abundant knowledge? (IS, p. 86.)

Again, through his principle of analogical circumstances, he was able directly to apply Christ's parables of the fig-tree and the growing corn:

. . . the two parables teach us different lessons, each

making that of the other complete. We should do all that we can do, and then leave the event to God with confidence. To provide for the future by any present act is wise and good; but to be anxious about the future, where no act of ours can affect it, is a weakness and a want of faith. The parable of the fig-tree teaches us the duty of the first, the parable of the growth of corn while men slept, teaches us the foolishness of the second. (IS, p. 189.)

In more theoretical criticism he was careful to oppose interpretations of Scripture which, because perverse, appeared unlikely to lead to moral edification. For example, he warned against " pushing too far our notion of God's personality." Men tended to be influenced by ideas of human personality when thinking of God and thereby might be led into errors about God's will for them. For this reason, Arnold maintained that one ought not to anthropomorphize God and should not " inquire into the relations of the Divine nature except towards its own works " (*Sermons*, III, 402-403). At the same time, he disapproved of " pantheistic doctrines " such as the idea of " a constitution of things favouring virtue and discouraging vice, and requiring men, as parts of the great whole, to act in conformity with it, and to support its tendencies, . . ." Although he recognized that such ideas were " little more than the strong recoil of anthropomorphism," and were less denials of truth than " awkward and obscure expression[s]" of it, he nevertheless suggested that they had " an injurious moral tendency, inasmuch as by removing all the analogies which might help us to conceive of our relations to God, they [could not] but destroy religious affections . . ." (*Sermons*, III, 397-98).

As a further aid to Christian believers in making use of the Scriptures as a guide to conduct, he urged the testing of religious views against the teachings and spirit of Christ. Observing that most men have a tendency to some particular " idol," fanaticism, or superstition in religious matters, Arnold maintained that these shortcomings (as well as that of unbelief) could be overcome by singleminded devotion to Christ. He suggested that in comparison to worship of Christ, attachment to estimable but lesser objects of worship such as truth, justice, charity, and benevolence would be recognized as spiritually inadequate (CLH, pp. 217-20). For this reason, he found particular comfort in the fact that all surviving teachings of Christ were available in the " one small volume of the four Gospels. . . ." From these might be gathered a " full specimen " of his teachings, the spirit of which was compassion, and the object, to save what was lost (CLC, pp. 242-43). If one remembered that Christ habitually employed parabolical language, he might then understand His words " in their true light and their true bearings . . ." and from them, ascertain the Divine will for himself.[37] From close attention to the " direct practical precepts " of Jesus as expressed in the parables and the Sermon on the Mount, Christians might expect to clear up the confusions and differences which had arisen as the result of undue attention to doctrines " supposed to be deduced by a fair process of reasoning from certain expressions in the Scriptures. . ." (MWA, pp. 450-51). The whole tendency of this advice is to facilitate the use of Scripture as a source of moral guidance.

Another aid to the effective application of the Scriptures was what Arnold called " an experimental knowledge of [their] power and living truth. . . ." In other words, he urged the trial of the truth of the main teachings of Scripture in everyday life, as a means of " possessing the earnest of the Spirit. . . ."[38] He was sure that such a trial would lead to an increasing ability to apply Biblical teachings in the whole range of human experience:

> The broad and principal commandments strike us imme-
> diately; or rather we are made familiar with them from our
> childhood, so that we know them at least, whether we
> practice them or no. But he who, first honestly labouring
> to fulfil these, turns over the volume of the Scriptures to
> learn the finer and more minute features of the Christian
> character, will find something applicable to every part of
> his daily living. . . . (IS, pp. 530-31.)

Because he was aware that in an age when Christianity had " lost many of its artificial supports," its moral influence on modern life might be in jeopardy, Arnold urged his readers to a " real and earnest love of its principles. . ." (*Sermons*, II, 164). This he sought to inculcate by his own teachings:

> Enter life as Christians, and you need not fear lest the
> world will hurry you on too rapidly. There is much to
> learn, much to admire, much to enjoy, much to do. Vast
> powers are at work, vast results producing; do not de-
> spise them, nor yet fear them. Walk amidst them, study
> them, use them; you will not be carried away with their
> intoxication; for on the one hand you see also what there
> is in them of weakness and unworthiness; whilst you see
> and know what is hid from other eyes . . . Christ's king-
> dom advanced in man's salvation. Never at any time,
> since the Gospel was first preached to mankind, were its
> peculiar qualities better fitted to the peculiar evils of the
> world. . . . For let the human mind go on as far as it will,
> and the wisdom of the Gospel still expands before it,
> satisfying its highest refinement as it humbled itself to its
> greatest ignorance. (IS, pp. 313-14.)

By such counsels he hoped to provide a stay for those who

in future years would grapple with the religious and political problems of their time.

ARNOLDISM AND THE LATER NINETEENTH CENTURY

The major results of Arnold's writings on the Bible are not to be seen in any immediate effect on the thought of his day. His essay on scriptural interpretation which he regarded as his most important production, was also the most misunderstood of his writings (*Life*, I, 287). Frequently his views were bitterly attacked by conservative Churchmen who objected to the principle of individual responsibility for moral application of the Scriptures as against interpretation according to ecclesiastical authority.[39]

This consequence is not surprising. Arnold addressed himself chiefly to the future and it was after his own day that the fruits of his teachings were chiefly to be seen. The main continuators of his work were four eminent and widely influential Englishmen, Matthew Arnold, Arthur Penrhyn Stanley, Benjamin Jowett, and Frederick Temple. Largely because each of these men eventually attained a wide hearing, the Arnoldian effort to retain a sense of " the true greatness of Christianity " (the phrase is used as a chapter heading in *Literature and Dogma*) without doing violence to the understanding became widely known in Victorian England. The result was what one writer of the 1890's called the " astonishing *growth* of Dr. Arnold's influence " in the fifty years after his death.[40]

Matthew Arnold's major writings about the Bible amply reflect the teachings of his father. One can find many aspects of *St. Paul and Protestantism* (1870), *Literature and Dogma* (1873), *God and the Bible* (1875), and *Last Essays on Church and Religion* (1877) which lend force to Matthew Arnold's poignant remark to Arthur Stanley that Dr. Arnold's death cut off the " sole source of *information* " of the Arnold family.[41] Along with the many appreciative references to the elder Arnold's work in Matthew Arnold's letters,[42] these parallels suggest that he greatly profited from the example before him of a man who " combined the deepest religious convictions with an accessibility to the light of modern ideas . . . rare indeed in the English clergymen of his day." [43]

Matthew came to think of his own work as something of a continuation and development of his father's teachings. In 1868 he noted with satisfaction his belief that the elder Arnold would have approved of the major part of his critical effort (*Works*, XIV, 171-72). On other occasions he spoke of specific works as reflecting his father's ideas or as extending Dr. Arnold's work to a wider sphere.[44]

Certainly Matthew Arnold was appreciative of the historical acumen which the elder Arnold manifested in the notes to his edition of Thucydides, in his *History of Rome*, and in his *Introductory Lectures on Modern History*, and which he also brought to bear on problems of Biblical interpretation. Some five years before the decade which Matthew devoted to writings about religion, he suggested that his father's great contribution to English religion was in " bringing such a torrent of freshness [to it] by placing history and politics in connection with it " (*Works*, XIV, 65). A few years later he observed that the elder Arnold's " historic sense " saved him from the provinciality of other English clergymen of his day and enabled him to become " wonderfully . . . European " (*Works*, XIV, 189).

No doubt Matthew's projected account of the " impulse which [Thomas Arnold] gave to the life and thought of the generation which felt his influence " (*Works*, XIV,

200) would have included a description of Dr. Arnold's work as Biblical interpreter, for the son stated elsewhere that his father (along with S. T. Coleridge) ministered to the Spirit of the Age in " the exploding of the old notions of literal interpretation in Scripture, and the introducing of a truer method of interpretation " (*Works*, XIV, 210).

That Matthew believed further advocacy of this " truer method " to be necessary may be seen by six aspects of his religious criticism which suggest that it is the full development of principles suggested by Dr. Arnold: (1) rejection of the idea of plenary Biblical inspiration; (2) emphasis on the ethical rather than the metaphysical significance of the Bible; (3) validation of religious doctrines by the teachings of Christ; (4) reference to experience (the " experiential test ") as demonstration of the efficacy of Christian teachings; (5) distrust of anthropomorphic conceptions of God's nature; and (6) considered employment of humanistic learning in Biblical interpretation. Obviously, in view of the wide diffusion of liberal religious ideas in nineteenth century England, no *unique* indebtedness can be demonstrated, especially since Matthew Arnold expressed interest on various occasions in the work of Spinoza, John Smith (the Cambridge Platonist), S. T. Coleridge, C. C. J. Bunsen, Ernest Renan, Arthur Stanley, and Benjamin Jowett.[45] Still, when Matthew's statements about the indebtedness are considered, we are forced to conclude that at least a contributory influence, a predisposition to accept similar ideas from other sources, must be admitted. Moreover, we know that Dr. Arnold's sermons in which his Biblical views were prominently set forth were to Matthew " the most delightful and satisfactory to read of all his writings." [46] Let us therefore now consider each of the six points of comparison separately.

We have already seen that the rejection of the doctrine of the plenary inspiration of the Bible was a major feature of the elder Arnold's criticism. Matthew Arnold's attitude on the same point may be briefly illustrated from *Literature and Dogma*:

> . . . recognition of the liability of the New Testament writers to make mistakes, both of fact and argument, will certainly, as we have said, more and more gain strength, and spread wider and wider. The futility of their mode of demonstration from prophecy . . . will be more and more felt. The fallibility of that demonstration from miracles to which they and all about them attached such preponderating weight, which made the disciples of Jesus believe in him, . . . will be more and more recognized. (*Works*, VII, 141.)

Dr. Arnold's conviction that the Bible should be read "not for truths but for lessons" was also that of his son, who emphasized the ethical rather than the metaphysical significance of the Bible. In the preface to *God and the Bible* Matthew Arnold wrote approvingly of his father's suspicions of "formal and technical" metaphysical speculations by theologians:

> . . . Dr. Arnold, who had a sound historical instinct, could tell at once, from the warnings of this instinct, that theology, which is a series of conclusions upon the history of the Bible, had apprehended that history all wrong; that it was faulty, therefore, in its very base, and so could not be a true theology, a science of the Christian religion, at all. (*Works*, VIII, xxvii.)

Matthew's agreement with his father's view that the Bible's chief value was that of a guide to conduct is patent in the following paragraph from *Literature and Dogma*:

A system of theological notions about personality, essence, existence, consubstantiality, is *artificial* religion, and is the proper opposite to *revealed*; since it is a religion which comes forth in no one's consciousness, but is invented by theologians. . . . The religion of the Bible . . . is well said to be *revealed*, because the great natural truth that "*righteousness tendeth to life*," is seized and exhibited there with such incomparable force and efficacy. (*Works*, VII, 50-51.)

For both men, the crown of the Biblical ethic was to be found in the personality and teachings of Jesus. The elder Arnold was intent that Christ "as set forth to us fully in the Scriptures" be put at the center of religion. Matthew Arnold's view can be seen in the following evaluation of the *logia* of Jesus:

. . . how admirably fitted are Jesus Christ and his precepts to serve as mankind's standing reminder as to conduct,— to serve as men's religion. Jesus Christ and his precepts are found to hit the moral experience of mankind, to hit it in the critical points, to hit it lastingly; and when doubts are thrown upon their really hitting it, then to come out stronger than ever. (*Works*, IX, 189-90.)

Dr. Arnold appealed to experience as proof of the efficacy of Christian teachings and wrote of "an experimental knowledge" of their power. He felt that belief in God's existence, if accepted as an instrumental concept, would "convince us every day more and more that we assumed its truth justly" (*Sermons*, III, 208). Matthew Arnold's use of the same form of persuasion is apparent in the following passage from *Literature and Dogma*:

. . . if, on the other hand, they ask: "How are we to *verify* that there rules an enduring Power, not ourselves, which makes for righteousness?"—we may answer at once: ... *by experience!* It *is* so; try it! (*Works*, VII, 325.)

Again, Matthew had some precedent in his father's work for his distrust of anthropomorphic conceptions of God's nature. Thomas Arnold disapproved of speculations about the precise nature of the Creator, although he thought something could be inferred from the demonstrable sense of moral obligation in man to live up to ideas of "truth, and justice, and excellence, and goodness ..." (Sermons, III, 402-403). Again, though apparently he did not hold "pantheistic" views himself, he was able to recognize some truth in the conception of "a superhuman archetype of virtue in the tendencies of nature" which theoretically, at least, provided "a sanction for man's actions existing out of himself ... a standard to which he is morally bound to conform his being." (Sermons, III, 398-99.) Matthew Arnold's more extreme views on this point may be seen in his celebrated definitions of God in *Literature and Dogma* and in *God and the Bible*: "*The Eternal, not ourselves, that makes for righteousness*" (*Works*, VIII, 26) and "*the stream of tendency by which all things fulfil the law of their being*" (*Works*, VII, 42).

Finally, the Arnolds were alike in their insistence on humanistic learning as a requisite to sound Biblical interpretation. Since both held the proposition that "language at its very best and greatest, is, and can be, but an asymptote of thought ... [that] ... *the law speaks in the tongues of men*," [47] it followed that they agreed on the uses of historical tact in distinguishing the essential from the accidental in Scripture. Dr. Arnold's views on clerical education have already been noted. They were such as to offset sectarian narrowness and perversity, to prevent any partial views of the Bible, and to make possible the "wary" handling which he felt to be necessary in interpretation (*Sermons*, III, xvi, 355-56). Matthew Arnold's opinions were similar.

In *Literature and Dogma* he proffered "*culture*" as the best means of assuring sound Biblical interpretations—"the acquainting ourselves with the best that has been known and said in the world, and thus with the history of the human spirit":

> To understand that the language of the Bible is fluid, passing, and literary, not rigid, fixed, and scientific, is the first step toward a right understanding of the Bible. But to take this first step, some experience of how men have thought and expressed themselves, and some flexibility of spirit, are necessary; and this is culture. (*Works*, VII, xii, xiv.)

In the preface to his final work of religious criticism, *Last Essays*, Matthew Arnold gave utterance to the conviction which most surely marks him as the intellectual heir and creative disciple of his father:

> I am persuaded that the transformation of religion, which is essential for its perpetuance, can be accomplished only by carrying the qualities of flexibility, perceptiveness and judgment, which are the best fruits of letters to whole classes of the community which now know next to nothing of them, and by procuring the application of those qualities to matters where they are never applied now. (*Works*, IX, 174.)

These words epitomize the "attempt conservative and attempt religious" comprised by *St. Paul and Protestantism, Literature and Dogma, God and the Bible*, and *Last*

Essays. The greater genius and literary gifts of the son should not prevent us from seeing that to a considerable, if not precisely determinate degree, this attempt was an outgrowth of Dr. Arnold's teachings.

The elder Arnold's influence is even more obvious in the life and works of Arthur Penrhyn Stanley (1815-81), the author of *Life and Correspondence of Thomas Arnold* (1844) and among the most ardent and accomplished of the Arnoldian disciples.[48] Having developed a fervent boyhood admiration for Arnold at Rugby, Stanley came to think of his teacher as the chief force in his whole intellectual and moral development. Many years after Arnold's death Stanley wrote as follows of the nature and force of that influence:

> The effect of his character, and the lessons of his teaching, have been the stimulus to whatever I have been able to do in the forty years since I left school; and his words come back to me as expressing better than anything else my hopes and fears for this life, and for the life to come.[49]

With " apostolic zeal " Stanley undertook to make the ideas of his master prevail. While holding a series of responsible and influential positions he was able to give Arnold's views wide dissemination. Thus he was successively Tutor of University College, Oxford (1843), Select Preacher to the University (1845), Secretary of the Royal Commission on University Reform (1850), Oxford Professor of Ecclesiastical History (1856-63), and Dean of Westminster (1864-81).[50]   He was, in addition, a considerable influence at court, a prolific writer for the leading reviews of the age, and for a time the chief spokesman for the liberal Broad Church party of Anglicanism. More than one of his critics would have agreed with the judgment of a contemporary who asserted that Stanley " made the Church of the future a present power " or with a half-humorous contemporary description of him as " the little man with such large ideas and with such powers of enlarging other people's." [51]

In most of his major works of Biblical interpretation he stated indebtedness to Dr. Arnold's views. In the preface to his *Sermons and Essays on the Apostolical Age* (1847), he acknowledged his debt to Arnold and explained the few direct references to his works by " vindicating once [and] for all, for the scholars of Arnold, the privilege and pleasure of using his works and adopting his thoughts without the necessity of specifying in every instance the source from which they have been derived." [52] In its acceptance of the findings of Biblical criticism, whether English or continental, and its insistence that the criticism did not destroy the grounds of religion, Stanley's work was thoroughly Arnoldian:

> If criticism destroys much, it creates more. If it cuts away some grounds from our faith, it reconstructs out of the chasm others incomparably more secure. If the sea of doubt has advanced along one part of our coast, it has proportionately receded from another. (P. 6.)

Stanley's later works also are grounded on Arnoldian principles. In particular, his *Lectures on the History of the Jewish Church* (three volumes, 1863-76) embody the principles of the essential historicity of the Bible, the need for a positive approach in Biblical interpretation, the theory of progressive revelation, and the emphasis on ethical content, which were prominent in Dr. Arnold's earlier work.[53] It was this work which Matthew Arnold praised because it fulfilled " the indispensable duty of edifying at the same time that it informed." He observed that in the lectures

Stanley had seized " a truth of criticism " by finding the Biblical narration to be a " substantially historical " work.[54] Such an approach was germane to Dr. Arnold's criticism.

The extent to which Stanley's later thought was marked by Arnoldian influence is also well illustrated by his reaction to two highly controversial works produced by English liberal theologians. Of the epoch-making *Essays and Reviews* (1860) which has been called " the delayed action upon Oxford of Thomas Arnold," [55] Stanley wrote approvingly because, as he said, the work reflected principles for which Arnold had stood. He found that the various essays were linked by the concept of theological development, one of the greatest achievements of nineteenth century theology. This concept had, he felt, received its " first and clearest statement " in England in Arnold's " Essay on the Right Interpretation and Understanding of the Scriptures " (1831).[56] Similarly, in spite of disapproval of his actions by his clerical superiors, Stanley took occasion to defend Bishop Colenso of Natal whose work, *The Pentateuch and Book of Joshua Critically Examined* (1862-79), had questioned the authorship and chronologies of the Mosaic books and had led to charges of heresy against its author.[57] Although Stanley disapproved of the negative emphasis in Colenso's work, he felt obliged in Convocation to oppose the censure of its author.[58] He felt that if the censures were passed, office in the Church of England would then become incompatible with Biblical criticism.

In his fearless defense of reason in religious matters, Stanley was clearly in the Arnoldian tradition. Well might Matthew Arnold write in his elegy on Stanley:

Even as my father, thou—

. . . .

Hast thy commission done; ye both may now
Wait for the leaven to work, the let to end.[59]

To a lesser extent, Dr. Arnold's Biblical views were influential on two other well-known Victorian clergymen,
Benjamin Jowett (1817-93) and Frederick Temple (1821-
1902). Both made their principal contributions to English
Biblical criticism in the controversial *Essays and Reviews*
(1860), a work which to conservative Churchmen like
Bishop Wilberforce seemed to be marked by " infidelity, if
not Atheism." [60] Neither Jowett nor Temple had been
schooled by Dr. Arnold but both had expressed admiration
for him and were acquainted with his works. Jowett, who
later was to become Master of Balliol and a celebrated
classical scholar, received his introduction to Arnoldian
ideas through Stanley, his fellow-student, Oxford colleague,
and lifelong friend. The effect of this introduction was
reinforced by Jowett's attendance at Arnold's Oxford lectures on modern history and by the appreciation of Arnold
by foreign thinkers with whom Jowett came into contact
during tours of the continent.[61] Jowett was a much more
independent thinker than Stanley, however, and far more
extensively grounded in speculative philosophy, especially
that of Hegel. Accordingly, he was rather critical of some
of Arnold's ideas, discriminating in his acceptance of others,
and in some instances was carried beyond views which
Arnold could have accepted. In particular, Dr. Arnold
would have declined to accept either Jowett's view that
one could not talk meaningfully of a physical Resurrection of Christ or his heavily positivistic emphasis on humanity as the most perfect revelation of God.[62] Nevertheless, despite Jowett's often repeated stricture on Dr. Arnold's
" peculiar danger," defined as " not knowing where his
ideas would take other people and ought to take himself,"

he could immediately add a revealing qualification: " Yet had he been living, how we would have nestled under his wings! " (*Abbott and Campbell*, I, 285.)

With his friend Stanley, Jowett undertook the project of translating and commenting on the Pauline epistles, a work " originally inspired by the example of Dr. Arnold " who had begun the same task before his death.[63] The result of the joint effort was Jowett's commentary on Thessalonians, Galatians and Romans (1855) and Stanley's commentary on Corinthians (1855). Of these two works, Jowett's was the more strongly objected to by conservative Churchmen in spite of its unusual success in revealing St. Paul's relations with the Hebraistic and Hellenistic cultures and in spite of the great learning which it displayed. In large measure, the objections were aroused by an essay, " On the Interpretation of Scripture," which Jowett published with his commentary.[64] In his essay, Jowett maintained the Arnoldian position that the Scriptures could best be understood by the methods of interpretation ordinarily used by classical scholars. The essay was republished five years later in *Essays and Reviews* where it had a wider circulation and marked its author as one of the " *septem contra Christum*," as conservative Churchmen tended to regard the contributors to that volume. The essence of Jowett's argument in the essay might well serve as a brief statement of Thomas Arnold's whole conception of the problem confronting the intelligent, thoughtful, and intellectually honest believer:

> . . . as the time has come when it is no longer possible to ignore the results of criticism, it is of importance that Christianity should be seen to be in harmony with them, . . . the Christian religion is in a false position when all the tendencies of knowledge are opposed to it.[65]

Moreover, in the same essay Jowett followed Arnold in rejecting plenary inspiration (pp. 14-22), espousing the theory of progressive revelation (p. 18), suggesting that sectarian differences could be lessened by sound Biblical interpretation (pp. 92-93), and maintaining that the ethical teachings of Scripture were its primary value (p. 98). Though in later life Jowett passed far beyond Arnold's concern with demonstrating the historicity of the happenings recorded in the Gospels, he came more and more in his thinking to approximate the other great tenet of the elder Arnold's thought, the Bible as a guide to practical conduct.[66] Evidently his general comment about Dr. Arnold's notes to his edition of Thucydides would seem to apply as well to Arnold's writings about the Bible: " When a great man undertakes the office of an interpreter, he throws a light on the pages which the mere verbal critic is incapable of communicating." [67]

Jowett dedicated the first two editions of his *Commentary* to Frederick Temple, his younger colleague and friend. Together the two men had been accustomed to discuss exegetical matters during the 1840's. During the same period, Temple, who had lectured on Lucretius, Comte, and Kant, jointly undertook with Jowett what was then a daring project for English clergymen, the translation of Hegel's *Logic*.[68] We may be sure that they also discussed the great religious questions which were then in the air and to which Dr. Arnold had addressed himself. Like Matthew Arnold, Stanley, Jowett, and Arthur Clough, Temple attended Balliol during the period when it was regarded by conservative Churchmen as an " heretical and Arnoldian college." [69] As a young man Temple had visited Rugby, but it was perhaps not until 1841 when Arnold came to Oxford to lecture that the younger man felt the full force of his personality. The effect was such that it was described by his biographer as " epoch in Temple's career." In particular, Arnold's teachings served to offset the attractions of Newmanism to Temple at this period. Later, upon reading Stanley's *Life of Arnold* in 1844, Temple declared that he found summed up there the ideas of all the Rugby men that he had known.[70] In later years Temple followed in Dr. Arnold's footsteps to become Headmaster of Rugby where he had a brilliant career from 1857 to 1869.

In recommending Temple for this position, Matthew Arnold wrote that " in commanding at once the respect and affection of those under his charge " Temple greatly re- sembled Dr. Arnold. On other occasions he noted like- nesses in the directness and force with which the two men approached religious questions. In the field of Christian education Temple seemed to him the *one* man who might do something of the same work as his father.[71] Temple himself frequently spoke of his recognition that Thomas Arnold was a great man and an exemplar to those who followed him.[72]

Temple's own indebtedness to Dr. Arnold is perhaps no- where more apparent than in his contribution to *Essays and Reviews*. His article in the controversial work was en- titled somewhat vaguely " The Education of the World." *

---

* The title tends to suggest that Temple was probably also indebted to G. E. Lessing's " Die Erziehung des Menschenge- schlechts " (1780) which grew out of the controversy surrounding the publication of the *Wolfenbüttel Fragments*. This essay also embodies the idea of progressive revelation analogous to the " schooling of mankind." The first two propositions of the work well sum up its central argument: (1) " Was die Erziehung bei dem einzelnen Menschen ist, ist die Offenbarung bei dem ganzen Menschengeschlechte," (2) "Erziehung ist Offenbarung, die dem

Actually its drift was far more religious than educational, for Temple argued by analogy with the human individual that the human race also underwent a process of moral growth and development. According to his theory, this proceeded through orderly stages of childhood (obedience to precept and law), youth (preponderance of feeling over understanding), and manhood (conduct governed by principle). Furthermore, each of the great races and cultures had a valuable contribution to make in the " schooling "; the Jews taught mankind the value of righteousness; the Greeks that of reason, measure, and beauty; the Romans, order and law; and Asia, spirituality and unworldliness. Temple argued that since man had (by 1860) reached a late stage of his spiritual development, it was time to " modify the early dogmatism by substituting the spirit for the letter, and practical religion for precise definitions of truth." His essay therefore de-emphasized dogma, asserted the importance of Christianity as an ethical system, and recognized the historical growth of religion.[73]

His views may be regarded as an adaptation of the idea of progressive revelation or spiritual " progress " which, it will be recalled, Stanley had found in its " first and clearest statement " in nineteenth century England in Dr. Arnold's essay on scriptural interpretation. Arnold has stated that since God did not " raise mankind at once to its highest

einzelnen Menschen geschieht: und Offenbarung ist Erziehung, die dem Menschengeschlechte geschehen ist und noch geschieht " (*Werke*, ed. Georg Wittowski [Leipzig: Bibliographisches Institut, n.d.], VII, 428). Writing of *Essays and Reviews*, Matthew Arnold suggested that Temple's essay contained nothing that the instructed " could not find in a far more perfect form in the works of Lessing." Similarly, he found Jowett's essay to be a repetition of Chapter VII of Spinoza's *Tractatus Theologico-Politicus* (1670) (" The Bishop and the Philosopher," *Macmillan's Magazine*, VII (January, 1863), 254.

state of moral perfection, any more than individuals are born at once to their maturity," the commandments given to men at one period did not necessarily accord with the enlightened state of their conscience at a later time. Men living in the later period might well become aware of the inconsistency of practices during the " childhood and youth of the human race " with moral principles of which they were aware (*Sermons*, II, 386-91).

In defending the publication of *Essays and Reviews* to his Rugby sixth-formers, Temple said that the book contained opinions " which had long been lurking in corners," and which in his opinion needed to be " dragged to light and faced." [74] In particular, the crucial question of Biblical inspiration was one which excited much of the clerical hostility against the work, finally resulting in its synodical condemnation in 1864. To the popular charge that the volume was " infidel," Temple replied that it was so only if Galileo and Dr. Arnold were infidels. For himself he declined " to call a book infidel because it refuses to shut up the discussion of whether the Biblical narrative is in all parts literally true " (*Memoirs of Temple*, II, 615-16). Elsewhere he suggested that it was Dr. Arnold who had pointed the way to the enormously important question of the " degree and limits " of Biblical inspiration, a question which he found to be inescapably confronting the entire Christian world (*Memoirs of Temple*, I, 304). Twenty years later in his Bampton Lectures, " The Relations Between Religion and Science " (1884), Temple again took up the question central to Dr. Arnold's criticism:

> . . . there is a real and great danger that the spiritual may be altogether obscured by the literal and the physical. We look back with astonishment on the Rabbinical interpretations of the Old Testament. . . . But we see something of

the same spirit in the attempt to maintain a verbal and even literal inspiration of the whole Bible, filling it not with the breath of a Divine Spirit, but with minute details of doctrine and precept often questionable, and whenever separated from principles of eternal law, valueless or even mischievous.[75]

Temple's rise in the Anglican hierarchy (he became Archbishop of Canterbury in 1896) may be taken to mark the wide acceptance of Arnoldian views about the Bible. The work of Temple along with that of Matthew Arnold, Arthur Stanley, and Benjamin Jowett not only reflected Thomas Arnold's teachings but was, indeed, the most effective means of their perpetuance. Through these men, Dr. Arnold accomplished the two main purposes of his far-sighted program: (1) the demonstration that the Bible, though not infallible, was not *historically* discredited by the inconsistencies of its human authors; and (2) the demonstration of the Bible's enduring relevance as a source of moral guidance. Ultimately, Arnoldian answers to the problems of Church and State would have to rest on this foundation.

THREE

Arnold and the Church

THOMAS ARNOLD WAS accustomed from an early age to judge the religious and social institutions of his time by the Gospel standard. The inevitable result was that he found them wanting. When as a boy of eleven he wrote of the "nefarious forgeries and worldly conduct of the Christian bishops" and the "vices and follies" of the lesser clergy, he gave good indication of the nature of the man of whom the child was the father.[1] Years later, in 1826, he wrote to a friend of a projected work on the Church:

> . . . the more I think of the matter, and the more I read of the Scriptures themselves, and of the history of the Church, the more intense is my wonder at the language of admiration with which some men speak of the Church of England, which certainly retains the foundation sure, as all other Christian societies do, except the Unitarians, but has overlaid it with a sufficient quantity of hay and stubble, which I devoutly hope to see burnt one day in the fire. I know that other churches have their faults also, but what have I to do with them? It is idle to speculate in *aliena republica*, but to reform one's own is a business which nearly concerns us. (*Life*, I, 51.)

His anxiety to call the attention of the clergy to the need

for Church reform originated in his fear that the Church
would be disestablished as a consequence of growing popular dissatisfaction with its inefficiency, exclusiveness, and
" priestly inutilities." [2] The seriousness of this eventuality
was heightened, in his judgment, by the need of a National
Church to evangelize the State and so to help to bring
about the Kingdom of God on earth. The unpopularity
of the Church was one of two problems facing Arnold.
The other was the unwillingness of English clergymen to
set their own house in order.

DANGERS TO THE CHURCH

The danger that the Church would be disestablished
arose from a powerful alliance of Benthamite political reformers and religious nonconformists aggrieved by political
and educational disabilities. Utilitarianism, of which Jeremy
Bentham, George Grote and the Mills were the chief ex-
ponents, was traditionally skeptical and inquiring by nature
and was bound to assess the value of all social institutions
according to their utility to society.[3] Through the influential *Westminster Review* owned by Bentham, the Utilitarians after about 1820 carried on a vigorous campaign for
Church reform or Church destruction as the disposition of
the individual critic tended to dictate.[4] Moreover, because
the Utilitarians were attuned to the Spirit of the Age and
were able to supply would-be reformers with both a com-
prehensible ideal in the " greatest happiness " principle and
with specific suggestions for legislative reform, they were
widely influential as legislators. It has been noted that
Macintosh, Brougham, Romilly, Joseph Hume, Grote, Roe-
buck, Macaulay, O'Connell, and Peel were all in sympathy
with Utilitarian ideas. In addition, the Utilitarian influence

extended to the editors of the London *Examiner, Chronicle,* and to many of the writers for the *Edinburgh Review.*[5] When one recalls that Bentham and Grote regarded the relation between Church and State as an alliance between " a standing army " of superstitious priests and " the sinister interests of the earth," [6] the seriousness of the threat to the Church becomes apparent.

Although not all advocates of Church reform were as radical as Bentham and Grote, most were sufficiently influenced by Utilitarian propaganda to approach the problem in a hostile and negative spirit. Among the scores of reform publications of the period which are illustrative of a sharply critical attitude towards the Church was one called *The Extraordinary Black Book* (1831). This publication " edited " by John Wade is exemplary of the reformers' hardheaded approach to Church questions and their unrelenting method of attack:

> . . . the administration of Church of Englandism to 6,500,-000 hearers costs nearly as much as the administration of all other forms of Christianity to 203,728,000 hearers.[7]

Wade offered a list of the incomes reportedly attached to English Church livings and suggested that when foreign stipends for equivalent duties were compared with them " the disparity in ecclesiastical remuneration appear[ed] incredible " (*Black Book*, p. 64). Wade also attacked the evils of nonresidence and pluralism (i.e., the holding of more than one Church living simultaneously). He estimated the proportion of nonresident to resident clergy at three to two and pointed out that a full third of the clergy held more than one living, with some cases of five appointments held simultaneously.[8] The implication of such findings was that the Church could not justify itself on the grounds of its contribution to the general good.

Opposition to the Established Church was strengthened by a large and growing population of religious nonconformists, many of whom were eager to see the influence and authority of the Church weakened if not destroyed. This feeling, partly attributable to sectarian emulation, was greatly intensified by the longstanding civil and educational disabilities suffered by dissenters. The most important of these disabilities were the payment of Church Rates and exclusion from Oxford and Cambridge. The dissenters could see little reason why they should pay any amount, however small, for the maintenance of buildings which they never used except, as was required by law, for weddings and funerals.[9] As Church Rates were levied up until the passage of Gladstone's Compulsory Church Rate Abolition Bill (1868),[10] the grievance remained an active one through Arnold's lifetime. The other leading disability was educational.

Because subscription to the Anglican Thirty-Nine Articles was required at matriculation and graduation at Oxford and Cambridge, dissenters were barred from use of the national universities and consequently from cultural advantages which they might otherwise have had. They were therefore often forced to rely upon continental or Scottish universities or to forego higher education. Frequently they were excluded from the pursuit of learned professions and, to some extent, from civil positions. This grievance existed all through Arnold's life and was only alleviated by the Oxford and Cambridge University Acts of 1854-56 and decisively settled by the Universities Test Act of 1871 which abolished religious tests for lay degrees and the holding of lay academic positions.[11] Prior to this relief, the antagonism of the dissenters tended to bring them into tacit agreement with the Utilitarian secularists that the Church should be disestablished.

The removal of other nonconformist disabilities proceeded slowly during Arnold's lifetime. The repeal of the Test Act in 1828 made it possible for dissenters to hold public office without first accepting holy communion in the Anglican Church.[12] In 1829, the Roman Catholic Relief Act was passed after years of agitation and over strong opposition of the Anglican bishops who voted thirteen to one in the House of Lords against the bill. This act may be taken as the first step in legislation which in 1869 culminated in the disestablishment of the Anglican Church in Ireland, a recognition of the injustice in its receiving the endowment of a National Church while ministering to only " a tenth part of the nation." A few years after Catholic " emancipation " the Irish Church Bill of 1833 was passed. This measure suppressed some of the Anglican bishoprics in Ireland and, in general, diminished the prerogatives of a Church established and supported against the wills of the people which it nominally served. Again, however, the measure was passed against the opposition of most clergymen.[13]

It was this clerical opposition together with the opposition of the Anglican bishops to the passage of the Parliamentary Reform Bill of 1832 which was a source of great danger to the Establishment. At a time when " reform was in the air," [14] inflexibility and stubborn refusal to give up ancient prerogatives of the Church appeared likely to lead to its dissolution. Instead of attempting to remove the sources of unpopularity by carrying out administrative reforms, many Churchmen launched attacks on the political reformers.

Particularly was this true of the Tractarian party which had formed to combat the "national apostasy" exemplified by the passage of the Irish Church Bill of 1833.[15] Under the leadership of John Henry Newman, a group of conservative Churchmen in 1833 began a momentous attempt to reassert the principles of ecclesiastical authority and tradition against the widespread movement of political and social reform which had begun to make itself felt in Church matters. This they sought to accomplish through articles in the *British Critic*, the Tractarian organ, and in a series of *Tracts for the Times*. In the former publication they attacked the legislative reformers in a series of articles which were less well informed and closely reasoned than fervent.[16] In the *Tracts for the Times* they promulgated the idea of the Apostolical Succession, "the true Episcopate as the condition of validity in the administration of the Sacraments, and the only sure guarantee for the preservation of right doctrine." By reviving the ancient idea of the *successio apostolica*, Newman hoped to "shake off the State."[17] In an age basically unsympathetic to the Church this seemed to the Tractarians to be the wise course, for they were not aware that the Ecclesiastical Commission rather than doctrinal bulwarks would be the means of saving the Church.[18]

Though Arnold and other liberal Churchmen could only have approved of the effect of Tractarianism in deepening the piety of individuals and in opposing a sense of spiritual reality to utilitarian materialism,[19] they could scarcely help feeling that the leaders of the Oxford Movement had put the Church on indefensible grounds. In a time when the chief need was a clear-headed reform of the anomalies of the Establishment before it was destroyed, Newman and Keble advanced views of the Church and the priesthood which could only further alienate the dissenters and the uncommitted who were already chafing at the exclusiveness of the Establishment. There was danger that important issues such as the needs for greater comprehensiveness, efficiency, and social efficacy would be obscured by the priestly emphasis of the *Tracts*. Moreover, the steadfast opposition of the Tractarians to prevailing ideas seemed likely only further to alienate public opinion from a Church already too unpopular for its own good. The point may be illustrated from the theses which Newman attributed to the liberals at Oxford and said that he opposed:

> . . . the Civil Power may dispose of Church property without sacrilege. . . . The Civil Power has the right of Ecclesiastical jurisdiction and administration. . . . Virtue is the child of knowledge, and vice of ignorance. Therefore, e.g., education, periodical literature, railroad traveling, ventilation, drainage, and the arts of life, when fully carried out, serve to make a population moral and happy. (*Apologia*, p. 277.)

The Tractarian " apotheosis of the past with a view to its control of the new mind " [20] was ineffectual in preventing further activity by those who saw Church reform to be an imperative need. Not all the proposals were as immoderate as those suggested by the Utilitarians, however. In 1832 Lord Henley publicized a scheme of Church reform in which he proposed to restrain the accumulation of pluralities, enforce the residence of clergymen, and adjust clerical remuneration. In addition, he made the important suggestion that new dioceses be created to enable the Church better to perform its function in areas in which the population had outstripped the facilities of the Establishment.

The latter measure was of great importance particularly

in London and the northern industrial cities where the growth of population had been rapid. As early as 1818, it had been known that Church facilities in many London parishes and in the dioceses of Chester and York were pitifully inadequate. In 1835 investigation in London revealed four parishes with a population of 160,000 persons and Church accommodations for only 8,000.[21] Arnold himself noted in 1833 that the Bishop of Chester had nominal supervision over 2,000,000 persons and a diocese 100 miles long (MW, p. 293). Under such conditions the need for increasing the administrative and pastoral machinery of the Church was acute.

This need was recognized in clerical legislation after 1835. In that year an Ecclesiastical Commission was appointed by the government to make recommendations for improvement of the Church's efficiency. These recommendations, made on the basis of a thorough study of the existing situation, were embodied in the Established Church Act of 1836 which provided for the redistribution of clerical incomes and the rearrangement of dioceses. Subsequent reforms from 1836 to 1840 dealt with episcopal incomes, pluralism, and the membership of bishops on the Ecclesiastical Commission which thereby became a body devoted to the administration and financial management of the Church. In large measure, it may be said that these reforms, carried out over the protest of conservative Churchmen and generally with the support of liberal Churchmen, were the means by which the Church was preserved against the forces threatening it in Arnold's time.[22]

The most notable of those who shared Arnold's views on the necessity of internal reforms and co-operation with the government were Richard Whately, Archbishop of Dublin, and Charles James Blomfield, Bishop of London. Whately, one of the Oriel Noetics whose associations with Arnold have previously been noted, supported the bill of 1833 which suppressed some of the Irish bishoprics.[23]

Although in the 1820's Whately had espoused a theory of the Church which was influential on Newman, he gradually shifted his position as to the necessity for a particular form of Church government, and in later life came to hold views similar to Arnold's on this point. After Arnold's death, Whately attacked the Tractarians in *Cautions for the Times* (1853).[24]

Bishop Blomfield, on the other hand, was the moving force of the Ecclesiastical Commission and was largely instrumental in retaining some clerical power for the Church in the guidance of the series of reforms already discussed. It was doubtless at his request that the Reform Government agreed not to send any measure to Parliament which had not previously been approved by the Commission.[25] Though he was very unpopular among conservative Churchmen, he was largely correct in his statement about his role in the carrying out of Church reform measures:

> They blame me for these measures, but they will hereafter confess that those very measures have been the saving of the Church.[26]

In later years Blomfield, along with Arnold, favored the Jerusalem Bishopric, which was a forerunner of modern ecumenical thinking about Church affairs and, to some extent, a following out of principles laid down in Arnold's theory of the Broad Church (Cornish, I, 266).

Aside from these men, Arnold had few powerful allies in his attempt to preserve the Establishment against the dangers which in the 1830's appeared to make its existence precarious. With his profound conviction of the value of the Church as an institution for the spiritual betterment of his country, however, he could scarcely avoid the difficult and largely thankless task of attempting its justification in the face of hostile criticism and its reform despite entrenched clerical conservatism.

A REFORM PROGRAM

Arnold's efforts to deal with the problems confronting him are to be seen in a series of essays and pamphlets written between 1826 and 1842. The most important of these are *Principles of Church Reform* (1833); " The Oxford Malignants," *Edinburgh Review*, LXIII (April, 1836); introduction and notes to *Christian Life, Its Course, Its Hindrances, and Its Helps* (1841); and *Fragment on the Church* (1842), published posthumously in 1844. These are supplemented by " On Letters of an Episcopalian," *Edinburgh Review*, XLIV (September, 1826); *The Christian Duty of Conceding the Roman Catholic Claims* (1829); notes on tradition and the Apostolical Succession in *Sermons*, volume III (1834) and periodical essays in *Englishman's Register* (1831), Sheffield *Courant* (1831-32), and Hertford *Reformer* (1839-41). Although these works are largely occasional in nature and specifically directed at a variety of ecclesiastical and political problems, they all are part of a program designed forcibly to present three main views: (1) that it was in the nation's best interests to retain the Church Establishment; (2) that the Church must be made more popular by administrative reform and the comprehension within it of dissenters; (3) that the Oxford Movement was only jeopardizing the further existence of the religious Establishment.

Arnold first considered the condition of the Church

Establishment in 1826 when he reviewed Richard Whately's *Letters on the Church by an Episcopalian.* In his book, Whately advanced a claim for the autonomy of the Church and advocated a policy of disestablishment without its disendowment. This course Arnold found to be gravely unsatisfactory because, as he pointed out, it would leave the State with "no religion at all." Furthermore, he observed that the plan was unrealistic in the supposition that the clergy as "State's Servants" would be allowed "to resign their commissions" and yet retain their emoluments. In place of disestablishment, Arnold suggested that the Church carry out administrative reforms which he felt would solve its problems.

The chief problem was the Church's unpopularity. Arnold wrote that it was only natural that the Anglican Church "should be taxed with indolence and indifference, and with thinking more of its dignities than its duties." [27] Its unpopularity arose from its failure to alter those practices which put it out of touch with the majority of the people. One such practice was the patronage of benefices by landowners. Because many parishes historically had been "coterminous with the estates of landowners who built churches for themselves and their dependents," the right of advowson, or perpetual appointment of a priest, was granted to the lord of the manor and became attached to his estate as a heritable privilege. During Arnold's lifetime, patronage was common and was only sharply limited after 1898 by the Benefices Act of that year. [28] Arnold suggested that the patronage system made Anglican clergymen far too attentive to the aristocracy and the Crown and not nearly attentive enough to the common people. Along with their "notorious spirit of Toryism" the clergy had even a habit of condescension toward the people which, reflected in the language of their tracts and sermons, destroyed any possibility of rapport with their parishioners. Arnold recognized another source of dissatisfaction with the Church in the widely condoned practice of holding multiple livings (MWA, pp. 224-25).

He suggested that there were also other serious faults in the English clergy. The worst was their tendency toward a "needless multiplication of the terms of conformity." By their insistence on exclusiveness, they had actually driven many into the ranks of the dissenters. Moreover, he found the means employed to ensure Anglican conformity ineffective in bringing about uniform teaching in the Church:

> . . . the fancied inconvenience of having the pulpits filled at different times with men of different opinions is greatly overrated . . . in point of fact they *are*, and ever must be so filled; for no articles of religion can ever embrace all, or a hundredth part of the topics which are discussed in public preaching: and the uniformity which subscription ensures, is much less important than the discordance, which it cannot prevent, in the tone of mind, in the moral opinions, nay in the very earnestness and seriousness of various ministers; so that the preaching of two men, both conscientiously subscribing to the same Confession of Faith may lead their hearers to the most dissimilar views of religious duty. . . . (MWA, pp. 227-28.)

He himself was of the opinion that the expression of differences on matters of doctrine was far less important than the agreement of most men on certain doctrinal points.[29]

Equally unsatisfactory to Arnold was the absence of any form of Church government which could represent the will of the people. Even the Church Convocations (prior to their suppression by the government in 1717) had served only imperfectly as a means of popular representation. By the 1820's Convocation had become " no better than a name" and the mass of clergymen and laity were left unrepresented in Church government. In Arnold's judgment, the making of the constitution of the Church more popular and effective was as necessary as the making of its terms of communion more comprehensive (MWA, pp. 229-35).

Beyond the making of these general recommendations he would not go in 1826, for he felt that an apprised public awareness of the major problems must precede intelligent reforms. First, the shortcomings of the Establishment must be admitted for what they were, without recourse to traditional catchwords. " Parrot-like phrases " such as " the venerable Establishment" must first be put aside. Arnold made this point in a telling analogy:

> " The venerable Establishment." We would ask, whether the venerable Cathedral Churches of that establishment have sustained injury from the cleaning, repairing, and removing of deformities, to which the taste and liberality of so many of our Deans and Chapters have been of late years so happily directed? or whether the ornaments added in the reigns of Elizabeth and James the First, were all so pure and so judicious, that it would have been barbarism and folly to meddle with them? (MWA, p. 234.)

Another well-worn formula received similar treatment:

> " The Constitution in Church and State! " Why, it is like the feet of the image in Nebuchadnezzar's dream, which were made part of iron, and part of miry clay; the State strong and sound, gradually perfected by the care of successive generations, carefully watched and continually repaired;—the Church patched up in a hurry three hundred

years ago, out of elements confessedly corrupted, and ever since allowed to subsist, unlooked to and unmended, as if, like the water of the Thames, it would grow pure by the mere lapse of time. (MWA, p. 233.)

Although in 1826 Arnold did not hope to see reform in his own lifetime, he was content, he said, to call attention to the problem and so prepare the way for reform:

. . . a little impulse is sometimes sufficient to set in motion the stream of public opinion, which, gathering force year after year, from continual accessions of experience and reflection, swells at last into an irresistible current, and sweeps away the stubbornest mudbanks of corruption and error. (MWA, p. 235.)

These militant words used when urging the cause of reform contrast sharply with the fervent prayer which he uttered on a later occasion when the Church appeared to be in peril:

Most heartily do I wish to see [the Church] reformed, at once for the sake of its safety and of its greater perfection; but reformed or not may God in His mercy, save us from the calamity of seeing it destroyed. (MW, p. 338.)

By 1831 Arnold saw that the changes for which he had called were more imminent than he had expected. Indeed, on the eve of the passage of the Parliamentary Reform Bill of 1832, public opinion was such that Arnold began to fear that the Church might be destroyed instead of reformed. Archbishop Howley upon arriving at Canterbury for his primary visitation was greeted by a mob which " hooted and pelted " him. The Bishop of Winchester was burned in effigy outside his palace. In late 1831 a mob of angry rioters actually burned the palace of the Bishop of Bristol.[30] These occurrences made it apparent to Arnold that, whatever the wisdom of his former writings on reform, something must now be done to allay public feelings about the Church. In the emergency he again turned to journalism and wrote a series of letters on the topic to the editor of the Sheffield *Courant*. In one of these he suggested a program of needed administrative reforms, but only after he had first scrupulously pointed out what he, following S. T. Coleridge, took to be a great advantage inherent in the Establishment:

> My conviction of the benefits of a Church Establishment arises from this: that thus, and thus only, can we ensure the dispersion of a number of well-educated men over the whole kingdom, whose sole business, *is to do good of the highest kind*; to enforce in their public teaching, the purest principles and practice that mankind has ever yet been made acquainted with; and to exhibit all these in their own persons in all their daily intercourse with their neighbors, instructing the young, visiting the sick, relieving, advising, and maintaining the cause of the poor; and spreading amongst all ranks the wholesome influence of a good life, a cultivated understanding, and the feeling and manners of a true gentleman. (MW, pp. 219-20.)

He argued that the existing Establishment should be retained because in its clergy, it had the best available means of performing this function.

Other Churchmen were similarly anxious that the Establishment be preserved. One of these was Lord Henley, who in 1832 made public his plan calling for various administrative reforms. To Arnold, some of the proposed reforms were desirable but, as he thought, insufficient. For one thing, he observed that Henley's measures failed to deal effectively with the worsening problem of religious dissent. In particular, the growing unwillingness of dissenters to pay Church Rates seemed to indicate a dangerous alienation from the Church. Accordingly, Arnold undertook to deal with the problem of dissent in a pamphlet whose chief purpose was, as he wrote Archbishop Whately, to show that administrative reforms alone were no longer enough to save the Church:

> Nothing, it seems to me, can save the Church but an union with the Dissenters; now they are leagued with the anti-Christian party, and no merely internal reforms in the administration of the actual system will, I think, or can satisfy them. (*Life*, I, 348.)

His procedure in *Principles of Church Reform* was, as the title suggests, rather that of establishing the general principles to be considered in reforming the Church than of advocating detailed proposals. Although he did set forth a program to comprehend dissenters in the Establishment and to improve the administrative efficiency of the Church, Arnold was quite willing to leave the working out of specific reforms to persons of "much greater experience and knowledge" than himself (MW, p. 260). The basic principles he stated as follows:

> These principles I believe to be irrefragable; that a Church Establishment is essential to the well-being of the nation; that the existence of Dissent impairs the usefulness of an Establishment always, and now from the peculiar circumstances threatens its destruction; and that to extinguish Dissent by persecution being both wicked and impossible, there remains the true, but hitherto untried way to extinguish it by comprehension; that different tribes should act together as it were in one army, and under one command, yet should each retain the arms and manner of fighting with which habit has made him most familiar. (MW, p. 259.)

Here it will be seen that he puts primary emphasis on inclusion of dissenters, for as he elsewhere observed, he was willing to " sink into nothing the difference between Christian and Christian " in order to win the dissenters away from the party of unbelief (i.e., Utilitarians and other radicals) and thereby weaken the opposition to the Establishment (*Life*, I, 390).

He based his argument for comprehension on the fact that religion involved metaphysical, moral, and political questions to which no single decisive answer could be given. In addition, differences of religious opinion were increased by the widely differing interpretations of Scripture among the various sects. For these reasons, it was futile to expect any uniformity of opinion or to attempt to enforce it by such means as were practiced in England. Both persecution and toleration had been unsuccessful in doing so (MW, pp. 271-76). The result was that the Established Church then contained both " the extremes of Calvinism and [of] Arminianism " (p. 326). Furthermore, the antagonistic power of dissent was then much augmented; for it had as its ally a vast " populace " or proletariat who were part of the greatly increased British population (MW, pp. 278-79). As he elsewhere observed, the failure of the Church to provide devotional and educational facilities for the masses of workers in the industrial towns made it easy to see why the Church was bitterly hated in the manufacturing districts:

Is it not because . . . the Church has allowed thousands and tens of thousands of its members to grow up in misery and in ignorance; and that a stepmother's neglect is naturally requited by something of a stepmother's unpopularity? (MW, p. 210.)

He concluded that the only effective defense against destruction of the Church was the inclusion of dissenters in a National Church which would "allow great varieties of opinion and of ceremonies . . .while it . . . worshipped a common God."

Arnold never doubted that inclusion could be effected. He pointed out that most English sects held in common the essential ideas of religion. All believed in God and in Christ, all regarded the Bible as God's sole revelation to men, and for the most part, all had the same ideas of right and wrong and agreed on what constituted sins. Even the Quakers, Roman Catholics, and Unitarians might in time by moderate treatment be induced to approximate orthodox belief, and so be won to the Anglican fold (MW, pp. 279-84).

He realized that certain changes in articles, creeds, and Church government would have to be made before comprehension would be possible, however. Articles and creeds would have to be made less exclusive. This he was perfectly willing to have done, believing as he did that formularies tended to stifle religious truth:

> I dislike Articles because they represent truth untruly, that is, in an unedifying manner, and thus robbed of its living truth, whilst it retains its mere literal form; whereas the same truth, embodied in prayers, or confessions, or even in catechisms, becomes more Christian, just in proportion as it is less theological. (*Life*, I, 361.)

He suggested that the real basis of union was not subscription to articles but the ability to use in common such "essential parts of Christian worship" as "addressing Christ in the language of prayer and praise." Hence as long as Unitarians, for example, fulfilled this requirement of worship, Arnold would make no attempt to discover whether the ideas of Christ's nature held by Unitarians approximated orthodox ideas on the same subject (MW, p. 285). Arnold's conviction that the heart of Christianity was its guidance of conduct thus allowed him to conceive of a Church whose composition would be anathema to his Tractarian opponents.

In a sermon on " Creeds " (c. 1832-34), Arnold deprecated the " minute dwelling upon every word of the Creeds " and recommended that they be used not as "a sort of declaration of war against those who may not agree with us in them " but rather as " a free and triumphant confession of thanksgiving to God " (*Sermons*, III, 276, 279). He thus anticipated the spirit of the Clerical Subscription Act (1865) which substituted a declaration of " assent " to the Thirty-Nine Articles and the Prayer Book for the previously exacted oath of literal acceptance.[31]

As for the form of Church government, Arnold maintained that it should be basically episcopal but greatly popularized by the institution of a series of reforms which would result in its increased efficiency and which would satisfy the longing of the people for participation in Church organization (MW, pp. 291-97). He felt the most pressing of these to be the greater inclusion of the laity in Church government. Because that government had been so exclusively administered by the clergy, a harmful separation between clergy and laity had come about. The very word " Church " had lost its inclusive meaning and had come to apply only to Bishops and priests. From this came two unsatisfactory results: the administrative powers of the Bishops had to be greatly restricted in order to prevent clerical " tyranny," and the laity's desires for participation in their Church government led many of them to become dissenters.

He observed that claims for sacerdotal authority (i.e., those advanced by the Tractarians) were largely responsible for the existing situation:

> . . . from a superstition about what men fancy to be the divine right of the Episcopacy, the Church has practically all but gone to pieces, from the want of any government at all. (MW, p. 291.)

To Arnold, one of the great weaknesses of the Church was its divorce from ordinary life. He frequently lamented an otherworldliness which preached heavenward orientation at the very moment when people were starving. At the same time he consistently opposed cutting "life into slices." [32] What was needed was a thorough interpenetration of secular and spiritual life, an idea which eventually led him to his theory of the Christian State. As a step in the direction of it, he advocated the extension of lay influence in matters of Church government (MW, p. 291). He conceived one important means of accomplishing this to be the institution of Bishops' councils composed partly of laymen. Arnold envisioned the functions of these groups as juridical, legislative, and advisory:

> . . . a bishop should be incapable of acting without his council, and this council should consist partly of lay members, and partly of clerical, to be appointed partly by himself and partly by the ministers and lay elders of the several parishes in his diocese. A court would thus be formed, to which the maintenance of discipline might be safely entrusted, and ministers of scandalous life might be removed from their benefices without the tedious and ruinous processes imposed upon the bishop, if he is anxious to do his duty in such cases. (MW, p. 294.)

Arnold referred to the complicated system of ecclesiastical courts which through most of the Victorian period made it extremely difficult to maintain clerical discipline through legal means because of the multiplicity of courts to which any one case might be appealed. The procedure for prosecuting offenders was greatly simplified by the Clergy Discipline Act (1892) which provided for trials by the Bishop and a board of Assessors (Cornish, II, 357).*

Arnold also suggested that general diocesan assemblies be instituted to meet annually in order to enact general diocesan regulations and, perhaps most important of all at this period, to " present the Church to [the people] in a form at once imposing and attractive " (MW, p. 294). In this manner, he hoped to make the Church truly *national* and thus in the interests of all to preserve. His recommendation anticipated modern diocesan conferences, the first of which was held in the Anglican Church in 1871.[33]

He also considered how an additional barrier to the evolution of a *national* Church might be overcome. He was profoundly aware that dissenting clergymen lacked the " rank and tone " which he thought necessary to the ministry, and that they were characterized by a " narrowness of view," and " want of learning, and a sound critical spirit." [34] In his judgment they could hardly serve as full ministers of the Church. He therefore suggested that they be appointed as assistants to the regular Anglican minister of the parish

---

* Cf. the unsuccessful attempt by Lord Sandon in 1871 to conduct through Parliament a Parochial Councils Bill which would limit the powers of the clerical incumbents by creating statutory councils of parishioners (S. C. Carpenter, *Church and People, 1789-1889* [London: Society for Promoting Christian Knowledge, 1933], p. 366). A similar provision, the Parochial Church Councils [Powers] Measure, was passed in 1921 (Herbert Hensley Henson, *The Church of England* [Cambridge: Cambridge University Press, 1939], p. 179).

in which they were working. To the possible objection by Anglicans that this would sanction a ministry neither learned nor orthodox, Arnold replied that dissenting ministers, whether sanctioned or not were, in fact, already preaching. He argued that it was far worse to have them as enemies of the Establishment wholly outside its influence than as a functioning part of it and so, subject in some measure to it. He supposed that the prospect of sharing in the government of the Church would be sufficient inducement to keep the dissenters from objecting to the comprehension scheme (MW, p. 295).

Similar considerations led him to suggest the use of the Anglican parish church by those who were dissenters prior to comprehension. This he thought would lead to greater unity and, at the same time, bring the new Churchmen into ennobling contact with the " beautiful and venerable " aspects of the Establishment, especially as these were to be seen in the churches (MW, p. 307). He saw no reason why preferences for varying forms of worship need interfere with this plan:

> There is no reason why all should not be gratified without quarreling with each other; why the organ should not sound at the morning service, and be silent at the evening: why the same roof which had rung at one part of the day with the rich music of a regular choir, should not at another resound with the simpler but not less impressive singing of a mixed congregation. (MW, p. 308.)

In the conclusion of his pamphlet, Arnold recognized the likelihood of objections to his plan and attempted to anticipate certain criticisms which he supposed might be brought against it. To the criticism that his plan was too radical, he answered that it was necessary because of the extreme danger in which the Establishment was placed by hostile sectarianism. He further granted that some might call his plan impracticable, but pointed out that it would be necessary to subject it to trial to prove it so. He contended that a partial reform would be ineffective to meet the Church's needs:

> . . . if the reform of the Church be impracticable, its destruction unhappily is not so, and *that* its enemies know full well. It may be that a patchwork reform will be deemed safer as assuredly it is easier; it may be too, that after such a reform has been effected and has left the great evils of the Church just where it found them so that its final destruction shall be no less sure, the blame of its destruction will be laid by some on the principle of reform, and we shall be told that had no pretended improvements been attempted in it, it would have stood for ever. So it is that no man is ever allowed to have died from the violence of his disease; but from the presumption of his physician, whose remedies tried at the eleventh hour, he was too weak to bear. (MW, p. 319.)

He was substantially correct as to the nature of the criticism with which his pamphlet was to be taxed. A writer in the *Quarterly Review* commended him for working out a theory of comprehensive reform but termed the plan itself, " impracticable." [35]

Arnold later admitted that the remedies which he proposed were more extensive than they would have been had he not thought " that the Church Establishment was in extreme danger." Nevertheless, he reaffirmed his belief that his original proposals were in themselves " right and good " (*Life*, I, 336). In the " Postscript " to his pamphlet he had stated essentially the same opinion. To explain his position he again used the analogy of a physician prescribing:

Jephson finds that his patients will adopt a very strict diet, when they believe themselves to be in danger; but he would be very indiscreet if he prescribed it to a man who felt no symptoms of indisposition, for the man would certainly laugh at him, although perhaps the diet would do him great good, if he could be induced to adopt it. (MW, p. 322.)

Certainly there was one party in the Anglican Church which was unlikely to accept Arnold's prescriptions. His views of Church reform were strongly opposed by the Tractarians. Newman, after reading Arnold's pamphlet, wrote ironically to a friend that Arnold would require an additional Sabbath, for " surely there will be too many sects in some places for one day." [36]

On his part, Arnold was an inveterate opponent of the teachings of Keble, Pusey, and Newman. He always regarded the Oxford Movement as marked by religious superstition and bigotry paralleled only by that of the Judaizers who hampered the efforts of St. Paul.[37] Consequently, his expressions against the "Newmanites" were many and vigorous.

He first came into opposition to High Church tendencies over the question of whether Roman Catholics should be admitted to Parliament. In 1829 a "Catholic Emancipation" bill which provided for their admission was before the nation. The passage of this measure was bitterly opposed by John Keble and other High Churchmen who feared that if passed, it might strengthen " Romanism at the expense of the Church of England." [38] To Arnold, however, the measure seemed wholly just. He therefore undertook to lessen the strong clerical opposition to the bill. In *The Christian Duty of Conceding the Roman Catholic Claims* (1829), he addressed himself particularly to the clergy and argued that it was their duty as Christians to support the Catholic Relief Act. The two main points of his argument were (1) that justice and Christian duty compelled the admission of Catholics to Parliament, and (2) that "the path of duty [was] the path of wisdom," i.e., that such admission would probably tend to "purify the Catholic religion in Ireland from its greatest superstitions, and gradually to assimilate it more and more to Protestantism " (MW, p. 6).

Several years intervened before any open theological conflict with the party of Keble and Newman developed, however. During this period, the Tractarians gradually settled on their central doctrines of the Apostolical Succession and the necessity of a priesthood to insure the efficacy of the sacraments as the strongest defenses of ecclesiastical authority against secular encroachment. At first, Arnold was unable to take the new movement very seriously, for its tenets appeared to him too unreasonable to gain wide acceptance (*Life*, II, 2). With the appearance of the first two volumes of the *Tracts for the Times* (1834-36), however, he became aware of the real force of the Oxford Movement and particularly of the degree to which its central doctrines threatened his own ideas of an inclusive National Church in which the laity had a large part (*Life*, II, 4). In addition, it seemed likely to divert attention from the need for greater social efficacy of the Church.

For this reason, he felt compelled to speak out against the High Church doctrines and, of course, against the productions of the Tractarian leaders, Keble, Pusey, and Newman. Of these three men, Arnold knew Keble best, for he had been Arnold's schoolfellow at Corpus. It was he to whom Arnold had turned for advice during an early crisis of belief (*Life*, I, 22). Later, despite growing differences of opinion, Thomas Arnold asked Keble to be Matthew Arnold's godfather. Finally, however, the friendship was for a time almost completely broken off because of antagonisms created by religious controversy. That Keble was planning a friendly visit to Fox How in 1842, a visit which was prevented by Arnold's death, suggests both the strength of the original attachment and the concern of both men that it not be broken by acrimonious disputes.[39]

The acquaintance of Arnold and Pusey was also a respectful one; each was well aware of the unusual abilities of the other. In 1834 Arnold wrote the conservative Churchmen deprecating his alliance with the Tractarians and suggesting that there were still " many points of unison " between them. As late as 1838, after the Oxford Movement was well under way, he sought information from the great Tractarian about the views of the early Church fathers on Biblical prophecy. For his part, Pusey did not hesitate to recognize Dr. Arnold's talents which he said were greater than his own. On the other hand, he never agreed with Arnold's scriptural views or with his ideas about the Church and, in general, found Arnold wrong in measuring Christian antiquity " by a modern standard." [40]

With this opinion Pusey's principal associate in the leadership of the Oxford Movement, John Henry Newman, would certainly have agreed. Newman and Arnold met on two occasions, in 1828, and again in 1842 while Arnold was in Oxford delivering his lectures on modern history. Although Arnold was bitterly opposed to the ideas espoused by Newman and heartily approved of actions taken against him in 1841 by the University authorities at Oxford, he did recognize the distinctiveness of Newman's piety and the force of his personality. Newman, though certain that

Arnold's liberalism was heretical, could not but admit Arnold's impressiveness as a person and his moral effectiveness as a teacher.[41]

In 1833, the very year of John Keble's "National Apostasy" sermon which Newman resolved to take as the beginning of the Oxford Movement,[42] Arnold published his *Principles of Church Reform* which, in addition to noticing the need for comprehensive changes in the Church, also attacked the High Church claim for the necessity of the episcopacy in the government of the National Church (MW, p. 330). About the same time, he considered the Tractarian claim for the necessity of a priesthood to ensure the efficacy of the sacraments. This claim he found to be without any Biblical or historical authority. Furthermore, he condemned the doctrine because of its effect in making something other than faith in Christ necessary to worship. To Arnold, the mediation of any priest was blasphemous (*Sermons*, III, 370).

He was therefore greatly annoyed by the ambiguity in the Tractarian phrase "the power of keys." This he defined as nothing more than "a declaratory power of pronouncing an absolution which God bestow[ed] and not the minister."[43] Whenever possible, he employed the term "minister" instead of "priest" and emphasized the function of clergymen in interpreting the Scriptures for the moral guidance of parishioners. This he described as a ministry "derived from apostolical teachings" in sharp contrast to the spurious Tractarian claim for an Apostolical Succession (*Sermons*, III, 383).

Despite his strictures, however, he saw Tractarianism in the early 1830's grow more influential. By 1834 he found himself on the defensive against growing conservative tendencies at Oxford. One such tendency was represented by the circulation at the University of a petition against the admission of dissenters. To this, Arnold replied in a counter-petition for the admission of all Christian dissenters except Unitarians, whose denial of the divinity of Christ seemed to him grounds for exclusion. At this time he reasserted his acceptance of nonsectarian principles and the belief that Christian teaching could be given " without touching on those particular questions on which the Church and the mass of Dissenters [were] at issue." [44]

In this opinion he was supported by Renn Dickson Hampden (1793-1868), one of the Oriel Noetics in whose behalf Arnold became involved in his bitterest controversy with the Tractarians. In 1834 Hampden, an Oxford don, published a pamphlet, " Observations on Religious Dissent " advocating abolition of religious tests and the admission of dissenters to Oxford. He was soon attacked for his views in the *British Critic* whose " abuse," as Arnold said, he had " the honour of sharing " with Hampden.[45] In the following year, Hampden further aroused the ire of the Tractarians by advocating the substitution of a declaration of assent to the Anglican Articles for the unqualified subscription then required.[46]

In view of these actions, it is not surprising that Hampden's appointment as Regius Professor of Divinity in 1836 was sharply challenged by the conservative Churchmen. His Bampton Lectures, *The Scholastic Philosophy in Its Relation to Christian Theology* (1832), were submitted to scathing review by Newman in " Elucidations " which appeared to show Hampden's religious unorthodoxy. In the same year, Pusey issued a pamphlet setting forth his concurrence with Newman's findings. These works were instrumental in obtaining the censure of Hampden by the Convocation of Masters of Arts of Oxford in 1836.[47]

One of the results of this censure was " The Oxford Malignants " (April, 1836), Arnold's most outspoken attack on the Newmanites. The title of this article (assigned by the editor of the *Edinburgh Review*) accorded well with its angry tone. In the essay, Arnold's disapproval of Tractarianism found vent in righteous indignation at what he took to be the unjust treatment of Hampden.

" The Oxford Malignants " opens with a recital of the various honors which had been awarded to R. D. Hampden prior to his condemnation at the hands of the Convocation. Arnold observed that these honors were conferred by the University and with the attestation by prominent officials in the University that Hampden was of sound religious faith. After the King's Government had " believed the University's testimonial " and had, as a result, preferred Hampden to the honor of Regius Professor of Divinity, this preferment was opposed in " one of the most extraordinary courses of agitation ever yet witnessed even in the annals of party malignity." [48] Arnold then proceeded to discuss the declaration issued by a committee organized to oppose Hampden. In this declaration Hampden was charged with having systematically set forth mischievous principles in his lectures. Utilizing the fact that these lectures were given in 1832 and not noticed as unorthodox until 1834, Arnold undertook to cast doubt on the justice of the charge. The passage bears quoting as an indication of the vigor of Arnold's counteroffensive:

> It is monstrous, it is almost incredible, that a charge of " mischievous principles " should be founded upon Dr. Hampden's Bampton Lectures of 1832; and not only this, but that these mischievous principles should be described as " SET FORTH SYSTEMATICALLY! " Mischievous principles " SET FORTH SYSTEMATICALLY," in a course of eight ser-

mons preached successively in the University pulpit, before the Vice-chancellor and all the Dignitaries and Tutors of the University,—and no proceedings instituted, no censure passed, no accusation made,—but on the contrary, the preacher subsequently receiving from the University the highest degree in divinity—that degree which is virtually a professorship of theology—the University's commission to give lectures to its students in every branch of that faculty—receiving again the office of Head of a Hall—and lastly, the Professorship of Moral Philosophy! Such was the University of Oxford's censure upon eight sermons full of " SYSTEMATIC MISCHIEF "—preached in her own church,—and in the presence of her highest authorities (Whitridge, pp. 217-18.)

His point was more strongly enforced in a subsequent passage:

But the marvel is greater still. This charge against Dr. Hampden's Lectures, made by five individuals, has been adopted and sanctioned by seventy-six others—all of them masters of arts at the least—all describing themselves as persons "engaged and interested in the religious instruction of the University." All the five accusers, and an immense majority of the seventy-six sanctioners of the accusation, were as much engaged and interested in the religious instruction of the University in 1832, as they are now in 1836. A reference to the Oxford calendar of 1832 will prove this at once to those to whom it is not notorious. Was there ever an accusation involving its unhappy promoters in such a dilemma of infamy? Compromisers of mischievous principles in 1832, 1833, 1834, and 1835,— or slanderers of a good and most Christian man in 1836— disqualified for the office of religious instructors, upon their own showing, by four years of either dulness or indifference, during which they could not understand, or did not notice, what was "mischievous"—or else by one month of audacious and unprincipled calumny! We leave it to the nation to decide for which of these merits it will continue to respect and confide in the greater part of the eighty-one graduates, fellows and tutors who have signed the declaration against Dr. Hampden. (Whitridge, pp. 218-19.)

Arnold further disapproved sharply of the methods employed by Newman and Pusey in "elucidating" Hampden's statements. He observed that both writers quoted statements out of context and deliberately ignored Hampden's distinction between scriptural truths and the technical language in which those truths were expressed in the Thirty-Nine Articles (Whitridge, p. 223).

Finally, in a blistering summary of what he took to be the vagaries of the High Church party, Arnold accused its members of fanaticism and zeal for unworthy objects:

> . . . the fanaticism of the English High Churchman has been the fanaticism of mere foolery. A dress, a ritual, a name, a ceremony; a technical phraseology; the superstition of a priesthood without its power; the form of an Episcopal government, without the substance; a system imperfect and paralyzed, not independent, not sovereign, afraid to cast off the subjection against which it is perpetually murmuring. Such are the objects of High Church fanaticism—objects so pitiful, that if gained ever so completely, they would make no man the wiser or better, they would lead to no good, intellectual, moral, or spiritual,— to no effect, social or religious, except to the changing of sense into silliness, and holiness of heart and life into formality and hypocrisy. (Whitridge, p. 230.)

He was convinced that as long as Tractarianism prevailed in England, the reforms which he thought necessary to the survival of the Church would remain unaccomplished. The "Newmanites" were adamant against both administrative reforms and comprehension of dissenters. He therefore continued his attack on the Oxford Movement. In the introduction to his fourth volume of *Sermons* (1841) he undertook a treatment of the *Tracts for the Times* with the purpose of showing that they reflected both unscriptural doctrines and a defective sense of history. The quotation from S. T. Coleridge which Arnold took as an epigraph to this work is indicative of his general position:

> As far as the principle on which Archbishop Laud and his followers acted went to reactuate the idea of the Church, as a co-ordinate and living power by right of Christ's institution and express promise, I go along with them; but I soon discover that by the church, they meant the clergy, the hierarchy exclusively, and then I fly off from them in a tangent. For it is this very interpretation of the church, that, according to my conviction, constituted the first and fundamental apostasy; and I hold it for one of the mistakes of our polemical divines, in their controversies with the Romanists, that they trace all the corruptions of the gospel faith to the Papacy.[49]

Arnold was wholly in accord with Coleridge that the word "Church" did not mean merely the clergy and the ecclesiastical hierarchy. He therefore strongly opposed the Tractarian doctrines which emphasized priestly authority. The most important of these were (1) the Apostolical Succession, and (2) the necessity of that succession to ensure the efficacy of the sacraments. These doctrines Arnold found to be "totally unsupported by the authority of Scripture " (CLH, p. xxxvi).

Further, he maintained that the leaders of the Oxford Movement were seriously limited by a defective sense of history which made them unreliable guides on religious questions. For example, Newman's judgment in his "Letter to Dr. Jelf" that the Oxford Movement was "something better and deeper than satisfied the last century" was misleading because it suggested that the tendencies of the eighteenth century were "wholly evil" (CLH, p. vii). In Arnold's opinion, this judgment exemplified the failure of the Tractarians to make statements about history "with reserves and exceptions" (CLH, p. vii) as true students of history should. Even worse, Newman and his friends had overestimated the periods of history in which their own doctrines were predominant and had underestimated other periods:

> . . . if their system was not supported in all its points by Scripture, it had at least the warrant of Christian antiquity. Thus Mr. Newman and his friends found that the times which they disliked had professed to rely on Scripture alone; the times which they loved had invested the Church with equal authority. It was natural then to connect the evils of the iron age, for so they regarded it, with this notion of the sole supremacy of Scripture; and it was no less natural to associate the blessings of their imagined golden age with its avowed reverence for the Church.[50]

Arnold maintained that a glorification of the past, in company with an ill-acquaintance with the present, had put the High Churchmen out of all touch with the *Zeitgeist*:

> Thus previously disposed, and in their sense or apprehension of the evil of their own times already flying as it were for refuge to the system of times past, they were over-taken by the political storm of 1831, and the two following years . . . all things seemed combined against them: the spirit of the period which they so hated was

riding, as it were upon the whirlwind; they knew not
where its violence might burst; and the government of the
country was, as they thought, driving wildly before it,
without attempting to moderate its fury. Already they
were inclined to recognize the signs of a national apostasy.
(CLH, pp. ix-x.)

He suggested that if the Tractarians had understood their
own century, they would have looked " for their remedy
not to the second or third or fourth century but to the
first . . . not the Church of Cyprian, or Athanasius, or
Augustine, but the Church of St. Paul and St. John "
CLH, p. xxi). The High Church adherents to patristic
Christianity and a " continuous " ecclesiastical tradition
failed to recognize what he elsewhere called the " wide
gap " in surviving Christian writings between the Apostles
and Justin Martyr (FC, p. 60). Moreover, the Tractarian
appeal to the " authority " of the first four or first seven
centuries falsely suggested that the merely historical authority of Christian commentators was a decisive one
(CLH, pp. 472-73).

Certainly it appeared that the priestly movement with
which he was contending distracted attention from urgent
social needs of the nineteenth century. Believing that the
Church should be committed to the moral and physical
betterment of the people, he could not but lament the practice of Newman's followers in " substituting unrealities for
realities " (*Life*, II, 151):

When we look at the condition of our country: at the
poverty and wretchedness of so large a portion of the
working classes; at the intellectual and moral ideas which
certainly exist among the poor, but by no means among
the poor only. . . . can any Christian doubt that here is

the work for the church of Christ to do; . . . And does he really apprehend the perfection and high calling of Christ's church . . . who comes forward to preach to us the necessity of apostolical succession. (CLH, pp. lxv-lxvi.)

The problems were rather to be met, he thought, by an adaptation of the usages of the past to present needs. For Arnold there was no contradiction in the proposition that the immutable Christian religion could best be brought home to Englishmen by modifications in the mutable Christian Church:

The truths of the Christian religion are to be sought for in the Scripture alone; they are the same at all times and in all countries. With the Christian church it is otherwise; the church is not a revelation concerning the unchangeable and eternal God, but an institution to enable changeable man to apprehend the unchangeable. Because man is changeable, the church is also changeable; changeable not in its object . . . but in its means for effecting that object. . . . (CLH, pp. xliii-xliv.)

To Arnold the duty to reform was clear. Whatever the opposition, the Church had to be made ready to meet the challenge of its day and the needs of those who in future years would be determining the course of English public life.

AFTERMATH: BROAD CHURCH LIBERALISM

Arnold's writings on Church questions were widely read in his own time. *Principles of Church Reform* went through four editions within the first six months of its appearance in 1833. Despite this wide circulation of the pamphlet, however, it cannot be said that his program of reform was influential in his own day. His recommendations were doubtless too radical to be acceptable to most Churchmen, and his advocacy of extensive reforms and, at the same time, of the continued need for the Establishment, insured that his suggestions would be unfavorably received by both the conservative and the liberal parties. Dissenters were offended by Arnold's strictures on their sectarian narrowness and Churchmen by the " latitudinarianism " of his scheme to include dissenters in the Church of England.[51] His other writings in this field had no better reception. Perhaps the most that could be said for the contemporary effect of his pamphlets and essays was that by means of them, the need for administrative reforms in the Church was forcibly asserted to clergymen by a clergyman.

In later years, certain of his views were approximated by legislation, the passage of which should be attributed only partly to the effect of his teachings. Other ideas have had to wait for widespread acceptance until our own century which has seen such developments as the Enabling Act (1919), increasing lay participation in Church government, and the joint Anglican-Free Church report, *Church Relations in England* (1950).[52] Although it would be unwise to speak of such distant reflections as showing Dr. Arnold's influence, they do suggest that his thinking was far ahead of that of his age. Accordingly, it is not surprising that Victorian liberals younger than himself responded enthusiastically to his preachments. In particular, the effects of his teachings about the Church can be seen in certain aspects of the work of Matthew Arnold, Arthur Stanley, Archibald Campbell Tait, and Frederick Temple.

On several occasions Matthew Arnold remarked that in his writings about the Church, he was conscious of functioning as his father's continuator. As he himself suggested, once sufficient allowance were made for " the change of

times and modes of action," his own " scope " was not so
different from Dr. Arnold's as it appeared (*Works*, XIV,
157). In 1869, while writing to Gladstone about the vexing
questions surrounding the status of the Irish Church, he
reiterated Thomas Arnold's views about the value of an
Establishment and suggested his father's prior interest in
Gladstone's early views on the Church.[53] Again, in a letter
to his mother, Matthew acknowledged that he was indebted
to Dr. Arnold for ideas incorporated into his published
works.[54] In addition to the works noted in Chapter II,
these include *Essays in Criticism* (1865), *Culture and
Anarchy* (1869), *Mixed Essays* (1879), and *Irish Essays
and Others.* (1882). Two main aspects of these writings
especially reflect the principles of Dr. Arnold: (1) their
views concerning the Established Church and its relations
to religious dissent; and (2) their insistence on the social
mission of the Church.

We have seen that Dr. Arnold strongly favored an
Established Church which made possible the residence of
a learned clergy throughout the realm and thus afforded
a decided cultural advantage to the nation. He also recognized that such a National Church could do much to counteract sectarian narrowness and to ennoble dissenters by its
" beautiful and venerable " character. Matthew Arnold's
similar attitude on this point can be illustrated from *Culture and Anarchy*, in which he pointed out the advantages
of a church which had " the main current of national life
flowing round [it]." To belong to such a church was
likely to be " a lesson of religious moderation, and a help
towards culture and harmonious perfection " (*Works*, VI,
xix-xx). On another occasion he advanced a view much
like the elder Arnold's argument for the use in common of
parish churches by Anglicans and dissenters:

The consecration of common consent, antiquity, public establishment, long-used rites, national edifices, is everything for religious worship. " Just what makes worship impressive," says Joubert, " is its publicity, its external manifestation, its sound, its splendour, its observance universally and visibly holding its sway through all the details both of our outward and of our inward life." (*Works*, VI, 175.)

Matthew Arnold also followed Dr. Arnold in advocating a Broad Church in which dissenters could play a part. One of the major objects of *St. Paul and Protestantism* was the demonstration to the nonconformists that because they had based their church organizations on an indefensible reading of the Bible, there was no good reason for continued separation from the Establishment.[55] In " Puritanism and the Church of England " Arnold made it clear that his ultimate aim was the comprehension of all Christian dissenters in the National Church:

[There] are proposals " to be made by the Church of England for the union of *Protestants*." Who cannot see that the power of joint life . . . would be far greater and stronger if it comprehended Roman Catholics too? And who cannot see, also, that in the churches of the most strong and living Roman Catholic countries,—in France and Germany,—a movement is in progress which may one day make a general union of Christendom possible? (*Works*, IX, 168-69.)

The possibility of such union was based on a conception of the Church as " *a national society for the promotion of goodness* " (*Works*, IX, 230). Again, Dr. Arnold had held a similar view, as can be seen in his definition of the Church as " a society for the putting down of moral evil " or " the moral improvement of mankind " (MWA, p. 447). Such

broad definitions would permit the union of those who differed widely on matters of doctrine. In addition, Matthew
Arnold, like his father, asserted the need for loosening the
" theoretical " tie of religion by altering the terms of subscription to the Thirty-Nine Articles (*Works*, IX, 230-37).

Matthew Arnold followed Dr. Arnold in his approach
to the involved problem of Anglo-Irish relations. Thomas
Arnold had emphasized the *Christian* duty of dealing fairly
with the Irish nonconformists. Similarly, in his essay entitled " Irish Catholicism and British Liberalism," Matthew
Arnold considered the questions of Irish politics as partly
religious issues:

> Questions of good government, social harmony, education,
> civilisation, come forth and ask to be considered; and
> very soon it appears that we cannot possibly treat them
> without returning to treat of religion. Ireland raises a
> crowd of questions thus complicated. (*Works*, X, 94.)

No less than Thomas Arnold, he favored the establishment
of the Roman Catholic Church in Ireland as a means of
making the Catholics " larger minded and more complete
men " (*Works*, VI, xli-xlii).

Finally, Matthew Arnold's religious writings reflect the
principles of Dr. Arnold in their insistence on the social
mission of the Church. In an address to the London clergy,
the younger Arnold warned that the alienation of the
working classes from the Church was its most formidable
danger. He argued that unless the clergy gave up their
" obsequiousness to the landed and propertied and satisfied
classes " and " superstitious worship of existing social facts "
they might well expect the eventual disestablishment of the
Church. Accordingly, he called attention to the need of
establishing the *kingdom*, " an immense renovation and

transformation of our actual state of things. ...." By making themselves "simple instruments for the public good," clergymen might hope to enable the Church to endure.[56]

The elder Arnold's work was also carried on by Arthur Stanley, A. C. Tait, and Frederick Temple, three liberal Churchmen who were part of a larger group of religious liberals which after about 1850 came to be designated as the Broad Church movement. The name seems to have been chosen to describe the tendency of the liberals to favor toleration of religious differences and to de-emphasize the importance of formal doctrine. In sharp contrast to the Tractarians and other High Churchmen, the Broad Church party was generally receptive to the findings of modern Biblical criticism, favorably disposed to proposals for reform of the Church in the direction of increased lay participation of its government, and deeply concerned that the Establishment be maintained. Along with S. T. Coleridge, Dr. Arnold was unquestionably one of the important sources of this movement.[57]

Of the continuators of Thomas Arnold none was more committed to the Broad Church position than Arthur Stanley whose "signal merit" (according to Matthew Arnold) it was to show by his own life that the position, widely accepted among the laity, was also tenable for clergymen (*Works*, XV, 96). Stanley was a persistent fighter in the cause of religious tolerance. In 1850 he wrote an article for the *Edinburgh Review* in which he rejoiced in the "comprehensive principle of the Church of England." This principle he illustrated in his own conduct when as Dean of Westminster he invited a Unitarian scholar to an Anglican communion service held for the joint committee undertaking the Revised Version of the Bible, an invitation which received considerable adverse notice in the religious press of the time.[58]   A prolific writer for reviews of the period, Stanley often surprised both his friends and his opponents by speaking out in favor of free expression of religious views, whether or not those views were his own. He was equally likely to make what he considered justified criticisms of his own Church and party. On one occasion he advanced a reform proposal which in its comprehensiveness is worthy of Dr. Arnold. In an essay entitled " The Church and Dissent " Stanley argued that relations between the religious communions could best be served if Anglican ministers first reformed their own liturgy, then ministered to all, irrespective of denomination, and finally, exchanged pulpits with their brothers in Dissent.[59]   Throughout his career he directed his efforts towards making the Church of England the truly National Church which had been the ideal of his teacher. As he pointed out, the advantages of a common Christianity had been " powerfully urged " by Dr. Arnold.[60]

Stanley also took up the views of Dr. Arnold about subscription to the Anglican Articles of Religion. In 1840 Arnold expressed his view that the terms of subscription should be greatly relaxed for both clergy and laity (*Life*, II, 211). In the same year Stanley promoted a petition to this effect which was presented to the House of Lords, where, however, it was rejected (*DNB*, XVIII, 932). Like Dr. Arnold, Stanley subscribed to the Articles only on his expressed inability to accept some portions of them.[61] Recognizing the unsatisfactoriness of this course of action, he campaigned in later life for less exacting terms of clerical subscription. Of greater importance in this respect was his pamphlet, " Letter to the Lord Bishop of London on the State of Subscription in the Church of England and in the University of Oxford " (1863), which had the sanction of

Gladstone and the interest of Queen Victoria. In this work Stanley advanced the argument, also used by Dr. Arnold, that an exacting subscription tended to lower the intellectual quality of the candidates available for ordination. In large measure, his recommendations were taken in the Clerical Subscription Act (1865) which substituted a declaration of assent to the Articles for the older and more rigid practice of literal acceptance of all parts of the doctrines set forth in them.[62] In these efforts Stanley proved once more that his former teacher was indeed a major influence on his life and works.

Stanley was greatly assisted in the work of liberal Churchmanship by Archibald Campbell Tait (1811-82) who had been his tutor at Balliol, Oxford, and who in later years became Headmaster of Rugby (1842-49), Dean of Carlisle (1850-56), Bishop of London (1856-68), and Archbishop of Canterbury (1868-82). Although Tait's independence of mind and, in later years, his growing personal conservatism, sometimes brought him into disagreement with Stanley and other Arnoldian liberals over such matters as Biblical criticism,[63] he was in many of his views about the Church a thoroughgoing Broad Churchman and a follower of Dr. Arnold. Tait was not a Rugbeian, nor does he appear to have been personally very closely acquainted with Arnold. Nevertheless, Stanley very soon succeeded in passing on to him his own enthusiasm for Arnoldian ideas. These evidently accorded well with those which Tait had begun to form from readings in Carlyle and in German philosophy and theology, for he became one of Dr. Arnold's strongest admirers.[64] In particular, Tait's opposition to the Oxford Movement and its aftermath, and his concern for improved relations between the Church and Dissent place him in the Arnoldian tradition.

Tait was the author of the momentous censure of New-man's Tract 90 which in 1841 led to the breaking off of Tractarianism. In thanking Tait for sending a copy of the censure to Rugby, Dr. Arnold expressed his gratification that the action had been taken but noted that his own objections to Newman's work were on moral rather than theological grounds. To Arnold the tract showed " utter perversion of language " such that if it were followed, one could subscribe religious articles while holding " the very opposite opinions " (*Life of Tait*, I, 86-87). His own opinions, like those of Stanley, were that the conditions of subscription should be eased rather by legislation than by casuistry.

Tait's appointment of Stanley as his Examining Chaplain in 1856 shows his continued loyalty to the liberal cause in later years. In at least two respects so does Tait's part in the authorship and administration of the Public Worship Regulation Act (1874). This law was Arnoldian in spirit in that it sought to prevent priestly complication of religious observance and ceremonial additions to the existing order of worship. In Disraeli's words the Act was passed " to put down Ritualism." Although Tait's enforcement of the law made it rather more prescriptive and stringent than Arnold would have approved, it did work towards the Arnoldian purpose of excluding possible distractions from the ethical heart of religion. Moreover, certain provisions of the Act were aimed at the simplification of the clerical judiciary, a goal long before pointed out by Dr. Arnold.[65]

Finally Tait's concern for the improvement of relations between the Church and Christian dissenters shows his affinity with Dr. Arnold's religious ideals. Like Dr. Arnold he was reproached with Erastianism and with too great concern for the masses of the population rather than for the clergy. Nevertheless, though priestly critics might refer to him as " archbishop of the laity," he never gave up his belief—also that of Dr. Arnold—that the Church was not equivalent merely to its ordained members.[66] Nor, indeed, was he willing to overlook the possibility of co-operation with Christians outside the pale of that Church. One illustration of Tait's efforts to promote favorable relations between Anglicanism and the dissenting sects is very much in line with Dr. Arnold's opinions. In 1876, in the face of considerable adverse criticism from Churchmen, Tait held a conference of Anglican and non-conformist leaders for the purpose of discussing the possibility of joint efforts against " the progress of irreligious thought in England " (*Life of Tait*, II, 502). Such endeavors made it obvious to Tait's contemporaries that he was of the " Arnoldian School." [67] His work suggests that it was not merely in the field of Christian education that Tait set himself to maintain " that system which Dr. Arnold [had] begun " (*Life of Tait*, I, 112).

To a similar degree, the ecclesiastical career of Frederick Temple reflects the earlier work of Dr. Arnold. Temple, who went on from Balliol to become successively Headmaster of Rugby (1857-69), Bishop of Exeter (1869-85), Bishop of London (1885-96), and Archbishop of Canterbury (1896-1902), was greatly indebted to Dr. Arnold's religious and educational ideas. Apparently, passing years merely added to a loyalty formed in his college days. In 1897, near the end of his own life, he found in Arnold the distinguishing mark of " the truly great [man] ": " his greatness is more and more appreciated as we move further and further away." [68] Temple's work in the Church reflects his acceptance of Arnoldian principles in four main ways: (1) its emphasis on the need for administrative reform of

the Church; (2) its attention to the improvement of relations with dissenters; (3) its opposition to ritualism; and
(4) its attempt to increase the social efficacy of the Church.

As an Anglican prelate, Temple was able to support the
passage of measures for the administrative reform of the
Church. He was chairman of a committee in the House
of Lords which laid the groundwork for the passage of the
Pluralities Act Amendment Act (1885) and the Clergy
Discipline Act (1892). These measures were directed at
the solution of problems incident to pluralism and the
prosecution of clerical offenders, issues which had earlier
concerned Thomas Arnold. Other parallels with Dr. Arnold's work for administrative reform of the Church may
be seen in Temple's opposition to the patronage system, his
work in popularizing Church government, and his advocacy
of the subdivision of dioceses.[69]

Temple also followed Dr. Arnold in efforts to improve
the relations of the Church with dissenters. Important in
this respect was Temple's support in the House of Lords
of the Universities Test Bill (1884), which opened the
national universities to dissenters, and of the Law of Burial,
opening the churchyards to dissenters (1876). His attack
on the anthemas of the Athanasian creed was also occasioned by his desire to lessen the antagonism between
Churchmen and dissenters.[70]

Like Dr. Arnold and A. C. Tait, Temple was strongly
opposed to ritualism and the more priestly aspects of Anglo-
Catholicism, which by the latter half of the nineteenth century had become a powerful force in Church life. In 1886,
as Bishop of London, Temple specifically repudiated the
doctrine of the Apostolical Succession taught " as a means
of separating the clergy from the laity " and cited the
opinion of Dr. Arnold (*Memoirs of Temple*, II, 10-11).

Despite considerable criticism from religious conservatives and the press, Temple consistently pronounced against additions to the authorized ritual of the Church. His own emphasis, like that of Thomas Arnold, was on increasing the social efficacy of the religious establishment. Accordingly, he directed attention to the condition of the working class and was himself influential in the fields of philanthropy and poor relief.[71]

In these respects, Temple, no less than Matthew Arnold, Arthur Stanley, and Archibald Tait, carried forward the central idea of Thomas Arnold's thought about the Church: that it must be a vital force in the everyday lives of all Christians. Arnold looked to an awakened Church as the "soul" of the Christian Commonwealth, the ultimate means by which he hoped to see the Kingdom of God established on earth.

FOUR

Arnold and the State

ONE GREAT QUESTION was often on the lips of Thomas Arnold. " Why," he asked, " amongst us in this very country, . . . is the mighty work of raising up God's kingdom [stopped] . . . [the work] of bringing every thought, and word, and deed, into the obedience of Christ[?]" (*Sermons*, I, 104). It was a question designed to move his hearers to action. To Arnold, the obstacles to the realization of Christ's kingdom were so apparent that he spent his life in an attempt to remove them. His work in scriptural interpretation was aimed at the removal of one great difficulty, unawareness of the relevance of Biblical teachings to modern life. The Church reforms which he sought would have ended another difficulty, the exclusion of many Englishmen from the Established Church. A third difficulty was exclusively secularistic thinking about public affairs. It was this obstacle which Arnold sought to overcome by making religion operative in English political life.

THE NEED FOR THE SPIRITUAL CRITIQUE

Certainly Dr. Arnold could have seen ample evidence in the 1830's and 1840's that Christianity was not the ruling force in the lives of many of his contemporaries. Five main tendencies made this obvious: (1) the denial of the relevance of religion to political questions; (2) the general insensitivity to the sufferings of the poorer classes, together with a corresponding failure to see the logical outcome of neglecting them; (3) the excess of partisan spirit in all national affairs; (4) the extension of the British Empire through the use of force and chiefly for commercial gain; and (5) the lack of any adequate system of Christian education, particularly for the middle class.

The denial of the relevance of religion to political life came both from the Utilitarians, who argued that religion had been superseded by man's intellectual advances, and by Churchmen who held its interests to be otherworldly and hence not concerned with the direction of political affairs. Bentham, the founder of Utilitarianism, was of the opinion that religion occupied " a principal place among the causes of most human evils." In partnership with George Grote he published a work in which he maintained that religion was not only totally useless but actually harmful to society. James Mill, another Utilitarian leader, supported an agnostic view by stating that nothing could be known of the cause of the world except that it could not be the work of a good and intelligent creator.[1] As might be expected, these men, who were all ardent political reformers, did not base their programs of political action on the religion which they disavowed. Because of their influence on legislators, they had the means of embodying their views in the law of the land.

Even Whigs like Macaulay who did not consider themselves to be supporters of the Utilitarian system sometimes adhered to the principle of laissez-faire, " the most vital part of Bentham's legislative doctrine." [2] In 1839 in his essay " Gladstone on Church and State " (to which Dr. Arnold replied in his *Introductory Lectures*, pp. 45-66), Macaulay held that as a matter of common sense the government ought to undertake not much more than political, i. e., administrative, duties.[3] Since the "main end" of government was "the protection of the persons and property of men," he favored its involvement in the attainment of other ends (such as Christian education) only when this did not lessen its efficiency in carrying out its primary aim. Thus where Arnold believed the government should provide for the religious education of the masses, Macaulay favored a policy of "let alone."[4]

In unspoken alliance with the Utilitarians and the laissez-faire theorists were those English Churchmen who held that the complete autonomy of the Church was desirable. Though these men were as opposed to Utilitarian doctrines as Arnold, they unintentionally aided the secularists by declaring themselves in favor of sharply limiting the Church's sphere of influence. Illustrative of this view was Richard Whately's *Letters on the Church by an Episcopalian* (1826), which John Henry Newman acknowledged to be influential on his own thinking about the relations between Church and State.[5] In essence, Whately's position was that the mere fact that the same persons belonged both to the national society of the State and to the society of the Church did not prove the identity of the two societies.[6] He therefore favored the disestablishment of the Church and its withdrawal from politics to the realm of its own internal administration and devotional activities. Similarly, the State would be relieved of the responsibility of insuring the sound administration of the Church or the Christian conduct of public affairs. In Arnold's opinion, such reasoning could only forward the advent of secularism in government.

A second main problem which Arnold faced was the general failure of Englishmen to abide by Christian principles in the relationships between the social classes. In particular, this failure took the form of upper and middle class insensitivity to the sufferings of the poverty-stricken, politically impotent, and exploited " working " class. The oppressed, on the other hand, also abandoned Christian principles and listened to counsels of violence and revolution.

The situation was made acute by a series of events partly attributable to England's participation in the Napoleonic Wars. The war had brought on the need for greater farming efficiency in the country and had led to the enclosure of small freeholds and lands which had been farmed in common. Small farmers unable to compete with the improved methods employed by the wealthy land-owners were often forced out. Furthermore, as they were usually poorly compensated for their lands, many became paupers. The decay of cottage industries consequent upon technological advances in industrial production of textiles and other goods further contributed to " the long-drawn-out disaster with which the nineteenth century opened." [7]

Those who declined bare subsistence on doles provided by the government and who moved to the great industrial centers often found themselves in worse condition than before. There, crowded into towns whose populations had perhaps doubled since the beginning of the century,* they were all too likely to suffer from inadequate housing, poor sanitation, and dangerous working conditions. Faced by

---

* The populations of Leeds, Sheffield, and Birmingham all increased twofold between 1801 and 1831 (Bernard N. Schilling, *Human Dignity and the Great Victorians* [New York: Columbia University Press, 1946], p. 2).

the prospect of eking out starvation wages with the labor of women and children of their families and by the ever-present danger of typhus, cholera, and typhoid fever, the toilers lived out their lives of " eating, drinking, working, and dying." In short, the conditions of the urban workers were those which inspired Kingsley's " Cheap Clothes and Nasty " and Hood's " Song of the Shirt." [8]

In the face of such conditions, the responsibilities of the aristocracy and the middle class were, from Arnold's point of view, perfectly clear. By all the dictates of the Gospel, they were obliged effectively to relieve the plight of their fellow human beings. Unfortunately for this view, however, there were tendencies at work to restrict religion to its " proper sphere " (i. e., devotional activities). Authorities other than the Biblical one were adduced to support the existing practice. In a time when the ruling class was doing little to solve the problems created by the industrial revolution, economists came forward saying that " nothing was after all the best thing to do." [9] According to the writings of Adam Smith (1723-90), T. R. Malthus (1766-1834), and David Ricardo (1772-1823), and their more *doctrinaire* followers, the condition of the working class was irrevocable because of the operation in the economy of the " laws " of self-interest, free competition, supply and demand, population, and wages. To those of humanitarian tendencies, political economy compounded of a " selection and exaggeration " of the ideas set forth in Smith's *Wealth of Nations* (1776), Malthus' *Essay on Population* (1798), and Ricardo's *Principles of Political Economy and Taxation* (1817) became indeed " the dismal science." It was all too convenient for the capitalists of the time to be told that they had only to seek their own economic ends in order to further the general good. By such an argument, low wages, intolerably long working hours, dangerous working conditions, and child labor could all be justified. Since the pursuit of private interest was theoretically to the common advantage, the government was obliged not to interfere with the free competition among individuals to sell their own labor. Although laissez-faire was the most hated of terms to Arnold and his followers, it was less objectionable to many Victorians.

A typical approach to the solution of the problems of the poor was that taken by Lord Brougham, Charles Knight, and other members of the Useful Knowledge Society. In manuals prepared for workers, these authors sought to explain to the proletariat that the interests of labor and capital were essentially the same, since by furthering the accumulation of capital, labor made greater sums available for wages in accordance with the concept of a " wages fund." [10] Malthusians expounded another aspect of the " Wages Fund " theory. They pointed out that since the price paid to any individual for his labor was determined by the number of competing individuals, population must be limited. [11] To those crowded in the cellars of Manchester these admonitions could have been no more satisfying than those of William Paley, who in his *Reasons for Contentment Addressed to the Labouring Public* had earlier advised toilers to be reconciled to their appointed lot. [12]

Additional support for a policy of laissez-faire could be found in the ineffectual Poor Laws enacted by the government. To a great extent, these seemed only to worsen the condition of the lower class. From 1795 to 1834, the notorious " Speenhamland Act " (so-called from its origin at a meeting in that town of the magistrates of Berkshire in 1795) was in effect. By the provisions of this unhappy law, wages were supplemented out of parish rates up to a minimum level based on the price of bread. The result was the pauperization of most workers because of the unwillingness of their employers to pay the minimum wage. In addition, many small landholders were ruined by the heavy Poor Rates by which the paupers were supported. In a later effort to solve the same problem, the Whigs in 1834 passed a law which ended automatic relief to all applicants and set up the workhouses familiar to readers of *Oliver Twist* (1838). Here thousands suffered as the administrators, seeking to make pauperism undesirable, "made workhouse life miserable as a matter of policy." [13]

Because of their political impotence, the workers appeared to have no lawful means of improving their situation. Although the Parliamentary Reform Bill of 1832 aroused hope that they might one day attain a voice in the government, the measure itself "merely shifted the power from one class that used the people for its own ends to another." [14] Until they could obtain political power, there was the ever-present danger that they might be incited to violence. Many persons began to share Carlyle's conviction that the future held a "steady approach to democracy, with revolution (probably *explosive*) and a *finis* incomputable to man." [15] Certainly in the struggles of the workers towards better working conditions, Dr. Arnold could have found ample reason to deplore the lack of attention to Christian principles.

The two great related movements of Trade Unionism and Chartism appeared in Arnold's time to be heading in the direction of outright insurrection. Born in the era of governmental repression following the Napoleonic Wars, the trades unions were a continuing source of anxiety on the early Victorian scene. Their potentialities for violence could hardly be ignored after 1830, when a vast uprising of nonunion agricultural workers throughout the southern counties wreaked havoc on farm machinery and other implements which had reduced the demand for labor. If an unorganized mass of laborers could defy the government for a time, what might be expected of their brethren of the industrial north? The severity with which such outbreaks were repressed could not lessen the fears aroused by the formation of such bodies as the National Association for the Protection of Labor (organized 1830). The succeeding decade which brought pitched battles between employers and member unions heightened the general uneasiness and helped to gain wide acceptance for the concept of the class war.[16]

Chartism, another working class movement, was even more threatening to the peace of England than Trade Unionism. The former, unlike unionism, was a political movement which sought to gain Parliament's assent to a program of universal manhood suffrage, use of ballots, equal electoral districts, payment of members of Parliament, abolition of property qualifications for voting, and annual Parliaments. On three occasions, 1838, 1842, and 1848, the Chartists presented petitions to Parliament only to have them rejected. On each occasion the rejection was followed by strikes, sporadic insurrections, and governmental repression. Until it was finally crushed by governmental forces in 1848, the movement created widespread public anxiety.[17] Because Feargus O'Connor and other Chartist leaders fostered class hatred in their followers, the movement deeply troubled thoughtful Englishmen who wished to see Christian principles operative at all levels in the difficult readjustment of class relationships which was taking place.

This readjustment was often made vastly more difficult

by yet a third main problem which confronted Arnold in his attempt to approach political questions from the Christian viewpoint. This was the intensely partisan spirit with which all political and social questions were considered. Because the issues seemed to be crucial and the dangers threatening society to loom large, the time was characterized by a fervid sectarianism. Panaceas for complex problems were advanced and supported with " vigour and rigour " (to use Matthew Arnold's phrase). The result has been well described by J. S. Mill in " On Liberty ":

> Every truth which men of narrow capacity are in earnest about, is sure to be asserted, inculcated, and in many ways even acted on, as if no other truth existed in the world, or at all events none that could limit or qualify the first. I acknowledge that the tendency of all opinions to become sectarian is not cured by the freest discussion, but is often exacerbated thereby; the truth which ought to have been, but was not, seen, being rejected all the more violently because proclaimed by persons regarded as opponents.[18]

The problem was greatly intensified when those speaking to the people were not well-educated men of Mill's stature but political journalists not much less ignorant than those to whom they wrote. Frequently unable to distinguish charlatanry from statesmanship, the poor tended to fall under the domination of adventurers whose desire for power or whose grudge against the existing order was their chief motive for action.[19] Even lower class spokesmen of real ability like William Cobbett could not be expected always to see the need for preserving ties with the past in the transition from aristocracy to political democracy. Despite his purpose of diverting the working classes from violence to agitation for Parliamentary Reform, Cobbett in

his *Political Register* (1802-35) exhibited an inflammatory
" recklessness of statement and violence of diction "[20] which
characterized many other journalists of the period whose
aims were more revolutionary. From sources such as Feargus O'Connor's *Northern Star* or from Richard Carlile, the
radical publisher, unrestrained propagandizing could be expected. The result was that, by Arnold's time, there was a
great need for calm appraisals of catchwords and party
fervor and for the testing of proposed solutions to social
problems against some nonpartisan standard. The need, in
short, was for the " spiritual critique." [21]

Looking beyond the shores of Great Britain in the 1830's
and 1840's, Dr. Arnold also had good reason to lament the
absence of such a standard and such a critique in the
nation's foreign and colonial affairs. During this period,
the immensely popular Lord Palmerston pursued an aggres-
sive policy of power politics and imperialism which led
Bulwer to observe that when Palmerston talked of diplom-
acy he never failed to talk also of ships of war. Certainly
he did not hesitate to employ the British fleet in support of
national prestige or commercial interests. Several times
during the two decades his intervention in the affairs of
other nations appeared to make war inevitable, but through
good fortune (or, as some thought, good *bluff*), his " happy
go lucky jingoism " prevailed.[22]

Unfortunately, the rapid growth of the Empire was not
without its problems for British settlers. Among the various
hardships fought by the colonists of Australia and New
Zealand, for example, was that of living in areas serving
as dumping grounds for convicts " transported " from England. In 1840 Australia obtained a temporary suspension
of transportation to the continent. During a four year
period thereafter, 16,000 prisoners were sent to Tasmania.

Despite the protests of free settlers, the practice was continued into the 1860's.[23] In the eyes of those who were deeply concerned about moral conditions in these new domains, the existing colonial and penal policies left much to be desired.

The general attitude toward the methods to be used in colonial expansion during this period is reflected in the fact that from 1801 to 1854 the Secretary of State for War also had control over the colonies. In the 1830's threats of military force (along with negotiations and bribery) were important to the great success of the English in obtaining commercial rights in the Middle East.[24] Similar methods employed in the Far East were equally fruitful. In 1842 attempts by the Chinese government to resist the importation of opium by British traders eventuated in a " war " with the result that England gained Hong Kong, a tribute of six million pounds, and the right to enter Chinese ports for trading purposes.[25] Truly, neither the day of David Livingstone's admonitions as to the duty of spreading Christianity among the " inferior " races nor that of Kipling's " White Man's Burden " had dawned.[26]

Arnold also faced the problem of the lack of any adequate system of Christian education, especially for the middle class. He was deeply concerned that in a professedly Christian kingdom, vast segments of the population never received Christian instruction. In default of this, they were offered " useful " knowledge of a wholly secular character. In 1825 Lord Brougham, Lord John Russell, James Mill, and other prominent philanthropically minded Whigs and Radicals had formed a society for the diffusion of useful knowledge. This purpose they sought to accomplish in a series of publications which included the *Library of Useful Knowledge* and the *Penny Magazine*, appearing between 1825 and 1846, when the society came to an end. The productions of the society were chiefly devoted to the " objects, advantages and pleasures of science " (as Brougham entitled the opening treatise) and were designed to fulfill a general aim of making " the most useful and the most exalted truths of science easily and generally accessible." [27] Their good organization and employment of eminent writers resulted in their success in providing some educational experience to the lower and middle classes. From Arnold's point of view, however, the society's work was misguided in its deliberate exclusion of Christian education from its ends.[28]

Brougham and his associates were also busy with other educational programs designed to extend the benefits of education to those who would otherwise be without them. In 1820 the first mechanics' institute was established in London. The idea was quickly seen to be a practicable, if imperfect, approach to popular education and was widely copied. By 1850 the number of such institutes had grown to over 600 and the number of students to more than 100,000.[29]

In the field of secular higher education, Brougham and others were responsible for the foundation of London University (1828). This institution was designed to serve students who were either too poor to attend Oxford or Cambridge or who were unwilling to sign the Anglican Articles as a prerequisite to a college degree. The new institution was granted a royal charter in 1836 which allowed it to confer degrees in any field of learning except theology.[30] Despite the protests of clergymen who objected to the exclusively secular emphasis of the University, it regularly granted degrees in the 1840's and after. The growing tendency among the secularist philanthropists was to solve the nation's educational problems by eliminating religious teaching and " leaving the various churches to settle their differences apart from the State." [31]

The passage of the Reform Bill of 1832 heightened the danger incident to the lack of adequate Christian education by giving the franchise to a whole new class of poorly educated voters, the middle class. Some forward-looking individuals pointed to the continent where in Prussia the government had undertaken the systematic education of both middle and upper classes in day schools. In England, however, the best schools were the boarding public schools devoted solely to the education of the aristocracy and upper middle class.[32] Middle class education was largely divided between endowed and private schools, many of which were pursuing a " commercial " curriculum and which consequently came to be called " commercial " schools. These were often conducted by unlicensed laymen whose competence to teach was at least questionable. Perhaps only readers of *Hard Times* would be fully prepared for the emphasis put on the rote learning of factual material in a course of study which might typically include the catechistic learning of the thirty-five subjects surveyed in *An Easy Introduction to the Arts and Sciences* (1821).[33] Certainly from such a course of study would not come the ideal citizens of the Christian State, or the solutions to the political problems of Arnold's time.

CHRISTIAN POLITICS

Arnold approached these problems in a series of essays, pamphlets, and sermons written between 1827 and 1842. The most important of these are the postscript to *Principles of Church Reform* (1833), *Fragments on Church and*

State (1827-41, published posthumously in 1844 as appendices to the second edition of *Fragment on the Church*), and the Inaugural Lecture and Lecture VI of *Introductory Lectures on Modern History* (1842). These are supplemented by *The Christian Duty of Conceding the Roman Catholic Claims* (1829), " The Social Progress of States " (first appendix to the edition of Thucydides, 1830), Letters to the Hertford *Reformer* (1837-41), " On the Divisions of Knowledge " (a lecture before the mechanics' institute at Rugby, 1838), Preface and sermons 29-33 of *Sermons*, volume II (1831), 11 and 20 of *Sermons*, volume III (1834), and sermons 24, 28-30, and 38-40 in *Christian Life, Its Course, Its Hindrances, and Its Helps* (1841). Dr. Arnold's general aim in these works was the extension of religion into political life. His specific topics of discussion were the following: (1) the theory of the Christian State; (2) the duty of the upper and middle classes to alleviate the situation of the poor, and of the lower class to abstain from violence; (3) the need for a Christian nonpartisan approach to political questions; (4) the relevance of Christian values to foreign policy and colonial relations; and (5) the need for an adequate system of Christian education, especially for the middle class.

The work to which he looked forward as the chief employment of his old age was the writing of a treatise on Christian politics. He did not live to reach old age, however, and his work remained fragmentary.[34] But because he embodied some of the ideas of this partially completed work in many of his other writings, it is possible to see that he followed lines laid down in Aristotle's *Politics*, Hooker's *Laws of Ecclesiastical Polity*, and Coleridge's *Constitution of Church and State*.* Certainly he accepted

* Arnold once cited Edmund Burke's " Speech on the Unitarian

the Aristotelian view that any true state " must pay attention to virtue " and not exist merely for mutual protection
or enrichment of its citizens. Hooker's great work added
the " high ideal of a Christian State, whose other name is
Church. . . ." Finally, in Coleridge's work, Arnold found
a condemnation of the view that " religion is not within
the province of the civil magistrate." [35] These ideas became
an integral part of his political views.

Arnold's political theory was based on the conviction
that there was no valid segregation of secular and religious
affairs. His theory of the Christian State was, in fact, one
result of his unwillingness, as Thomas Hughes put it, to
" cut life into slices." In advocating the adoption of his
theory as a guide to political action, however, Arnold preferred to point out the identity of ultimate ends of both
Church and State. He employed this means in the " Postscript " to his Church reform pamphlet. As he understood
it, the end of the Church was the " promotion of man's
highest possible perfection and happiness." This, he thought,
could be accomplished only through moral and spiritual
improvement which would bring him to a " state of goodness and wisdom." The end of the State was the same:

> Now this is precisely the object of civil society also: that
> is, of the State. Our physical wants may have led to its
> actual origin, but its proper object is of a higher nature;
> —it is the intellectual and moral improvement of mankind,
> in order to [sic] their reaching their greatest perfection,
> and enjoying their highest happiness. This is the object
> of civil society or " the State " in the abstract; and the
> object of any particular civil society or state is still the

Petition " (1792) in support of his view of the state (LMH, p. 68),
but appears not to be primarily indebted to the great eighteenth
century statesman.

same, but limited to certain local boundaries which mark the particular subdivisions of the society of mankind. (MW, p. 331.)

In pursuit of this common goal, each had an attribute needed by the other. The Church was without the power which the State had and the State was without the wisdom which the Church had (LMH, p. 66). Since the goal of both was the same and each had need of the other, Arnold argued that the two must unite for " the effective removal of all evil, and promotion of all good " (*Life*, II, 190-91).

Once fully enlightened by the spiritual knowledge of the Church, the State became, in effect, a new entity, a " kingdom of Christ " and an earthly manifestation of the Universal Church. Its form, however, was not that of the old, limited Church but that of the new evangelized body politic:

> The spirit of the Church is transfused into a more perfect body, and its former external organization dies away. The form is that of the State, the spirit is that of the Church; . . . in a sense in which " Church " denotes the outward and social organization of Christians in any one particular place, it is no longer a Christian Church, but what is far higher and better, a Christian kingdom. (MWA, p. 464.)

The effectual result of the union was, as Arnold put it on another occasion, that " the State in its highest perfection becomes the Church " (MW, p. 332). Such was the lofty ideal of the " high state " which guided his own political thinking and that of his followers.

He was under no illusions as to the ease with which the fusion could be effected. The Christian State was rather an ideal to be approached than an immediately realizable goal or a description of actuality:

I regard the theory of government, maintained in my Lecture, to be a theory which we can in practice only partially realize. This I quite allow with regard either to the present, or to any future, which we can yet venture to anticipate. It is a theory which, nowhere perfectly realized, is realized imperfectly in very different degrees in different times and countries. It is not to be forced upon a state of things not ripe for it, and therefore its most zealous advocates must often be content to tolerate violations of it more or less flagrant. All this is true; but yet I believe it to be the true theory of government, and that by acknowledging it to be so, and keeping it therefore always in sight, we may be able at last to approach indefinitely near to it. (LMH, pp. 46-47.)

On the other hand, Arnold believed that the English Reformation had placed the country in a position peculiarly favorable to the attainment of his ideal. Through the Act of Supremacy (1534), the English had broken down a great barrier to the union of Church and State by asserting the royal headship of the Church. This he took to be the " assertion of the supremacy of the Church or Christian society over the clergy." [36]

He regarded an unduly limited idea of the proper function of the State as a great bar to the realization of the Christian commonwealth. For example, a view of the function of the State as " the protection of men's bodies and goods " actually implied a separation of Church and State (MW, p. 466). He therefore contended that the very sovereignty of the national government implied that it must control the education, habits, and principles of its subjects. Once it accepted such a view of its responsibilities, it was, in effect, already a Church:

. . . a Christian government acting in the name of a Christian people, is bound to shape its practice and its institutions according to Christian principles, that is, in every thing that relates to moral good; it is bound to do the exact business of a Church. . . . (MW, p. 450.)

From Arnold's point of view, the State was as bound to provide for the " constant and public dissemination of Christian principles amongst all classes of its people " as it was to provide for the administration of justice or to maintain national security. On one occasion, he likened the State to an educator who could not merely " teach his own science effectually " but must also consider all parts of the pupil's nature whether moral, intellectual, or physical (LMH, pp. 48-49). Since he believed that the very sovereignty of the State implied that it must provide for the cultivation of the higher faculties of its citizens, he opposed any attempt to restrict its responsibility merely to the " lowest part of our compound natures " (MWA, p. 495). The consequences of such a restriction seemed to him evil precisely because no account was taken of that faculty of man which, in his judgment, ought to be governing man's actions:

> For suppose for instance, that a nation as such is not cognizant of the notions of justice and humanity, but that its highest object is wealth or dominion, or security. It then follows that the sovereign power, in human life, which can influence the mind and compel the actions of us all, is a power altogether unmoral; and if unmoral, and yet commanding the actions of moral beings, then evil. (LMH, p. 13.)

Arnold urged his view of the nature and function of the State as the answer to most of the problems of his day. One of his last letters to the Hertford *Reformer* expresses his belief that the penetration of religion into political and social life was far more important than the acceptance or rejection of any specific measures:

> Undoubtedly, I wish that men held on political subjects those opinions which I believe to be true. But this is by no means my most earnest wish on the matter. What I wish for above all other things, is that men would talk, write, and act on political subjects in the fear of God; as if they were forthwith going to stand before His judgment. Even so talking, writing, and acting, they might and often would be in great error; still if ever we are to come to any generally sound knowledge about public matters, it can be only gained by this previous moral improvement in our way of studying them. (MW, pp. 517-18.)

Once bring political and social institutions to the religious test, however, and the duty to reform becomes clear. Arnold showed by his writings that he did not think that the Christian could stand aloof from politics. In his pamphlet on the Roman Catholic claims Arnold wrote of the scriptural basis of his political critique:

> [The Christian Scriptures] discourage the notion so common amongst religious bigots, that there is something profane in political institutions with which the servants of God should not intermeddle. On the contrary, the apostles teach that these political institutions are God's appointed means of governing the world, and that he so highly regards them as to invest them with one of his own attributes, the dispensation of good to the well disposed, and of punishment to the evil doer. If they are perverted from fulfilling these purposes they are faulty and require amendment, and every servant of God should use his best endeavours to restore them to their designed purity. (MW, p. 29.)

Accepting, as he did, this idea of the moral duty of reform, and further holding a definition of "State" as "our relations to other men according to God's ordinance" (LMH, p. 279), Arnold could not help being disturbed by the political and social situation of England during the 1830's and 1840's. "The condition of England" seemed to show that men were acting on principles far from religious. Above all, Arnold was fearful of a great social convulsion similar to the French Revolution which might destroy much that he considered worthwhile in English life, along with the abuses which provoked it.

The dominant social evil was "the widening rift between the upper and lower classes." [37] The problem seemed daily to worsen so that, to use Arnold's words, "while one half of society was moving forward, and the other half sinking backward, the distance between them in feelings and habits was continually becoming greater" (MW, p. 181). Arnold held a theory of the "social progress of states" which allowed him to describe English social change as the passage from an ascendancy of wealth to one of numbers. According to this theory, there was grave danger that the change might be violent. Since he believed that social change itself was inevitable, he concerned himself with making "the passage from the old system to the new as easy and imperceptible as possible" (MW, p. 116). In order to make it so, he realized that he would have to get concessions from both wealth and numbers. The former would have to be aroused to humanitarian activity, the latter to reason and love for the inherent good in the old order. Above all, both would have to "talk, write, and act on political subjects in the fear of God."

He so keenly felt the failure of many persons to do so that in 1831 he established a newspaper with the expressed intention of avoiding the errors of many journals of the era. The *Englishman's Register* began publication less than a year before the Reform Bill of 1832 was passed. Readers of the new journal found that its editors, Arnold and his nephew, John Ward, advocated a program of " Christian reform." In other words, they favored improvement in the condition of the poor but opposed violence and faction (MW, p. 118). As could be seen from some of the editorials in the *Register*, Arnold hoped to avoid the errors made by the extremists of both parties by staying on a middle road to reform. On one occasion he spoke of their oversimplified explanations of the cause of social problems as a great aggravation of the trouble:

> The anti-reformers have spoken as if all the sufferings of the poor were the result of inevitable necessity, and assert that the rich, far from being in any degree the cause of them, have done their best to relieve them. The ultra-reformers represent the rich as tyrants and the poor as slaves, and they speak of them as the natural enemies of each other, and tell the poor in plain terms that all their sufferings come from the oppression of the rich, and that it is their own fault if they do not at once remedy and revenge them. Thus one party tries to lull the consciences of the rich, and encourages them in their errors and neglect; while the other appeals to all the bad passions of the poor, and disposes them to regard with suspicion every attempt of the rich to do them good as if it were the mere stratagem of an enemy. (MW, p. 119.)

Like many of the journals of the reform era, however, Arnold's newspaper had too brief a life to enable it to attain significant influence on the public. Stanley ascribed its " natural death " after only nine issues to three causes: Arnold's lack of leisure properly to supervise the editorial work, his financial inability to support printing costs, and his unwillingness to assume a more popular program than that of " Christian reform " (*Life*, I, 285). Fortunately for Arnold's cause, the editor of the Sheffield *Courant* copied some of the editorials from the *Register* and thus extended the range of Arnold's influence. Later, in 1831-32, Arnold wrote a series of thirteen letters on " The Social Condition of the Operative Classes " for the *Courant*. In these he illustrated his belief that the aim of contemporary journalists should be " to calm and enlighten the poor; to interest and arouse the rich " (MW, p. 175).

He undertook to reach his objective by two principal means: a thoroughgoing criticism of the excesses of party journalism and oratory, and a nonpartisan analysis of the causes of the social distress. His effort might well be thought of as an attempt to present the problems as they really were.

In one of his Rugby sermons, Arnold told his boys to belong only to the party of Christ. To no other cause were they to commit themselves so completely that it alone determined their friends and enemies (*Sermons*, III, 193). Possibly it was his own attempt to hold membership in the Christian party which led to his dissatisfaction with the catchwords of political agitators. Arnold was not only afraid that the partisan journalists and orators were inflaming public opinion; he was afraid that truth would be lost in clamor:

> The people are just as much slaves when they follow
> blindly the violence and faction of an unknown writer in
> a newspaper, as when they are bribed and overawed by
> property and political influence. I wish the people to be
> really independent; that is, to think and judge calmly for
> themselves; not to be agitated and clamor without think-

ing, just as their favourite newspaper sets them on. I am a thorough friend to knowledge, and therefore, I detest excitement and violence; for these utterly obscure the truth, and make a man ready to talk and act upon everything while he knows nothing. (MW, pp. 172-73.)

He found that all too frequently the agitators distracted attention from the principal issues about which they should be speaking in order to stir up class hatreds:

. . . real and intelligible causes of the present distress . . . because they do not serve the ends of agitators . . . are passed over in silence, whilst the changes are rung upon the vague words—" Corruption," "Misgovernment," "Tyranny," " Pampered oligarchy," " Borough-mongering faction," etc. Truly it is hard to decide whether they who use this language are more wicked or more ignorant; for though their tone and spirit abundantly show that truth is not their object, their excessive shallownesss must wholly acquit them of having discovered it, and then wilfully suppressing it. But popular principles are too sacred to be abandoned in disgust because of the vileness of their advocates; and I hope to labour unceasingly in the great work of reform, notwithstanding the baseness and folly by which it is obstructed under pretence of advancing it. (MW, p. 177.)

This " baseness and folly " he hoped to offset by the inculcation of a spirit of patient and sober inquiry into the causes of the social disorders. He regarded such a spirit as more likely to be beneficial than acceptance of any contemporary nostrum:

. . . if I can only set an example of fair and calm inquiry, concealing nothing, palliating nothing, exaggerating nothing,—if I can lead men to consider their grievances wisely,

as well as to feel them keenly—to look into the causes of
them, and so to dismiss that soreness and fierceness with
which they now regard their supposed authors; if, in short,
I can but in any degree improve the temper and sober the
judgment with which men now study political questions,—
neither shall I have written in vain, nor will you, I am sure,
repent of the space in your paper which you have allowed
me to occupy. (MW, p. 173.)

The same spirit born of Arnold's determination to " talk,
write, and act on political subjects in the fear of God "
made him take up the difficult task of convincing the ill-
educated tradesmen of Sheffield of their need for that
wisdom which was chiefly the fruit of good education and
political experience. He suggested that the many appeals
to the " intelligence of the working class " had actually
done more harm than good to that class:

When, therefore, I hear so much said of the intelligence
of the working classes, and of the enlightened state of
public opinion, I feel very much as I should do if any ill-
judging friends were to overwhelm a clever and intelligent
child with compliments, and make him think himself as
wise as his teachers. I should say that these friends were
taking the very way to hinder him from ever being as wise
as his teachers,—by teaching him to think so too soon, and
thus to slacken his efforts, or to misdirect them. (MW,
p. 205.)

His case in point was that of William Cobbett, a " clever "
but " ill-educated " man, who in Arnold's judgment, was
quite unreliable as a guide to political action, chiefly as the
result of his faulty education. Arnold concluded that the
same inadequacy made the working class as a whole as yet
unready to supply the nation's political guidance. He was

sure that the common people would not be helped to
political maturity by the journalists of the time:

> As long as they listen readily to any one who appeals to
> their passions, and turn away from him who addresses
> their reason, so long must they necessarily remain half
> instructed; for truth can only be attained by overcoming
> prejudice, just as virtue can only be attained by the con-
> quest of our selfish passions. (MW, p. 206.)

Arnold's own analysis of the causes of the " condition of
England " was calculated to focus attention on the historical and sociological causes of the social distress and
thereby to facilitate intelligent reform. His approach was
characteristically flexible. The agreement of his readers
with every point of his analysis was less important to him
than that they should " consider freely and fairly those
questions on which they [were] no better than the veriest
parrots and slaves " (MW, p. 173). He even made a
lesson of the compressed form in which he was obliged
to present his analysis. If his readers had difficulty compre-
hending the involved problems in the brief space of a single
presentation, they were to remember how great must have
been the difficulty facing persons held responsible for the
problems " without the aid of experience to enlighten them,
. . . to see beforehand to what their conduct was leading."
The implication was the blanket condemnations of these
persons were unwarranted.

He found five " real and intelligible causes " of the social
distress: the war with France; the " natural " tendency of
" wealth to become richer, and of poverty to become
poorer "; the separation in the interests of the social classes,
resulting from differences of wealth; the Poor Laws; and
the " excess of aristocracy " (MW, pp. 175-76).

According to his analysis, the chief unfavorable effects of the war were increases of British population, commerce, and manufactures to " an unnatural and therefore mischievous excess." In a subsequent paper, Arnold discussed the Malthusian theory that population tends to outgrow the means of subsistence. He agreed with this theory, which he said was known quite as well to Aristotle and other ancient philosophers as to Malthus. His deep concern with the problem of overpopulation was one of the sources of his interest in colonization, which is discussed below.

As for the problems incident to the enormous growth of British industry during the Napoleonic Wars, none concerned Arnold quite so much as that of the plight of the " operatives " who manned the machines in the new and growing factories. His indignation at the exploitation of workers by their employers is apparent in the following rather Carlylean passage:

A man sets up a factory and wants *hands*: I beseech you . . . to observe the very expressions that are used, for they are all significant. What he wants of his fellow creatures is the loan of *their hands*; of their heads and hearts he thinks nothing. These *hands* are attached to certain mouths and bodies which must be fed and lodged: but this must be done as cheaply as possible; and accordingly up starts a miserable row of houses, built where ground is cheapest, that is, where it is least desirable to get it; built as close as possible, to have more of them on a given space, and for the same reason without any sort of a garden or outlet attached to them, because the comfort and enjoyment is quite independent of the serviceableness of the *hands*. But further . . . these *hands* are not only attached to mouths and bodies, but to reasonable minds and immortal souls. The mouths and bodies must be provided for, however miserably, because without them the hands cannot work: but the minds and souls go utterly unregarded. (MW, pp. 209-10.)

Similarly unfortunate was the plight of the small trades-man and farmer who, during a period when England had been " living, as it were, the life of three hundred years in thirty," had been unable to keep up with technological developments and had been forced out by competitors. Arnold took this plight to be the result of the second main cause of the social distress:

> It is an universal rule, whether in morals, in knowledge, or in money matters, that " much will make more," and that " little is apt to become less." The small farmer was driven out of the market by the large farmer; the small tradesman by the great one; the small home manufacturer, who eked out the produce of his farm or of the labour in the fields, by the spinning or straw platting, or lace making, of his wife and daughters, in the winter evenings, could not stand against the united powers of capital and machinery. (MW, pp. 180-81.)

The result was that these unsuccessful independent busi-nessmen were forced into the growing class of those who could sell nothing but their labor. As a consequence of the additions to the labor force, the value of labor itself fell (MW, pp. 179-81).

A third main cause of the distress was a separation in the interests of the social classes resulting from differences of wealth. Arnold suggested that the effect of wealth was to make men more able to procure " intellectual pleasures." Poverty, on the other hand, made the same pleasures " un-desired and unattainable." Consequently, the two classes " sympathized with and understood each other less " (MW,

p. 176). They were therefore all the more ready to become enemies of one another.

Arnold was sharply critical of those aristocrats who resisted the tendency of farmers in improved financial situations to seek social betterment. He only regretted that the condition of the agricultural laborers had not been similarly improved. What was needed, he suggested, was not social equality but mitigated inequality:

. . . whilst the Jacobin would reduce all ranks to the lowest level, the high Aristocrat would reduce all but his own. To both is the doctrine of the good and the wise utterly opposed. Our business is to raise all, and to lower none. Equality is the dream of a madman or the passion of a fiend. Extreme inequality, or high comfort and civilization in some, co-existing with deep misery and degradation in others, is no less also a folly and a sin. But an inequality where some have all the enjoyments of civilized life, and none are without its comforts,—where some have all the treasures of knowledge, and none are sunk in ignorance, that is a social system in harmony with the order of God's creation in the natural world,—and which can alone fulfil His purposes for man as a reasonable and a spiritual being, as capable of serving and glorifying his Maker here, and enjoying with Him hereafter an eternal communion. (MW, p. 182.)

Arnold regarded the Poor Laws as still another cause of the social distress. He suggested that although they were likely to be salutary or at least harmless in ordinary times, they tended in a " diseased " state of society to encourage " a want of exertion in the poor." The laws also resulted in an unfortunate attitude toward the poor on the part of the wealthy. Both the compulsoriness and the impersonality of the arrangement led to unfortunate results:

> . . . the rich are galled by a burden of a compulsory
> charity, their feelings are hardened; and, accustomed to
> look on their neighbors as on paupers supported at their
> expense, they lose towards them all sense of equality and
> brotherhood. (MW, p. 176.)

Nevertheless, since their malfunction was only one of a
number of evils, he denied that the mere abolition of the
Poor Laws alone could do other than harm (MW, p. 189).

A fifth and final cause of the social situation was that
which Arnold described as " the excess of aristocracy in
our whole system, religious, political, and social." He
observed that this excess, which derived from causes origi-
nating early in English history, had tended " silently and
unconsciously, to separate the higher classes from the
lower in almost every relation of life." This separation he
found reflected even in the separate dialects of the two
classes:

> . . . it is an enormous evil, yet one for which no one is to
> blame, that the rich and poor in England have each what
> is almost a distinct language; the language of the rich,
> which is, of course, that of books also, being so full of
> French words derived from their Norman ancestors, while
> that of the poor still retains the pure Saxon character in-
> herited from their Saxon forefathers. (MW, pp. 176-77.)

He was speaking of an excess, however. The aristocracy
as such, he regarded as able to render valuable service to the
nation. He suggested that, along with the Church, the
aristocracy was able to prevent England from becoming
truly, as the French had said, "a nation of buyers and
sellers" (MW, pp. 213-14).

Arnold's careful study of the causes of the social problems of the time brought him at last to the far more diffi-

cult question, "*how things are to be mended.*" He observed that much of the folly of the time arose from a
failure to understand how that question differed from a
mere inquiry into the causes of the social evils:

> There are mistakes enough afloat as to the causes of our
> present evils, and yet here we have actual facts to in-
> vestigate; they may be tangled and confused, it is true,
> yet we know that as the result is before our eyes, a careful
> tracing of things backwards will bring us at last to the true
> cause or causes of it. But in projecting remedies we are in
> a manner bridging chaos . . . we may hope, we suppose,
> fairly argue, and reasonably conclude; but with regard to
> the future, we cannot *know*. (MW, pp. 182-83.)

He would have had the journalists who spoke arrogantly
realize that only their short-sightedness prevented their
seeing obstacles to their proposals.

From his viewpoint, the major shortcoming of most
contemporary reform proposals was their emphasis on a
merely partial view of national welfare. He found several
proposed remedies to be inadequate because of their common failure to consider all the implications (including
religious ones) of the social problems:

> Every newspaper, every tract, every pamphlet . . . every
> active member of a club or union, has got a remedy at
> hand for the evils of the time. There is Mr. Owen [the
> radical socialist], formerly the proprietor of the great
> cotton factory at New Lanark, who would begin society
> from the very beginning and make us all men of different
> nature from what we are now. There is Mr. Carlile [the
> secularist publisher] of the Rotunda, who would make all
> things straight by merely persuading every man to get
> rid of his conscience, and labour, talk, write, and fight,

if needful, to advance his own interest and gratify his own passions; a doctrine which says in plain English, " every man for himself and the devil for us all." Others talk only of " the drones of society," of making those who live in idleness disgorge the wealth which they are daily sucking out of the poor man's labour: and especially of stripping parsons, pensioners, and stock-jobbers, by which last terms, Mr. Cobbett [the Tory spokesman for the lower class] means " *those who have got any money in the funds* [i.e., governmental securities]." (MW, p. 184.)

His own opinion was, as he said on another occasion, that the only single remedy which could be found to adequately meet the problems of the time was " a general and earnest application of the principles of the Gospel to our dealings with each other, not only as individuals, but as classes of society " (*Sermons*, II, 352).

Arnold also criticized the reformers of his time for failing to see that the co-ordinated application of several efficacious measures would be more likely to bring favorable results than any single measure. He pointed out that no one remedy would be likely to end social evils arising from various causes. For example, emigration might well ease the problem of overpopulation for a time but would leave attendant evils untouched:

. . . how [would emigration] affect the moral evils of our condition: how . . . raise the moral and intellectual character of the poor, to bring them and the rich nearer to one another? (MW, p. 188.)

He therefore suggested a comprehensive approach to the problem of social reform.

Arnold warned that the necessity for clear thinking about social reform had not ended with the passage of the Reform

Bill of 1832. For one thing, there was danger that radicals might get too much influence in the government. He insisted that the government clearly distinguish between the cause of social reform and social revolution and renounce both the " revolutionary " proposals of the Utilitarians who wanted to see the Church destroyed, and those of " political fanatics " like the Owenites or Saint Simonians who wanted to tamper with property rights (MW, pp. 237-39).

Furthermore, Arnold maintained that the working class lacked the education needed to give them political wisdom. Consequently there was great danger that they might fall under the sway of demagogues:

> It was the last humiliation of the dying lion in the fable that he was kicked by an ass: and surely the bitterest enemies of England could desire no worse shame to befall her, than that she should have broken to pieces the iron sceptre of Napoleon, only to be trampled . . . by the brute feet of demagogues and libellers—the shallowest, the vilest, and the falsest of their tribe, who have ever yet arisen to be the curse of their own times, and the mingled scorn and detestation of posterity. (MW, p. 241.)

The agitation incident to the Chartist movement seemed to confirm his worst fears for the social well-being of the country. In 1839 he addressed letters to the Sheffield *Courant* in which he continued his advocacy of Christian politics. He traced the ability of the Chartist cause to endure to the principle of laissez-faire in business and industry. This had led to the exploitation of workers and finally to their willingness to listen to the revolutionary counsels of the Chartist leaders (MW, pp. 476-78). The result was extreme danger to the institutions of British society from men who were virtually in the condition of slaves and, not surprisingly, had begun to think like slaves (*Life*, II, 136). What was needed was a re-direction of attention to fundamental issues:

> This is the real problem; it is how to keep more than twenty millions of human beings in such a state . . . that . . . they shall have sufficient physical comforts, and a share of political rights, and some degree at least of intellectual and spiritual cultivation. All these are the just portion of free men. (MW, p. 498.)

Again Arnold would base particular reform proposals on a thorough description of the problem and the causes from which it arose. He sought first to arouse public interest in a fact-finding society to gather information on the condition of the laboring classes.* When the facts had been gathered, he planned to present them to the public without any attempt to advocate particular remedies (MW, p. 483). This approach to the reform question is perhaps Arnold's most distinctive contribution to the literature on the " condition of England " question. In an age which was all too ready to fashion panaceas, he advocated a thoughtful and factually based study of social problems:

---

* Arnold's attempt to enlist Thomas Carlyle in such a society was only partially successful. In 1840 he wrote Carlyle admiring the latter's history of the French Revolution. Arnold said that from reading the book he could tell that Carlyle understood " the real nature and magnitude " of the problems arising from the condition of the lower class (Arnold Whitridge, *Dr. Arnold of Rugby*, p. 236). Carlyle replied to the letter offering to do whatever he could if the society came into existence: " As for me, with little money, little health, with in fact, no resources whatever except what lie within myself, all I can say is, if such a society should ever come to existence it would be one of the highest duties and a really precious pleasure for me to do in it whatsoever my best ability were equal to " (Whitridge, p. 240). This, however, was somewhat less than Arnold had hoped for.

That could be no deep and wide-spreading disorder in the political system, for which a common observer like myself, with no particular sources of information at his command, could confidently recommend a cure. It is, in fact, the common error committed by unprofessional men,—by those who are laymen, if I may so speak, with regard to the subject which they are discussing,—that not contented with calling attention to the evil, they venture also to prescribe a remedy for it. (MW, p. 479.)

Arnold's difference from the other " laymen " who undertook to treat the question was in his realization of the limits imposed on him by his ignorance. Later, in the era of the great British reform commissions, a similar method of careful inquiry as a preparation for action became an integral part of public life.

From even such independent study of the problem as he was able to make, however, Arnold was as convinced as he had been eight years before that it was to be solved by the co-ordinated application of several remedies rather than by one alone. If there was no one sure remedy, there were at least several " things practicable and beneficial " which were likely to improve the situation. He thought that the Church could do much to help. It might well subdivide parishes and appoint more ministers and lay-deacons to staff them so as to extend to the vastly increased urban population " the benefits of what may really be called society." An additional benefit could be gained by giving to each of the new units a popular local legislative body which, even if it acted only upon relatively unimportant matters, would at least exert a " softening and civilizing " influence on the population at large. By sharing in the government, the people would come to have a new respect for law and order. Above all, such a measure would help to end the intolerable situation of " a mass of human beings poor and ignorant, wandering often from one place to another to find work,—unmissed in the place they leave,—unnoticed in that to which they migrate " (MW, pp. 498-500).

He realized that other reforms were needed as well. Characteristically, however, he conceived of his primary function as that of pointing the way to intelligent reform rather than that of proposing specific measures. He suggested that something must be done to restrain the accumulation of property in single hands and to extend its benefits to the needy population as a whole. He was no more specific about how this was to be accomplished than he was about the means of ending that " enormous evil " the national debt, from which he thought evils such as the Corn Law question actually derived (MW, pp. 501-502). In the letters to the Hertford *Reformer*, as elsewhere, he conceived of his most valuable contribution to British politics as the fostering of the approach to social questions " in the fear of God ":

> . . . I am by no means sure that I could inform any one rightly upon the " poor-law, commerce, corn, or taxation," although I, like others, have my opinions on these points; but I am quite sure, that in advising men to seek for political information by setting about the study of politics in a pure, a lofty, a loving, and a holy temper, I am putting them on the right track to gain it. (MW, p. 519.)

Again, his diffidence about proffering solutions arose from his knowledge of his own limited experience and insufficient information.

It must not be supposed, however, that Arnold's diffidence extended to subjects on which he considered himself well qualified to speak more specifically. He was a well-traveled man with considerable experience as an educator. When, therefore, he turned to matters of colonization and empire on the one hand, and to national education on the other, he spoke with authority.

From about 1830 until his death, Arnold was profoundly interested in British colonization as a means of relieving the pressure of overpopulation, particularly in the urban manufacturing areas. Even earlier, however, he had written on the subject primarily from another motive. This, which was never wholly absent from his later work, may best be seen in an early essay, " The Effects of Distant Colonization on the Parent State," a work for which he received the Oxford Chancellor's English Essay Prize in 1815. Here his intention of making colonization a powerful means of advancing Christianity is apparent:

> Colonization must ever continue to take place till the earth is peopled, in compliance with a necessary law of nature. God's blessing was early pronounced upon it, and therefore it must be in itself capable of doing good. Happy are they who make themselves the instruments of producing it; who crave the honour of being the channel of so much happiness to the world. That for our own country this glory may be reserved is a pardonable prayer. It will be the crown of all her triumphs, the consummation of all the bounties which Providence has vouchsafed to her. And our hope is not without foundation. There yet lives within us that mighty spirit by which we have delivered Europe. Surely it will not be less powerful to create than to destroy; and in the room of that vast fabric of evil which it has overthrown, to build up a more noble and lasting temple of good. (PE, p. 145.)

In addition to the " glory and happiness of diffusing

the light of the gospel amongst poor and blinded pagans "
(PE, p. 144), Arnold saw other advantages to colonization.
By means of it, national commerce could be increased.
Even more important, it might serve as a means of lessening
overcrowded conditions in the mother country:

> . . . a country is happier with one million of people, all of
> whom are provided with a competent maintenance, than
> it would be with an infinitely greater number, of which a
> large proportion are pining in want. (PE, p. 123.)

He suggested, however, that most of the causes which
would make such emigration necessary could, in fact, be
remedied by timely political and social action. He pointed
out the heavy responsibility incurred by a government
which elected to send its citizens abroad rather than to care
for them at home. Just as in the case of persons who had
been transported for criminal offenses, emigrants were still
the responsibility of the government.* It was up to that
government to be sure that they were cared for physically
and morally (PE, pp. 124-25).

Some years later, in 1829, Arnold actually wrote of the
possibility of emigrating to the British colony in western
Australia. He was greatly dissatisfied with reports which
he had received of moral conditions in the settlements in
Australia and New Zealand. It seemed likely that they
might be improved if only more well-educated permanent
settlers could be found:

> My notion is, that no missionaryzing [sic] is half so bene-

---

* Arnold's prediction that large colonies distant from the mother
country would eventually become independent nations has proven
to be correct in the twentieth century shrinkage of the British
Commonwealth of Nations. Cf. LMH, p. 351, where he speaks of
distance as " an insuperable obstacle to political union."

ficial as to try to pour sound and healthy blood into a young civilized society: to make one colony, if possible, like the ancient colonies, or like New England—a living sucker from the mother country, bearing the same blossoms and the same fruits, not a reproduction of its vilest excrescences, its ignorance, and its wickedness, while all the good elements are left behind in the process. No words can tell the evil of such colonies as we have hitherto planted, where the best parts of the new society have been men too poor to carry with them or to gain much of the higher branches of knowledge; or else mere official functionaries from England, whose hearts and minds have been always half at home, and who have never identified themselves with the land in which they were working. (*Life*, I, 263-64.)

Arnold turned his eyes to America also. In his *Englishman's Register* he printed some letters received from a Rugby laborer who had been able to improve his situation vastly by emigrating to the United States. Arnold suggested in an editorial that because labor was scarcer in the new nation than at home, others also might be able to profit from emigration.[38] Although he did not think that any one measure would be enough to correct the social ills of the time, he did regard the resettlement of the poorer laborers as likely to be beneficial.

In maintaining this view, however, he found it necessary to counter the criticisms of working class leaders who identified such resettlement with the transportation of convicts:

When . . . I hear a Chartist leader protest against emigration and call it transportation, I hear the language not of freemen but of slaves; of persons bound to the soil . . . who . . . when distress and scarcity come . . . have no choice but to starve and die. (MW, p. 493.)

Arnold himself could see no injustice in resettling those in poor straits (MW, pp. 199-200). Indeed, many might enjoy benefits as American citizens or British colonists which would greatly improve their lot. From such advantages, however, they were barred by agitators who played on their fears and their ignorance of geography in order to oppose resettlement (MW, p. 200).

Despite his interest in colonization and emigration, however, Arnold consistently opposed the use of military force as a tool of imperial expansion. At a time when the " jingoism " of Lord Palmerston was much admired, Arnold called attention to the positive evil as well as the futility of England's military adventures in the Orient and Middle East and her threatened war with France. He bitterly deprecated British military support of the Chinese opium trade:

> ... this war with China ... seems to me so wicked as to be a national sin of the greatest possible magnitude and distresses me very deeply. Cannot any thing be done by petition or otherwise to awaken men's minds to the dreadful guilt we are incurring? I really do not remember, in any history, of a war undertaken with such combined injustice and baseness. Ordinary wars are to me far less wicked, than to go to war in order to maintain smuggling, and that smuggling consisting in the introduction of a demoralizing drug, which the government of China wishes to keep out and which we, for the lucre of gain, want to introduce by force; and in this quarrel are going to burn and slay in the pride of our supposed supremacy. (*Life*, II, 206.)

Similarly Arnold could not approve of English intervention in Middle Eastern affairs which in 1840 almost resulted in war with France. Palmerston's ministry had supported Turkey in its quarrel with Egypt, then a French protectorate. In the midst of much popular enthusiasm for British military feats before Acre, Arnold's sober warning of the consequences could scarcely have been very welcome:

> History is full of wars undertaken on slight grounds, and as foolish as they were wicked. But taking all things into account, the increased sense of the evils of war, now so generally prevalent, the actual difficulties of the country, the object aimed at, and the enemy selected, Lord Palmerston's war with France, should such a calamity unhappily take place, will stand, I verily believe, unmatched in the records of human folly. (MW, p. 508.)

Arnold had elsewhere stated his belief that war was a state of " fatal intoxication," which in addition to checking all social progress in a nation, also greatly increased the danger of its falling under a despotism (MW, p. 109). In 1840 he argued that the poor state of the British economy was utterly unfit to support a war. In addition, he anticipated considerable danger from the expanding Russian empire if England and France became enemies. Only as long as the two allies stood ready to " strike at the life of Russia through her vulnerable heel . . . the Crimea " could the world be free from the " evil spirit of Russian ambition " (MW, pp. 510-11).*

The basis of Arnold's interest in the fortunes of British imperialism was his conception of a far-flung Christian dominion " over palm and pine." Through the agency of the Empire, the blessings attendant on the Christian State

---

* Arnold's words anticipate British and French strategy in the Crimean War (1853-56) when the allies, anxious to avoid " the folly of the march to Moscow," invaded the Crimean Peninsula. In 1841 Arnold predicted that Russia's " future influence on the condition of Europe and of the world would be far greater than that which it exercises now " (LMH, pp. 45-46).

were to be extended beyond England's borders. His method of effecting his object was the inculcation of a sense of duty. The strong were obligated to assist the weak:

> . . . distinctions between race and race, like those between individuals, involve a duty which men have been unhappily very unwilling to practice. They who are most favoured by nature owe their best assistance to those whose lot is most unpromising; they who have advanced the furthest in civilization are bound to enlighten others whose progress has been less rapid. (MW, pp. 110-111.)

Arnold had hope that in time the evils of chauvinism and nationalism might be overcome. Once men had learned " to enlarge the circle of their regards " and had conquered the " narrow and unchristian feeling " of national jealousy, they might realize their common membership in the brotherhood of man:

> Exclusive patriotism should be cast off, together with exclusive ascendancy of birth, as belonging to the follies and selfishness of our uncultivated nature. Yet, strange to say, the former, at least, is sometimes upheld by men who not only call themselves Christians, but are apt to use the charge of irreligion as the readiest weapon against those who differ from them. So little have they learned of the spirit of that revelation which taught emphatically the abolition of an exclusively national religion and local worship, that so men, [sic] being all born of the same blood, might make their sympathies coextensive with their bond of universal brotherhood. (MW, p. 111.)

He hoped to achieve this lofty object by Christian education, the same means by which he attempted to improve the moral and intellectual welfare of the English working class. Writing in 1835 to his friend Dr. Hawkins, Provost of Oriel, he spoke of the "*idea*" of his life as the constructing of "a truly national and Christian Church, and truly national and Christian system of education" (*Life*, II, 14). This he could hardly expect to achieve solely by his work with Rugbeians who were, for the most part, members of the aristocracy and upper middle class. He therefore sought to extend the influence of Christianity into the field of popular education.

In 1831 he spoke ruefully of the "mass of imperfect and ill-digested knowledge" exhibited by the poor as little better than the "deep and general ignorance" from which they had freed themselves (MW, p. 212). In his judgment, the "teaching" proffered them by the journalist and the orator was unlikely to fit them for citizenship in a Christian nation. Arnold maintained that the lack of any more responsible instructors was the cause of the predominantly unchristian character of the working class. Because of their uneducated condition, the people found little to value in British religious and political institutions which, accordingly, they could not be counted on to preserve:

> Thousands of men grew up devoid alike of physical comforts and of intellectual and moral culture; and now we are reaping the fruits of it. Having no property of their own, they hate property,—having no means of intellectual enjoyment, they are driven to seek the pleasures which we have in common with brutes, having never been made Christians, their undisciplined natures are incapable of valuing Christianity, and their evil passions tell them to hate it. (MW, p. 211.)

He advocated philanthropically supported libraries and museums to aid in educating those who could not afford to attend schools. Public spirited men who made the facilities available should, he suggested, place them under the management of some society of working men. In this way, the poorer classes could obtain not only an education but some respect for public property. Both were needed if the poor were to be raised intellectually and spiritually (MW, p. 216).

Similarly, when the middle class gained the political franchise in 1832, Arnold was profoundly concerned that they be educated to use it rightly. In a letter to the Sheffield *Courant*, he addressed himself directly to the new voters, warning them about their now increased responsibilities:

> We are all aware of the growing power of the middling classes of society, and we know that the Reform Bill will at once increase this power and consolidate it. But power, like every other gift bestowed upon us by God's Providence, is not a mere gratuity, but a trust; it is given us to do good with it; and therefore, it is far better both for ourselves and others that we should not possess it at all, than that we should not know how to use it. (MW, pp. 226-27.)

He was far from sure that the existing system of middle class education was capable of bringing the people to the required knowledge, however. It had two serious defects: there was no assurance that its teachers were qualified to teach and there was some doubt that the right subjects were being taught.

The so-called "commercial" schools of the day were ordinarily conducted by unlicensed laymen. Arnold pointed out that the difficulty here was the lack of assurance that these men were intellectually or morally qualified to serve as teachers. Unlike the schools for the wealthy, the commercial schools were not conducted by clergymen, and hence there was no guarantee that middle class pupils would be taught by men possessed of " that union of intellectual and moral qualifications " which Arnold believed to be characteristically present in the English clergy. To make matters worse, there were no local universities for the graduates of commercial schools to attend. A consequence was that the schoolmasters had no particular incentive to train their pupils carefully, and no way of gaining a professional reputation by the prowess of the pupils. Arnold found that most of the teachers became dependent on their local patrons and were thus forced to a position of servility.

Because he considered good schools to be a powerful means of contributing to man's intellectual and spiritual good, he advocated governmental action to provide middle class schools and colleges capable of rendering to the middle class benefits analogous to those enjoyed by the wealthy in the public schools and universities (MW, pp. 228-30).

Arnold saw no remedy for the second defect of the commercial schools. He could only call attention to their failure to teach subjects which he considered essential to the very meaning of education. He granted that they were often well equipped to give excellent training in natural science or engineering but refused to admit that such training fitted the students to be good citizens or good men:

> I have little doubt that boys will be sufficiently taught all that they require for their particular calling; and scientific knowledge is so generally valued and confers a power so immediately felt, that I think its diffusion may be safely reckoned on. This, however, has nothing to do with the knowledge which the Reform Bill calls for. A man may be ever so good a chemist, or ever so good a mechanic, or

ever so good an engineer, and yet not at all the fitter to
enjoy the elective franchise. (MW, pp. 231-32.)

He thought the difficulty arose from widespread failure
to realize that man has two businesses in life, a particular,
and a general, calling. In training men to perform the
duties of their particular occupations, the commercial
schools were accomplishing but half the job. In addition to
such professional education, the people needed liberal education to prepare them for their general calling as citizens
and men.

Other educational reformers in the field were not in
agreement with Arnold on this point. The Useful Knowledge Society was a powerful sponsor of secular education
on the popular and university levels. Although he was in
general sympathy with the aim of the society to improve
the level of popular education, he regarded all the efforts
of Brougham and his group as vitiated by one serious lack;
the *Penny Magazine*, the mechanics' institutes, the University of London—all were centered not on religion but
on science. It was this mistaken emphasis, as he saw it,
which kept the secularist philanthropists from meeting one
of the fundamental needs of the lower classes, moral education. The idea of a purely secular education seemed to him
to have serious implications for the future of both education and religion.

Accordingly, about 1831, Arnold wrote to an officer of
the Useful Knowledge Society expressing his hope that
the *Penny Magazine* might be given a more " avowedly
Christian tone " (*Life*, I, 285). The governing committee
of the society had a vastly different notion from Arnold
of what studies were " useful," however. Neither Arnold's
offer to subscribe money nor his willingness to contribute

articles to the *Magazine* could induce them to broaden the basically utilitarian scheme of the journal enough to admit treatment of moral subjects from a Christian point of view. They were so firmly resolved to exclude religious matters from their program that they could not entertain his argument that neutrality to Christianity was really equivalent to hostility toward it.[39] Throughout the remainder of his life, Arnold was obliged to carry on his program of Christian education without the aid of a society whose educational potentialities he correctly estimated as very great.

He was only slightly more successful in his association with London University. In 1835 he was offered a Fellowship in the Senate of the new University by Spring Rice, then Chancellor of the Exchequer. Arnold gladly accepted the post in hopes of realizing his ideal of an educational institution which should be guided by Christian though nonsectarian religious principles. Although the majority of his colleagues in the governing body of the University were opposed to religious tests of any kind, Arnold felt that one, at least, was necessary. He therefore proposed that candidates for the B.A. degree be required to pass an examination in Scripture history and in the Greek version of one of the Gospels or the Book of Acts. By this means he hoped to retain what seemed to him the necessary tie between education and religion (*Life*, II, 10-11).

In view of his assurances that nonsectarian examinations were possible and that he stood ready to help prepare them, the Senate of the University reluctantly passed a resolution in 1837 calling for such examinations " as a general rule." Later, the measure was rescinded and the examinations were placed on a voluntary basis " to be followed by certificates of proficiency." [40]

To Arnold, however, who believed that " a knowledge

of the Christian Scriptures must form a part of the merely intellectual education of all persons in Christian countries," the change to the voluntary scheme robbed the University of much of its potential for good. Accordingly, after unsuccessful efforts to have the matter reconsidered, he withdrew from a body which thereafter served as a melancholy reminder to him of the growing force of secularism in education (*Life*, II, 88, 112).

He found the same force to be operative in the new mechanics' institutes which were springing up in England in the 1830's. When, in 1838, he was invited to address the institute in Rugby, he took occasion not merely to commend its function in providing education for those who would otherwise be without it, but to point out a necessary shortcoming of all such institutions. He thought this arose from an overly limited philosophy of education:

> Physical science alone can never make a man educated; even the formal sciences (i.e., grammar, logic, arithmetic and geometry), invaluable as they are with respect to the discipline of the reasoning powers, cannot instruct the judgment; it is only moral and religious knowledge which can accomplish this. And if habitually removing such knowledge from the course of our studies, we exercise our thoughts and understanding exclusively on lower matters, what will be the result, but that when we come to act upon these higher points, in our relations as citizens and as men, we shall act merely upon ignorance, prejudice, and passion? (MW, p. 423.)

Furthermore, as moral and religious knowledge was the chief means of learning God's will for men, it was therefore more valuable to man than any other knowledge (MW, pp. 410-12). For this reason, it appeared to Arnold that secular and utilitarian studies alone would be incapable of fitting Englishmen to deal with national problems, problems which he thought were to be solved by adherence to religious principles in political life.

CRITICS, CHRISTIAN SOCIALISTS, AND EDUCATORS

Arnold's special gifts in the political field were those of a critic. In an age of the ready panacea and the rabble-rousing orator, he insisted on a careful description of social problems and a thorough inquiry into their causes as a prelude to remedial action. He opposed superficiality and one-sidedness. Nor was he willing to give unreserved allegiance to any one party, for his obligation was rather, as he saw it, to the party of Christ. Despite the merit of these views, however, Arnold had serious limitations as a guide to his time on political questions. Though he was quick to see the shortcomings in the reform programs of others, he was not adept at proposing substitutes which appeared workable enough to gain acceptance by his countrymen.

Nevertheless, his political idealism was exactly such as to appeal to the young men who came under his tutelage.* Indeed, it was through the work of his pupils that he "elevated the political and administrative functions into Christian vocations at every level of the State. . . ." [41]

Matthew Arnold's correspondence contains many references to his father's political and social ideas and to the bearing of these on his own work. In time, he came to realize his profound indebtedness to Dr. Arnold's views even when treating topics on which the elder Arnold had not written. Very early in his career he seems to have been greatly impressed with Dr. Arnold's refusal to lead a clois-

* During Arnold's tenure at Rugby, 1320 boys were admitted (*Rugby School Register* [Rugby, 1886], I, 232).

tered, academic life—a decision which gained for him the respect of "worldly men" who, according to Matthew, saw that "in the business of life he met them and beat them on their own ground." Later, upon publishing a controversial work, Matthew Arnold noted his indebtedness to his father's "pamphleteering talent" and suggested that he himself had inherited Dr. Arnold's "positive style of statement." On other occasions he described himself as a "continuator" of the elder Arnold's views on the State and, as he suggested, he could not touch upon the subject without realizing how much his opinions were drawn from his father's. In Matthew's correspondence with such public figures as Gladstone and Richard Cobden, he cited Thomas Arnold's earlier advocacy of views or courses of action which he then, a generation later, was recommending.[42]

In such works of Matthew Arnold's political and social criticism as *A French Eton* (1864), "The Function of Criticism at the Present Time" (1865), *Culture and Anarchy* (1869), *Mixed Essays* (1879), *Irish Essays and Others* (1882), *and Discourses in America* (1885), may be found evidence which suggests that Matthew Arnold's admissions of indebtedness were not merely actuated by filial piety. In three main respects these works reflect the teachings of the elder Arnold: (1) the idea of the State as the major agency in the moral and intellectual improvement of mankind; (2) the recommendation of disinterestedness in the consideration of social problems; and (3) the advocacy of better middle class education as an important means of increasing national welfare.

We have seen that Thomas Arnold's political criticism was based on his theory of the Christian State, in which all activities of public life were to be conducted according to Christian principles. For Dr. Arnold there was no separat-

ing political and religious questions. Essentially the same
view was held by Matthew, as can be seen in his remark
that " questions of good government, social harmony, education, civilisation " could not be treated without first
" returning to treat of religion " (*Works*, X, 94). For
Matthew Arnold, as for his father, the goal was that of " a
commonwealth whose political institutions were informed
by the Christian spirit." [43] Confronted by the terrible condition of the industrial laborers of his time, Dr. Arnold had
called on the government to lend its aid in ending the evil
consequences of laissez-faire (MW, p. 478). Similarly,
in *Culture and Anarchy* Matthew Arnold looked to the
State to end the " anarchy " of individualism, petty strife,
and class rivalry:

> We want an authority, and we find nothing but jealous
> classes, checks, and a deadlock; culture suggests the idea of
> *the State*. We find no basis for a firm State-power in our
> ordinary selves; culture suggests one to us in our *best
> self*. (*Works*, VI, 76.)

Just as Dr. Arnold conceived of the end of the State as
" the intellectual and moral improvement of mankind, in
order to [make possible] their reaching their greatest perfection, and enjoying their highest happiness " (MW,
p. 331), so Matthew Arnold maintained that more State
activity was essential to the religious, artistic, political, and
intellectual welfare of British civilization.[44]

Matthew Arnold was also his father's continuator in his
practice of " disinterestedness " in the consideration of
political and social problems. Dr. Arnold's party was that
of " Christian reform " rather than that of any existing
political interest. He strongly advocated that voters resist
attempts by demagogues and political journalists to sway

their opinions. Matthew Arnold's " The Function of Criticism at the Present Time " is a development of this line of
thought:

> . . . the critic has many temptations to go with the stream,
> to make one of the party movement . . . it seems un-
> gracious to refuse to be a *terræ filius*, when so many excel-
> lent people are; but the critic's duty is to refuse, or, if
> resistance is vain, at least to cry with Obermann: *Périssons
> en résistant.* (*Works*, III, 30.)

One example of such " resistance " may be seen in the same
essay in the use of the dehumanized journalistic phrase,
" Wragg is in custody," to deflate the empty rhetoric of
British politicians of both parties:

> *Wragg is in custody.* The sex lost in the confusion of our
> unrivalled happiness; or (shall I say?) the superfluous
> Christian name lopped off by the straightforward vigour
> of our old Anglo-Saxon breed! (*Works*, III, 26.)

It is the same type of attack which Thomas Arnold employed in his analysis of the catchwords of contemporary
political journalism.

Similarly, Matthew Arnold shared his father's belief that
on political questions immediate action was not necessarily
desirable. In his essay on " The Social Condition of the
Operative Classes," Dr. Arnold set himself the task of clarifying issues, of calling attention to problems, and of noting
the limitations of proposed remedies. Frequently he observed that he was less interested in getting agreement on
specific points than in obtaining agreement on principles.
With these views can be compared Matthew Arnold's
statement in " Irish Catholicism and British Liberalism "
that he was not a politician but merely " one of a dis-

interested class of observers who, with no organised and embodied set of supporters to please, set themselves to observe honestly and to report faithfully the state and prospects of our civilisation" (*Works*, X, 104). Like his father, Matthew Arnold favored the postponement of action until information was available to make that action intelligent and effective:

> Let us think of quietly enlarging our stock of true and fresh ideas, and not, as soon as we get an idea or half an idea, be running out with it into the street, and trying to make it rule there. Our ideas will, in the end, shape the world all the better for maturing a little. (*Works*, III, 39.)

Like Dr. Arnold, Matthew Arnold also worked toward the improvement of middle class education on a national level. Thomas Arnold's editorials on "The Education of the Middle Classes" show his concern about the inadequate system of education available to the class given the political franchise in 1832. Matthew Arnold devoted a quarter of a century to the inspection of middle class nonconformist schools and, in addition, gave evidence before the Taunton Commission (1864) then studying the condition of middle class education.[45] His professional experience made him fully aware of the shortcomings of the middle class schools. No less than his father before him, he was alarmed at the degrading tendency of such education:

> . . . the great mass of the middle part of our community . . . are both badly taught, and are also brought up on a lower plane than is right, brought up ignobly. . . . the training produces with fatal sureness the effect of lowering their standard of life and impairing their civilisation. It helps to produce in them, and it perpetuates, a defective type of religion, a narrow range of intellect and knowl-

edge, a stunted sense of beauty, a low standard of manners. (*Works*, XI, 61-62.)

His proposed solution to the problem also reflected Thomas Arnold's thinking on the matter. Dr. Arnold had sought to have the State provide educational benefits for the middle class analogous to the public school education enjoyed by the upper class (MW, p. 230). Similarly, Matthew Arnold held that the need should be met by the government's "establishment of public schools for the middle classes" (*Works*, XI, 123). Such a step he took to be preliminary to the "transformation" of the middle class and hence to the moral and intellectual salvation of English life.[46]

Thomas Arnold's teachings also bore fruit in the Christian Socialist Movement of 1848-54, especially through the work of Thomas Hughes, Arthur Stanley, and Arthur Hugh Clough.

Hughes (1822-96), who attended Rugby from 1833 to 1842, was the author of *Tom Brown's Schooldays* (1857), one of the several works (including Stanley's *Life of Arnold* and Matthew Arnold's "Rugby Chapel") by which Dr. Arnold's aims and character became widely popularized during the Victorian period. Hughes was a determined if not always subtle or intellectual continuator of Arnold's work. He was profoundly influenced by Dr. Arnold's *Sermons on Christian Life*, from which he read intensively between 1841 and 1844.[47] Upon reading Stanley's *Life of Arnold* in 1844, Hughes was strongly taken with Arnold's advocacy of democracy according to orderly principles, a view which is reflected both in Hughes's work with the Christian Socialists and with the Collectivist Movement. It was about this time that he began to con-

ceive of himself, along with Arnold and other liberals, as
one of the "humble agents of God's mission to the century." [48] Throughout his life, he understood this mission
as "the setting up of the kingdom of God on earth as the
practical goal of all . . . efforts." [49]

Accordingly, in 1848 he was glad to associate himself
with F. D. Maurice, Charles Kingsley, and F. W. Ludlow
in what came to be called the Christian Socialist Movement. This group of men was primarily concerned with
realizing the social mission of the Church through their
own work and through attempts to increase the social
sensitivity of those in places of power. Because of his great
vitality, his personal popularity, and his gift for journalism, Hughes soon became the center of the movement;
it was chiefly through him that Arnold "greatly influenced
the Christian Socialists." [50]

The chief purposes of the movement are summarized in
the first number of *Politics*, the "tracts for the times"
produced by the socialists:

> . . . to consider the questions which are most occupying
> our countrymen at the present moment, such as the Exten-
> sion of the Franchise; the relation of the Capitalist to the
> Labourer; what a Government can or cannot do to find
> work or pay for the Poor.[51]

Like Arnold, the members of the movement opposed the
separation of politics from Christianity and accordingly
sought to influence political action. Again like Arnold,
the socialists concerned themselves with the relations between the social classes. In his preface to Charles Kingsley's
Alton Locke, Hughes even made the exaggerated claim
that the combined efforts of the socialists and the trade
unionists between 1848 and 1856 had "entirely changed

the . . . relations of the working to the upper and middle classes." [52]

In fact, however, the socialists were not often completely successful in attaining their ends. Nevertheless, their evident good will and moderation did make possible their obtaining a charter from the government. Co-operative societies such as their own were given legal status in 1852 by the Industrial and Providential Societies Act. This end attained, each of the socialist leaders turned to his own field of special concern. To Thomas Hughes, bent on " the setting up of the kingdom of God on earth," this meant an attempt to bring the Christian religion into the industrial sphere where it seemed most lacking. Accordingly, with E. V. Neale, Hughes became one of the leaders of the Co-operative Movement in the industrial north of England. [53] There he carried into practical action Thomas Arnold's teaching that one " could not cut [his] life into slices. . . ." [54] It was in this work that Hughes came to be regarded as a " prophet " of the Co-operative Movement. [55] He was no less the old Rugbeian at work in society.

Hughes was assisted in this work by two more former students of Dr. Arnold, Arthur Stanley and Arthur Hugh Clough, both of whom were slightly connected with the Christian Socialist Movement. Stanley was the author of two articles published respectively in the socialist organs, *Politics for the People* and *The Christian Socialist*. [56] Outside these journals, however, one may find many parts of Stanley's voluminous works which reflect Thomas Arnold's thought. His continuation of the elder Arnold's efforts in the fields of Biblical criticism and Church reform has already been pointed out. His writings in the political and social field, though much less extensive, are equally Arnoldian. Especially so was his persistent unwillingness to give unreserved allegiance to any party (*DNB*, XVIII, 934); though the tone of his work sometimes grew strident in the bitter controversies of the age, his habitual position was that of detachment, somewhat like that recommended by Dr. Arnold in his Christian reform program. Moreover, Stanley completely endorsed Dr. Arnold's opposition to laissez-faire political economy and accepted his moderate socialism.[57] Also, after initial doubts, and with some minor qualifications, Stanley accepted Dr. Arnold's theory of the " high " or Christian State which he propounded as follows:

> It is not so much that Church and State are one as that the Church, in its highest sense, is equally above both Church and State. . . . (*Life of Stanley*, I, 384.)

In addition to propagating Arnold's political ideas at Balliol and editing his *Miscellaneous Works* which contain important treatments of this theory, Stanley made his own contributions to the subject in his *Essays Chiefly on Questions of Church and State from 1850 to 1870.* In looking back on Stanley's life and works, Benjamin Jowett mentioned as his double inheritance from Dr. Arnold, his theory of Church and State (with which Jowett could not agree) and " a noble impulse which he communicated to others " to live righteously. Clearly the " disciple " who as a boy had often written down Dr. Arnold's sermons from memory, and who after Thomas Arnold's death had felt himself cast upon " an island of memory," set himself early to work towards the lofty political ideals which his teacher had embodied in the theory of the Christian State.[58]

To a lesser degree, the results of Dr. Arnold's religious and political teachings can be demonstrated in the works of Arthur Hugh Clough (1819-61), the Victorian poet and intellectual usually taken by critics as the classic ex-

ample of the unsettling effects of Arnold's heavy emphasis
on moral responsibility and his questioning approach to
religious matters.[59] According to Stanley, Clough felt the
full strength of " that electric shock which Arnold communicated to all his better pupils." [60] Matthew Arnold, on
reading Clough's posthumously published letters and journals in 1865, observed that Clough had probably " felt . . .
too much " the force of the elder Arnold's personality and
teachings.[61] Certainly Clough, who was an outstanding student at Rugby, very early developed both an ardent admiration for his teacher, and a preoccupation with moral
and metaphysical questions which seems to have been
associated in his mind with that admiration. It is undeniable
that he spent many years of his later life in anxious specu-
lation and unhappy introspection about religious questions.[62] On the other hand, there seems little doubt that
Clough's religious " puzzling " at the hand of Oxford
philosophers and logicians like William George Ward also
contributed powerfully to the psychological damage usually
attributed to Clough's Rugby background.[63] Again, as has
been pointed out, Clough had a tendency towards emotional dependence which seems to have made him " the
most willing of victims " to the domination of strong per-
sonalities such as his mother, Dr. Arnold, Ward, and ultimately, Florence Nightingale.[64] On the whole, it would
appear that Dr. Arnold's responsibility for the subsequent
doubts and vacillations of Clough about moral and religious
issues is, at best, indeterminate.

That Clough did adopt certain of Arnold's social views
is, however, sufficiently clear. Like many Old Rugbeians,
he read his teacher's works closely and enthusiastically,
finding in the first three volumes of Dr. Arnold's *Sermons*,
for example, an " amazing quantity of wisdom and good

sense, and resolution and strength." [65] Perhaps most of all, he shared Thomas Arnold's unwillingness to shut his eyes to the sociological and spiritual " condition of England." [66] As early as 1844 Clough half-humorously wrote a friend that he had undertaken studies in Political Economy for the purpose of becoming " the apostle of ' anti-laissez-faire.' " [67] Later, his intense consciousness of widespread misery among the laboring class helped to make him discontented with the academic seclusion of his Oxford teaching post.[68] The same consciousness led him to associate himself with the Christian Socialist Movement, and, about the same period, to treat of social questions in a periodical essay published in the *North American Review*. In " Considerations of Some Recent Social Theories " (1853) Clough embraced one small aspect of Arnoldian social thought and preached a gospel of service and avoidance of evil.[69]

In Clough's later years, similar concerns appeared in exaggerated form in his " cab-horse " work for Florence Nightingale as secretary, general assistant, errand-boy, proofreader, editor, and author. Indirectly this may perhaps be related to the social concern which Dr. Arnold consistently fostered in his pupils.[70] Certainly Clough's part in such works as *Notes on the British Army* and *Suggestions for Thought to the Searchers after Truth among the Artizans of England* must have disappointed those who thought of him primarily as poet and man of letters. Such activities only serve to remind us, however, that the writer of " Say Not the Struggle Naught Availeth," " The Latest Decalogue," " Easter Day," and *Dipsychus* was, like many " disciples," capable of carrying the doctrines of a master to extremes which would be nearly unrecognizable to the originator. That Clough

habitually tried to follow the Arnoldian preachment of
extreme individual responsibility to follow one's convictions " though all the world were to follow the contrary "
seems clear. On the other hand, his failure to observe the
Arnoldian warnings against " morbid and unhealthy scrutiny about the exact nature of our feelings " and against
inquiries which made one's " spiritual state . . . depend upon
our power of metaphysical observation " could not be
more patent.[71]

Other results of Arnold's political teachings are to be
seen in the work of John Phillip Gell, W. E. Forster, and
William Delafield Arnold, all of whom concerned themselves with educational administration.

Gell (1816-98), a former Rugbeian, became Principal
of the projected College of Van Diemen's Land (later
Tasmania) at the behest of Arnold and there carried on
work which reflected Arnoldian principles. In 1839 the
governor of the colony consulted Arnold as to a candidate
for the educational office. Arnold unhesitatingly recommended Gell and wrote to the latter as follows:

> [Governor Franklin] wants a Christian, a gentleman, and a
> scholar,—a member of one of our Universities,—a man of
> ability and of vigour of character,—to become the father
> of the education of a whole quarter of the globe; and to
> assist, under God's blessing, and with the grace of Christ's
> Spirit, in laying the foundations of all good and noble
> principles, not only in individual children, but in an infant
> nation, which must hereafter influence the world largely
> for good or for evil. And I think that, if you could feel
> disposed to undertake this great missionary labour, you
> would work at it in the spirit of Christ's servant, and
> would become the instrument of blessings, not to be
> numbered, . . . (*Life*, II, 153.)

Arnold's interest in the proposed college was heightened
by his feeling that the mother country tended to neglect
the spiritual welfare of the colonies. Gell's acceptance of
a position in which he would be engaged in educating a
colonial population, many of whom were convicts, was
directly in line with Dr. Arnold's tenets of Christian
political responsibility.

In recommending Gell, Arnold had correctly estimated
his man. Mrs. Arnold remarked on one occasion that Gell
more nearly shared Thomas Arnold's "aims and capa-
bilities" than anyone she had known. Certainly Gell
ardently desired to establish a foundation inspired by the
Arnoldian ideal, "a stronghold of learning and a school of
Christian gentlemen." For four years he carried on a
campaign in the new colony for the establishment of a
national college which would be both Christian and nonsectarian. He was opposed by Franklin's successor as governor, Sir Eardley Wilmot, who thought "education without religion practical and desirable," and who eventually
even managed to have funds for the projected college excluded from the official budget. Eventually the plan for
a national college had to be abandoned.

Finally, in 1846, Gell was appointed Warden of the new
Christ's College of Tasmania supported by the Church of
England. There and in the associated public school of
the colony, he saw the partial realization of Arnold's principles of Christian education. Several years later, feeling
that he had accomplished his mission, he returned to England and took up the work of a parish clergyman successively at St. Mary's, Bryanston Square, London; St. John's,
Notting Hill; and Buxted, Sussex. In his later years his
work showed the orientation towards the needs of the poor,
the wide tolerance of religious differences, the interest in

liturgical reform, and the defense of a liberal Biblical criticism, all of which might be expected of one of Arnold's pupils.[72]

Particularly through Gell's work abroad, Arnold's ideas received wide dissemination. As late as 1883, one of Gell's former Tasmanian pupils wrote as follows of the force of Arnoldian ideals in the colony which Gell served:

> . . . through you and your influence, I was drawn to look closely into the character and teaching of . . . Dr. Arnold. . . . Here, at the Antipodes, and forty years after his death, he *speaks still*. . . . Far-reaching sympathy was with him an ever acting force and we have felt it. It comes from one Higher—It goes on working downwards; and it must, from its nature, draw upwards. Arnold's teaching and power, with God's blessing, will yet have a great harvest.[73]

Arnold's views on national education were also influential on William E. Forster, (1818-86), the author of the Elementary Education Act of 1870 which embodied some of Arnold's ideas. Forster, who was Arnold's son-in-law, served as Vice-President of the Committee of the Privy Council for Education from 1868 to 1874. Sir Joshua Fitch, who was personally acquainted with Forster, maintained that his convictions and policy had been affected by the Arnoldian tradition. Fitch found the Education Act of 1870 to be especially Arnoldian in several respects:

> . . . its large tolerance . . . its sympathy with the aspirations of the working classes for enlightenment and culture, the political insight which it exhibited, and above all, the determination of its author to enlist on behalf of a system of National Education the co-operation of good men of various religious creeds.[74]

In particular, the bill provided for elementary education

on a national scale without destroying the existing educational system. This mode of procedure was favored by Arnold, who had been concerned almost solely with middle-class education. The bill was also Arnoldian in its avoidance of the purely secularistic solution. It allowed religious teaching in the school, subject to the provision that objecting parents could require their children to absent themselves from any religious observance.[75] When he was importuned by the secularists to make the system a thoroughgoing nonreligious one, Forster gave a typically Arnoldian reply:

> If we did so, out of the religious difficulty we should come to an irreligious difficulty. . . . Surely the time will come when men will find out that on the main questions of religion they agree, and that they can teach in common to their children. . . . (Cornish, II, 279-80.)

By an amendment later added to the bill, a condition similar to that which Arnold had proposed for London University went into effect. Teachers were permitted to expound the Bible, but the use of sectarian formularies or catechisms was forbidden (Cornish, II, 282).

Dr. Arnold's political teachings were also reflected to some degree in the work of his fourth son,* William Dela-

---

* Some of the emotional and spiritual vicissitudes of Thomas Arnold, Jr. (1823-1900), Dr. Arnold's second son, may perhaps be traced to a sensitivity to ethical and social issues which seems to have been fostered by the elder Arnold's response to the " condition of England." But Thomas Arnold, Jr., despite his promising Oxford career and his subsequent display of ability as scholar and teacher, failed to produce significant work in the religious and social sphere (cf. Thomas Arnold, Jr., *Passages in a Wandering Life* [London: Edward Arnold, 1900], *passim*; T. H. S. Escott, " The Arnolds: a Study in Heredity," pp. 679-80; Kenneth Allott, " Thomas Arnold the Younger; New Zealand and the ' Old Democratic Fervour,' " *Landfall*, XV [September, 1961], 208-25).

field Arnold (1828-59), who rose to the position of Director of Public Instruction of Punjab, India (1856-59). After
an education at Rugby and Oxford (he left Christ Church
without taking a degree), William Arnold in 1848 enlisted
in the British Army for service in India. While there, he
became intensely interested in the educational and moral
problems of the colony, an interest apparently stimulated
by his early training and his continuing study of Dr.
Arnold's published works. He spoke of " the long range
of [Thomas Arnold's] Works " in his Indian quarters and
observed that he had come to esteem them even more since
leaving England. On first seeing the Himalayas, he was,
as he later wrote, reminded of his father. In the midst of
trying duties carried on far from home, he remembered
words from Rugby Chapel.[76]

In particular, William Arnold was deeply concerned at
this time with the moral issues of British imperialism and
with the problems raised in the colonies by the coexistence
of Christianity and other religions. Both appear without
much attempt at a definite resolution in his semi-autobio-
graphical novel, *Oakfield; or Fellowship in the East*, begun
in India and completed and published in England in 1853.
The principal conflict of the book is that between the
hero's ethical idealism and the existing manners and morals
of the social order in which he finds himself. The major
achievement of the author is that he successfully conveys
the impression of Oakfield's sincerity as he confronts the
moral and metaphysical ambiguities of his age. So apparent
was the " Arnoldism " of the work that when it appeared
under a pseudonym, a writer for the *Prospective Review*
discerned in it the characteristically Arnoldian desire " to
see the church and the world identified," and suggested

that it gave good hope " that Dr. Arnold's faith may yet become ascendant in the Church." [77]

William Arnold's concern about Indian questions also prompted him repeatedly to warn of the dangerous moral and political situation in the colony. Indeed, his earnestness about Indian affairs led Matthew Arnold to observe somewhat unfairly that if left in the army, William would someday " mount a tub in the barrack yard and prophesy to the regiment and the government of India, all the judgments they deserve." [78] In early 1857, with something of the prophetic attitude of his father, William wrote a series of letters to the Indian press pointing out the dangers incident to the creation of a native army. Shortly thereafter, the events of the Great Mutiny of that year proved the accuracy of his predictions. After the Mutiny was over, he wrote a series of articles for *Fraser's Magazine* (1857-58) which were instrumental in informing public opinion about the causes of the uprising and the responsibility of the British to resume control.[79] In these endeavors he clearly displayed his Rugby heritage.

The younger Arnold's educational politics indicate that he was guided by general principles of Dr. Arnold without attempting to adopt in India the specific measures more appropriate to England. One remembers Thomas Arnold's fervent prayer of 1833: " May God grant to my sons an unshaken love of truth, and a firm resolution to follow it for themselves." [80] William Delafield's official efforts to find out and follow the truth led him in 1858 to pronouncements which differed radically in policy from certain of his father's views at the same time that they may well have derived from Dr. Arnold's lifelong concern with social justice and his unremitting battle against bigotry and religious exclusion. In his *Memorandum on the Admission of the Bible as a Class Book into Government Schools,* the younger Arnold declared himself opposed to the popular movement to impose Bible teaching on the overwhelmingly Moslem school of Punjab. In effect, he held for secular instruction, which Dr. Arnold had vigorously opposed a generation before.[81] Nevertheless, in William Arnold's sense of the religious meaning of his vocation, his deep concern that colonial government realize its duty " to cultivate Men's Minds as much as possible," [82] and in his earnest efforts towards justice in colonial affairs, he was very much Dr. Arnold's son. His writings no less than the more polished expressions of Matthew Arnold, the vigorous journalism of Thomas Hughes and the Christian Socialists, and the stated principles of Gell and Forster, reflect the views of the great teacher who sent his pupils forth to transform society.

Rugby Curriculum under Arnold*

THE TERMS RAN approximately 1 September-20 December; 5 February-1 July. School was conducted Monday, Wednesday, and Friday, 7-11 A. M.; 2-5 P. M.; Tuesday and Thursday, 7 A. M.-1 P. M.; Saturday 7-11 A. M. Students were expected to attend Chapel services on Sunday.

FIRST FORM

Classical Division

1. Language: Latin Grammar and Latin Delectus.
2. Scriptural Instruction: Church Catechism and Abridgement of New Testament History.
3. History: Markham's England, Vol I.

Mathematical Division

1. Tables, Addition, Subtraction, Multiplication, and Division, simple and compound Reduction.

French Division

1. Hamel's Exercises up to the Auxiliary Verb.

* Adapted from Dr. Arnold's article "Rugby School" which first appeared in *Quarterly Journal of Education*, VII (1834) and here reprinted from MW, pp. 344-346.

SECOND FORM

Classical Division

1. Language: Latin Grammar and Latin Delectus; Eutropius.
2. Scriptural Instruction: St. Luke; Genesis.
3. History: Markham's England, Vol. II.

Mathematical Division

1. The work done in the first form repeated; Rule of Three, Practice.

French Division

1. Hamel's Exercises, Auxiliary Verbs, regular Conjugations, and some of the irregular.
2. Gaultier's Geography.

THIRD FORM

Classical Division

1. Language: Greek Grammar (Matthiae Abridgment); Valpy's Greek Exercises; Valpy's Greek Delectus; Florilegium; Translations into Latin.
2. Scriptural Instruction: Exodus, Numbers, Judges, I. and II., Samuel, St. Matthew.
3. History: Eutropius; Physical Geography, U. K. S.

Mathematical Division

1. Rule of Three.
2. Practice.
3. Vulgar Fractions.
4. Interest.

French Division

1. Hamel's Exercises, first part continued, Irregular Verbs.
2. Elizabeth, ou Les Exilés in Sibére.

LOWER REMOVE

Classical Division

1. Language: Greek Grammar, and Valpy's Exercises; Rules of the Greek Iambics; Easy Parts of the Iambics of the Greek Tragedians; Virgil's Eclogues; Cicero de Senectute.
2. Scriptural Instruction: St. Matthew in Greek Testament; Acts in the English Bible.
3. History: Parts of Justin; Parts of Xenophon's Anabasis; Markham's France to Philip of Valois.

Mathematical Division

1. Vulgar Fractions; Interest; Decimal Fractions; Square Root.

French Division

1. Hamel continued and repeated; Jussieu's Jardin des Plantes.

FOURTH FORM

Classical Division

1. Language: Æschylus Prometheus; Virgil; Æneid II. and III; Cicero de Amicitia.
2. Scriptural Instruction: Acts in the Greek Testament; St. John in the English Bible; Old Testament History.
3. History: Part of Xenophon's Hellenics; Florus, from III.21, to IV.11; History of Greece, U. K. S.; Markham's France, from Philip of Valois; Detailed Geography of Italy and Germany.

Mathematical Division

1. Decimals, Involution and Evolution, Addition, Subtraction, Multiplication, and Division of Algebra; Binomial Theorem; Euclid, Book I., Propositions I. to XV.

French Division

1. Hamel's 2nd Part, chiefly Syntax of the Pronouns; La Fontaine's Fables.

UPPER REMOVE

Classical Division

1. Language: Sophocles' Philoctetus; Æschylus; Eumenides; Homer's Iliad, I.II.; Virgil, Æneid, IV.V.; Parts of Horace, Odes I.II.III.; Parts of Cicero's Epistles.
2. Scriptural Instruction: St. John in Greek Testament; Deuteronomy and Epistles of St. Peter; Selections from the Psalms.
3. History: Parts of Arrian; Parts of Paterculus, Book II; Sir J. Macintosh's England.

Mathematical Division

1. Equation of Payments, Discount, Simple Equations; Euclid, Book I. from XV. to end.

French Division.

1. Translations from English into French; La Fontaine's Fables.

LOWER FIFTH

Classical Division

1. Language: Æschylus, Septem contra Thebas; Sophocles Œd. Tyr.; Homer's Iliad, III.IV.; Virgil's Æneid VI.VII.; Extracts from Cicero's Epistles, Parts of Horace.
2. Scriptural Instruction: St. John; Epistles to Timothy and Titus; Bible History from 1 Kings to Nehemiah, inclusive.
3. History: Parts of Arrian; Herodotus III., I. 38, 61, 67, 88, 116; Livy, Parts of, II. and III., Hallam's Middle Ages, France, Spain, Greeks, and Saracens; Physical and Political Geography of all Europe.

Mathematical Division

1. Exchange, Alligation, Simple Equations, with two unknown Quantities and Problems; Euclid, Book III.

French Division

1. Syntax and Idioms; A Play of Molière, to construe and then turn again from English into French.

FIFTH FORM

Classical Division

1. Language: Æschylus, Agamemnon; Homer's Iliad, V.VI. Odyssey, IX.; Demosthenes' Leptines, in Aphobum. I.; Virgil's Æneid, VIII.; Parts of Horace; Cicero in Verrem Actionis.
2. Scriptural Instruction: Epistles to the Corinthians; Paley's Horae Paulinae.
3. History: Parts of Herodotus and Thucydides; Parts of Livy; Hallam's Middle Ages; State of Society.

Mathematical Division

1. Quadratic Equations; Trigonometry; Euclid, to the end of Book VI.

French Division

1. Pensées de Pascal; Translations from English into French.

SIXTH FORM

Classical Division

1. Language: Various parts of Virgil and Homer; Some one or more of the Greek Tragedies; One or more of the private Orations of Demosthenes; Cicero against Verres; Parts of Aristotle's Ethics.
2. Scriptural Instruction: One of the Prophets in the Septuagint Version; Different Parts of the New Testament.
3. History: Parts of Thucydides, and Arrian; Parts of Tacitus; Parts of Russell's Modern Europe.

Mathematical Division

1. Euclid, III.–VI.; Simple and Quadratic Equations, Plane Trigonometry, Conic Sections.

French Division

1. Parts of Guizot's Histoire de la Révolution de l'Angleterre, and Mignet's Histoire de la Révolution Française.

Notes

INTRODUCTION

1. John Bowle, *Politics and Opinion in the Nineteenth Century* (New York: Oxford University Press, 1954), p. 91. Cf. G. M. Young, *Victorian England* (London: Oxford University Press, 1936), pp. 70-71; E. C. Mack, *Public Schools and British Opinion, 1780-1860, passim*; W. S. Knickerbocker, *Creative Oxford*, p. 84.

2. See the Bibliography.

3. Arnold Whitridge, *Dr. Arnold of Rugby*, still the best modern biography; Basil Willey, "Thomas Arnold," *Nineteenth Century Studies*, the best brief introduction to Arnold's ideas. See also Arthur Penrhyn Stanley, *Life and Correspondence of Thomas Arnold, D. D.*, and Reginald J. Campbell, *Thomas Arnold*.

4. John Middleton Murry, *The Price of Leadership, passim*; C. R. Sanders, *Coleridge and the Broad Church Movement*, pp. 91-122; Lionel Trilling, *Matthew Arnold* (New York: Norton Co., 1939), pp. 36-76; W. F. Connell, *The Educational Thought and Influence of Matthew Arnold* (London: Routledge and Kegan Paul, 1950), pp. 74-75, 278; William Robbins, *The Ethical Idealism of Matthew Arnold* (London: Heinemann, 1959), p. 58, *et passim*; James I. Osborne, *Arthur Hugh Clough* (Boston: Houghton Mifflin, 1920), pp. 15, 21-22; Asa

Briggs, *Victorian People*, p. 156, *et passim*; Frances J. Woodward, *The Doctor's Disciples, passim.*

5. *Apologia Pro Vita Sua*, ed. A. Dwight Culler (Boston: Houghton Mifflin, 1956), p. 52. The range of opinion may be illustrated by comparing the strictures of William George Ward (" Arnold's Sermons," pp. 298-364) with the praise of Arnold's foresight and religious vision by Frederick W. Farrar ("Thomas Arnold," *Living Age*, CXXXVII [1878], 433).

6. Cf. Yngve Brilioth, *The Anglican Revival* (London: Longmans, Green, 1925), p. 99; Charles E. Raven, " Prophets: I Thomas Arnold," *Pillars of the English Church*, p. 74.

7. Cf. Trilling, p. 56; Cyril K. Gloyn, *The Church in the Social Order*, pp. 98, 104.

8. The Rugbeian was William Temple, later Archbishop of Canterbury (A. Iremonger, *William Temple* [London: Oxford University Press, 1948], p. 93). Arnold's career at Rugby has been fully studied in Sir Joshua Fitch, *Thomas and Matthew Arnold and Their Influence on English Education;* Hugo Gutsche, *Thomas Arnold als Reformator des höheren englischen Schulwesens im 19. Jahrhundert* (Erlangen: Jacob, 1914); see also the discussions in the previously cited works by Whitridge and Mack, the preface by Fitch to the " Teachers' edition " of Stanley's *Life*, and Joseph J. Findlay (ed.), *Arnold of Rugby: His School Life and Contributions to Education* (Cambridge: Cambridge University Press, 1897). Cf. T. W. Bamford, "Discipline At Rugby Under Arnold," *Educational Review*, X (1957-58), 18-28.

CHAPTER ONE

1. *Life and Correspondence of Thomas Arnold*, I, 3 (hereafter cited as *Life*).

2. *Life*, I, 5; Norman Wymer, *Dr. Arnold of Rugby*, p. 23.

3. Arnold Whitridge, *Dr. Arnold of Rugby*, p. 6. Prideaux (1648-1724) advocated comprehension of dissenters and abolition of clerical pluralities (*DNB*, XLVI, 352-53).

4. See the Oxford edition published in 1839 by Thomas Tugg, II, 624.

5. Edward C. Mack, *Public Schools and British Opinion, 1780-1860*, pp. 73-74.

6. *DNB*, XXII, 28.

7. E. G. Selwyn, " Dr. Arnold as a Winchester Boy," p. 310.

8. Cf. Whitridge, p. 9; *Life*, I, 5.

9. Selwyn, p. 304.

10. *Life*, I, 5.

11. Whitridge, p. 8.

12. Selwyn, p. 14.

13. Wymer, p. 36.

14. Wymer, p. 31.

15. Thomas Fowler, *History of Corpus Christi College* (Oxford: Clarendon Press, 1893), pp. 302-03.

16. *DNB*, XII, 85.

17. *Life*, I, 19; Arnold cited this work in LMH, pp. 161-62.

18. S. C. Carpenter, *Church and People, 1789-1889* (London: Society for Promoting Christian Knowledge, 1933), p. 465.

19. Edward Copleston, *A Reply to the Calumnies of the Edinburgh Review against Oxford containing an Account of Studies Pursued in that University* (Oxford: J. Cooke and J. Parker, 1810), p. 154.

20. Copleston, pp. 139-41.

21. See the outline of 1827, MWA, pp. 442-43.

22. *Life*, I, 21; Wymer, p. 52.

23. Cf. Whitridge, p. 50; Wymer, p. 88; *Life*, II, 211.

24. *Works of Hooker* (Oxford: Clarendon Press, 1885), II, 511. The passage is from *Ecclesiastical Polity*, VIII, iii, 2. Arnold could not agree with Hooker's exaltation of a " priestly and ceremonial " religion, however. See *Life*, II, 66.

25. Arnold's readings in Butler may possibly have been begun while he was at Oriel College, 1815-19. Butler's *Analogy* (1736) was greatly admired by Oriel men at this time (W. S. Knickerbocker, *Creative Oxford*, p. 54). At the behest of R. D. Hampden, an Oriel don, the work was made a part of the Oriel B. A. examination in 1820 (Henrietta Hampden [ed.], *Memorials of Renn Dickson Hampden* [London: Longmans, Green, 1871], p. 16).

26. *Sermons*, II, 394.

27. Vernon F. Storr, *The Development of English Theology in the Nineteenth Century, 1800-1860* (London: Longmans, Green, 1913), pp. 45-58; Albert E. Baker, *Bishop Butler* (London: Society for Promoting Christian Knowledge, 1923), pp. 4-21.

28. Storr, pp. 57-58.

29. Baker, pp. 49-51.

30. *Analogy*, Introduction, paragraphs 6, 11-12 cited by Baker, p. 51.

31. CLH, p. 148.

32. Baker, p. 68.

33. Cf. CLH, p. 337; LMH, p. 133; *Sermons*, III, 135-36.

34. J. H. Newman, *The Idea of a University*, ed. Charles Frederick Harrold (London: Longmans, Green, 1947), p. 54.

35. David Rannie, *Oriel College* (London: F. E. Robinson, 1900), p. 181.

36. W. Tuckwell, *Pre-Tractarian Oxford* (London: Smith, Elder, 1909), pp. 2-5.

37. Storr, p. 94.

38. Tuckwell, pp. 258-59.

39. Thomas Mozley, *Reminiscences of Oriel* (London: Longmans, Green, 1882), I, 18 quoted by John Tulloch,

*Movements of Religious Thought in Britain during the Nine-
teenth Century* (London: Longmans, 1885), p. 43.

40. Storr, p. 96; Reginald Campbell, *Thomas Arnold*, p. 20.

41. Cf. W. G. T. Shedd (ed.), *Complete Works of Samuel
Taylor Coleridge* (New York: Harper's, 1853), V, 508;
Newman, *The Idea of a University*, p. 140; *Works of Matthew
Arnold*, ed. George W. E. Russell (15 vols.; London: Mac-
millan, 1904), VII, 351-52 (hereafter cited as *Works*).

42. Tuckwell, p. 59.

43. "Tracts on Baptismal Regeneration," *Quarterly Review*,
XV (July, 1816), 477. Davison is identified in *DNB* as the
author of this article.

44. L. E. Elliott-Binns, *Religion in the Victorian Era* (London: Lutterworth, 1946), p. 181.

45. Storr, pp. 187-89.

46. *Sermons*, II, 425.

47. *Life*, II, 223; the reference is probably to readings in
German theology of which, however, I have found no record.

48. Tulloch, pp. 48, 53; cf. *Works*, XIV, 104.

49. Tuckwell, p. 55.

50. Cf. *Life*, I, 47-48; *Apologia Pro Vita Sua*, ed. A. Dwight
Culler, p. 31.

51. Thomas Arnold, Jr., *Passages in a Wandering Life*
(London: Edward Arnold, 1900), pp. 19-22.

52. Tulloch, p. 62; *Life*, I, 47-48; Storr, p. 98.

53. William Blackburn, "Matthew Arnold and the Oriel
Noetics," *Philological Quarterly*, XXV (1946), 73.

54. *Life and Correspondence of Richard Whately*, ed. E. J.
Whately (2 vols.; London: Longmans, Green, 1866), II, 71.

55. Letter to R. D. Hampden, 17 February 1836, Hampden,
p. 63.

56. Harold Laski (ed.), *Autobiography* (London: Oxford
University Press, 1924), p. 125 quoted by Basil Willey, *Nineteenth Century Studies*, p. 148.

57. *Life*, I, 17; Wymer, p. 51.

58. Wymer, pp. 80, 147.
59. Willey, p. 69.
60. Wymer, pp. 148-49; *Letters of William and Dorothy Wordsworth*, ed. Ernest De Selincourt (Oxford: Clarendon Press, 1939), II, 627-28. Ernest Hartley Coleridge claimed that the gardens at Fox How were laid out by Sara Hutchinson (*John Duke Coleridge* [2 vols.; London: Heinemann, 1904], I, 45).
61. Henry Crabb Robinson, *Correspondence with the Wordsworth Circle (1808-1866)*, ed. E. J. Morley (Oxford: Clarendon Press, 1927), I, 290; II, 582, 704; Fredrika Beatty, *William Wordsworth of Rydal Mount* (New York: Dutton, 1939), p. 152.
62. Dedication "To William Wordsworth," in Augustus Hare and Julius Charles Hare, *Guesses at Truth* (2d ed.; London: Macmillan, 1838) quoted by C. R. Sanders, *Coleridge and the Broad Church Movement*, p. 131.
63. *Prose Works*, ed. William Knight (London: Macmillan, 1896), II, 229.
64. MW, p. 311.
65. R. J. White (ed.), *Political Tracts of Wordsworth, Coleridge and Shelley* (Cambridge: Cambridge University Press, 1953), p. xxvii.
66. Edith C. Batho, *The Later Wordsworth* (Cambridge: Cambridge University Press, 1933), pp. 214-15.
67. Matthew Arnold, "Memorial Verses," l. 63.
68. *Letters of the Wordsworth Family, 1787-1855*, ed. William Knight (Boston and London: Ginn and Co., 1907), III, 305.
69. Shedd, VI, 524.
70. MW, pp. 405, 422; *Life*, I, 440; II, 195.
71. Sanders, pp. 91-92; cf. *Life*, I, 440; II, 59, 195; Whitridge, p. 42.
72. "Personal Influences on Present Theology," *Essays, Reviews and Addresses*, I, 259.
73. C. R. Sanders in his study of Coleridge's influence on

liberal Anglicans says that Arnold was "scarcely a disciple of Coleridge and was very discriminating in his approach to Coleridge's teachings . . ." (p. 91). I agree with this judgment.

74. Cf. Willey, pp. 38-39; Alfred William Benn, *The History of English Rationalism in the Nineteenth Century* (2 vols.; London: Longmans, Green, 1906), I, 101, 253, 271; Lore Metzger, "Coleridge's Vindication of Spinoza: An Unpublished Note," *Journal of the History of Ideas*, XXI (June, 1960), 287; Shedd, VI, 386, 391, 442, *et passim*; *Biographia Literaria*, ed. George Watson (London: Dent, 1956), p. x, 261, 287-88.

75. *Life*, I, 403.

76. Rowland E. Prothero and G. G. Bradley, *The Life and Correspondence of Arthur Penrhyn Stanley* (2 vols.; New York: Scribner's, 1894), I, 111, 120.

77. See especially *Sermons*, I, 371.

78. Shedd, I, 456; cf. CLH, p. 461.

79. Storr, p. 322; Shedd, I, 188, 367.

80. Shedd, I, 351; VI, 263-64, 322-23; cf. *Sermons*, II, 424-27.

81. Willey, pp. 45-46.

82. Willey, pp. 46, 53-54; Shedd, VI, 77; Sanders, pp. 77, 114, 116.

83. Arnold's historical work has received thorough study in R. K. Barksdale, "Thomas Arnold as Historian." A later study to which I am indebted for its discussion of Arnold's philosophy of history is Duncan Forbes, *The Liberal Anglican Idea of History*. Other authorities which I have found especially helpful in my discussion of Arnold's relations to Niebuhr are G. P. Gooch, *History and Historians in the Nineteenth Century* (2d ed.; London: Longmans, Green, 1952); Storr; and Benn.

84. MWA, pp. 307, 330, 378, 383; *Life*, I, 45; HR, pp. vii-xi.

85. LMH, p. 157: ". . . the great object, as I cannot but think, is that which most nearly touches the inner life of

civilised man, namely, the vicissitudes of institutions social, political, and religious." Cf. MWA, pp. 382-93.

86. Gooch, p. 22.
87. *History of Rome* (1827), I, 451 quoted in *Life*, I, 46.
88. Forbes, p. 18.
89. Benn, I, 318.
90. Storr, p. 166.
91. CLC, p. 15.
92. Gooch, p. 18.
93. Francis Lieber, *Reminiscences of an Intercourse with Mr. Niebuhr the Historian* (Philadelphia: Carey, Lea and Blanchard, 1835), p. 61.
94. Lionel Trilling, *Matthew Arnold*, p. 45.
95. Storr, pp. 257-67.
96. *Sermons*, III, xiii-xiv; cf. HLR, II, 464.
97. FC, pp. 118-21.
98. John H. Finley, *Thucydides* (Cambridge, Mass.: Harvard University Press, 1942), p. 4.
99. Thucydides [*History of Peloponnesian War*], trans. Benjamin Jowett (2 vols.; Oxford: Clarendon Press, 1881), II, 248; I, 208.
100. Thucydides, i, 13, trans. Jowett, I, 10.
101. Forbes, p. 12.
102. Forbes, p. 20; cf. MW, p. 82.
103. MW, p. 82; Arnold did not deny that the work was "disfigured by some strange extravagancies."
104. *New Science*, trans. Thomas Goddard Bergin and Max Harold Fisch (Ithaca: Cornell University Press, 1948), p. 305.
105. R. A. D. Owen, *Christian Bunsen and Liberal English Theology* (Montpelier: Capital City Press, 1924), p. 22.
106. *Life*, II, 142. This view was evidently shared by Queen Victoria, for less than a year before Arnold's death she approved the Prussian government's choice of Bunsen to succeed von Buelow, the retiring ambassador to England (Owen, p. 10).
107. Thomas Arnold, Jr., p. 30.

108. Owen, p. 6.

109. Connop Thirlwall, Jr., *Connop Thirlwall, Historian and Theologian* (London: Society for Promoting Christian Knowledge, 1936), p. 19.

110. Owen, pp. 36-37.

111. Frances, Baroness Bunsen, *A Memoir of Baron Bunsen* (London: Longmans, Green, 1868), I, 389-90.

112. Bunsen disagreed with Arnold that a governmental commission was the proper means of effecting this reform, however. See Bunsen, I, 392.

113. Merton A. Christensen, "Thomas Arnold's Debt to German Theologians," p. 15.

114. Storr, p. 186; cf. *Life,* I, 435; CLH, pp. 481-91.

115. Christensen, p. 16.

116. Owen, pp. 52, 79, 82.

117. *Remains of Richard Hurrell Froude* (4 vols.; Derby, England: Henry Mozley and Sons, 1839), I, 371.

CHAPTER TWO

1. *Apologia Pro Vita Sua,* ed. A. Dwight Culler, p. 52.

2. Vernon F. Storr, *The Development of English Theology in the Nineteenth Century, 1800-1860,* p. 2.

3. Basil Willey, *Nineteenth Century Studies,* p. 54.

4. I am indebted to the following sources for this brief statement of a complex series of developments: Storr, Chapters 3-4, 7, 9-10; G. P. Gooch, *History and Historians in the Nineteenth Century,* Chapters 1-9; L. E. Elliott-Binns, *Religion in the Victorian Era,* Chapters 2, 7-9; A. W. Benn, *The History of English Rationalism,* Chapters 4, 7-8; R. H. Murray, *Science and Scientists in the Nineteenth Century* (London: Sheldon, 1925), Chapters 3 and 5.

5. *Henry Crabb Robinson in Germany,* ed. Edith J. Morley

(Oxford: Clarendon Press, 1929), p. 91; Robinson's comment is indicative of the inability of even very cultivated Englishmen to accept such a view at this date: ". . . could I but swallow this, I would mount the pulpit tomorrow."

6. H. P. Liddon, *Life of Edward Bouverie Pusey*, ed. J. O. Johnston and Robert J. Wilson (4th ed.; London: Longmans, Green, 1894), I, 73 (hereafter cited as *Life of Pusey*); cf. T. K. Cheyne's characterization of the work of Paulus and Gabler at Jena about 1800 as manifesting a " cold and superficial rationalism" (*Founders of the Old Testament Criticism* [London: Methuen, 1893], p. 31).

7. Storr, pp. 171-75.

8. Storr, p. 227; Elliott-Binns, p. 183.

9. Willey, *Nineteenth Century Studies*, pp. 221, 226.

10. Elliott-Binns, pp. 153-55.

11. Murray, p. 51; cf. Elliott-Binns, p. 154; J. Y. Simpson, *Landmarks in the Struggle between Science and Religion* (New York: G. H. Doran, n.d.), p. 174.

12. Lyell would not have accepted Darwin's principle of natural selection in 1830, however. See J. T. Shotwell (ed.), *Essays in Intellectual History Presented to James Harvey Robinson* (New York: Harper's, 1929), p. 75.

13. Storr, pp. 4-5.

14. Connop Thirlwall wrote in 1841 that there was not a single English theological journal which did not " studiously keep its readers in the dark as to everything that [was] said and done in German theology" (Connop Thirlwall, Jr., *Connop Thirlwall, Historian and Theologian*, p. 29).

15. Storr, pp. 178-79.

16. S. C. Carpenter, *Church and People, 1789-1889*, p. 466.

17. Introduction, p. xix quoted by John Tulloch, *Movements of Religious Thought in Britain during the Nineteenth Century*, p. 78.

18. Storr, p. 111; Tulloch, p. 76.

19. Basil Willey, *More Nineteenth Century Studies* (Lon-

don: Chatto and Windus, 1956), p. 139; cf. Yngve Brilioth, *The Anglican Revival*, p. 92; Storr, pp. 443-44.

20. C. R. Sanders, *Coleridge and the Broad Church Movement*, pp. 123, 269-70.

21. Tulloch, pp. 36-37. Arthur Stanley wrote that Hare's published *Charges* were marked by "incongruity of composition amounting almost to grotesqueness" ("Archdeacon Hare," *Victory of Faith* [1874], p. cix quoted by Sanders, p. 267).

22. Benn, I, 321; Storr, p. 114.

23. A. P. Stanley, *Life and Correspondence of Thomas Arnold*, II, 58, 60-61 (hereafter cited as *Life*); *Sermons*, III, xvi.

24. MW, p. 318; *Sermons*, II, 424.

25. Storr, p. 177. Van Mildert made the statement in his *Inquiry into the General Principles of Scripture Interpretation*.

26. Frances J. Woodward, *The Doctor's Disciples*, facing p. 25.

27. Arnold was founder and co-editor of the *Englishmen's Register*, a weekly journal which had a life of two months in 1831. For a fuller account of his journalistic activities, see Chapter Four.

28. *Life*, I, 317. He had hopes that the same essay would counteract both the "narrow views and technical phraseology" of the Evangelical party and the "principal errors" of the High Church party (*Life*, I, 286, 316).

29. See Arnold's comments on S. T. Coleridge's treatment of this "momentous question" (*Life*, I, 403) quoted in Chapter Two.

30. *Life*, II, 36-37; MW, pp. 409-11.

31. *Sermons*, I, 375-76, 434, 448.

32. On an earlier occasion Arnold had pointed out that historical fulfillment of prophecy itself could do nothing to prove the inspiration of the *record* of it (*Sermons*, II, 418-19).

33. CLH, p. 461. The understanding-reason dichotomy is a venerable one, probably "as old as Plato" (Sanders, p. 35).

34. Introduction, *Tom Brown's Schooldays* (London: Macmillan, 1902), p. xv.

35. Arthur P. Stanley, "The Theology of the Nineteenth Century," *Fraser's Magazine*, LXXI (February, 1865) quoted by Woodward, p. 54. The idea was a commonplace of German theology of the period (Merton A. Christensen, "Thomas Arnold's Debt to German Theologians," p. 17) and may have been drawn from the school of pietistic theologians of which Arnold's friend Christian Bunsen was a member. See the discussion of Arnold's friendship with Bunsen in Chapter One.

36. Willey, *Nineteenth Century Studies*, p. 66.

37. CLH, pp. 380, 385; IS, p. 191.

38. *Sermons*, II, 379, 426.

39. Cf. *Remains of Richard Hurrell Froude*, III, 359; W. G. Ward, "Arnold's Sermons," p. 360.

40. "Dr. Arnold after Fifty Years," p. 840.

41. R. E. Prothero, *Letters and Verses of Arthur Penrhyn Stanley* (New York: Scribner's, 1895), p. 74 quoted in *The Letters of Matthew Arnold to Arthur Hugh Clough*, ed. Howard Foster Lowry (London: Oxford University Press, 1932), p. 5.

42. Cf. *Works of Matthew Arnold*, ed. George Russell, XIII, 55-56, 180; XIV, 156-57, 183, 197; XV, 142 (hereafter cited as *Works*).

43. Willey, *Nineteenth Century Studies*, p. 264.

44. Unpublished letter from Matthew Arnold to his mother (27 November 1869) in possession of Mr. Arnold Whitridge; cf. unpublished letter from Matthew Arnold to Benjamin Jowett (25 May 187?) in Balliol College Library. Professor Arthur Kyle Davis has kindly permitted me to examine a typescript of this letter.

45. William Robbins, "Major Formative Influences," *The Ethical Idealism of Matthew Arnold*, pp. 55-70. See also Christensen, pp. 14-20; and Matthew Arnold's "Dr. Stanley's Lectures on the Jewish Church," *Macmillan's Magazine*, VII (February, 1863), 327-36 and "The Bishop and the Philosopher," *Macmillan's Magazine*, VII (January, 1863), 241-56.

46. Ernest Hartley Coleridge, *John Duke Coleridge*, I, 121.

47. Frederick W. Farrar, "Thomas Arnold," *Living Age*, CXXXVII (1878), 433.

48. F. J. Woodward has studied four of Arnold's pupils: Stanley, J. P. Gell, A. H. Clough, and W. D. Arnold (see *The Doctor's Disciples*). Of these only Stanley can be considered a significant and influential figure in the field of Biblical criticism and interpretation.

49. "Two Addresses by the Dean of Westminster.—II Arnold and Rugby," *Macmillan's Magazine*, X (July, 1874), p. 279.

50. W. S. Knickerbocker, *Creative Oxford*, p. 92; *DNB*, XVIII, 933-34.

51. Ellis Yarnall, *Wordsworth and the Coleridges* (New York: Macmillan, 1899), p. 198; Lucy Wake (ed.), *The Reminiscences of Charlotte, Lady Wake* (Edinburgh: Blackwood, 1909), p. 285; cf. *Works*, XIV, 297-98; XV, 96; Rowland E. Prothero and G. G. Bradley (eds.), *Life and Correspondence of Arthur Penrhyn Stanley*, II, 373, 455 (hereafter cited as *Life of Stanley*).

52. London: Griffeth, Farrar, Okeden, and Wise, 1890, p. v.

53. New York: Scribner's, I, 25-26, 36, 400.

54. Matthew Arnold, "Dr. Stanley's Lectures on the Jewish Church," pp. 327, 331.

55. Willey, *More Nineteenth Century Studies*, p. 139.

56. A. P. Stanley, "The Theology of the Nineteenth Century," quoted by Woodward, p. 54.

57. Elliott-Binns, p. 186.

58. *Life of Stanley*, II, 193.

59. "Westminster Abbey," ll. 167-70.

60. *Quarterly Review* (January, 1861), quoted by Willey, *More Nineteenth Century Studies*, p. 168.

61. Evelyn Abbott and Lewis Campbell, *Life and Letters of Benjamin Jowett* (2 vols.; London: John Murray, 1897), I, 86-87, 90, 108-10, 122, 150, 161.

62. Abbott and Campbell, I, 129, 150, 154; Edward Caird, "Professor Jowett," *International Journal of Ethics*, VIII

(1897), 43-44; James Robert Thrane, " The Rise of the Higher Criticism in England, 1800-1870 " (unpubl. Ph. D. diss., Columbia University, 1956), pp. 435-36.

63. Lewis Campbell (ed.), *The Epistles of St. Paul to the Thessalonians, Galatians, and Romans* (3rd ed.; London: John Murray, 1894), I, v; cf. Abbott and Campbell, I, 100; *Life*, II, 62.

64. Knickerbocker, p. 118. The title is reminiscent of Arnold's essay of 1831, " On the Right Interpretation and Understanding of the Scriptures."

65. *Epistles*, II, 43-44.

66. Willey, *More Nineteenth Century Studies*, pp. 156-60.

67. Thucydides, trans. Jowett, I, ix.

68. *Memoirs of Archbishop Temple by Seven Friends*, ed. E. G. Sandford (2 vols., London: Macmillan, 1906), I, 78-79, 87.

69. *Life of Stanley*, I, 191.

70. *Memoirs of Temple*, I, 161; II, 462; unpublished letter from Matthew Arnold to his mother [n.d.] in possession of Mr. Arnold Whitridge.

71. *Memoirs of Temple*, I, 153; *Works*, XIV, 112; 215-216; cf. XVII, 76, 173-74.

72. *Memoirs of Temple*, I, 153, 239; speech at Rugby (February, 1897) quoted by Arnold Whitridge, *Dr. Arnold of Rugby*, p. xx.

73. Willey, *More Nineteenth Century Studies*, pp. 141-42; Thrane, pp. 444-47.

74. "Archbishop Temple," *Edinburgh Review*, CCIII (April, 1906), 441.

75. *The Relations Between Religion and Science* (London: Macmillan, 1885), p. 241.

CHAPTER THREE

1. Norman Wymer, *Dr. Arnold of Rugby*, p. 36.

2. Basil Willey, *Nineteenth Century Studies*, p. 54.

3. Earl W. McGee, " The Anglican Church and Social Reform, 1830-1850 " (unpubl. Ph.D. diss., University of Kentucky, 1950), p. 50.

4. Yngve Brilioth, *The Anglican Revival*, p. 95; cf. A. V. Dicey, *Lectures on the Relation between Law and Public Opinion in England during the Nineteenth Century* (London: Macmillan, 1926), pp. 168-69.

5. David Roberts, " Bentham and the Administrative State," *Victorian Studies*, II (March, 1959), 197; Dicey, p. 169.

6. *The Analysis of the Influence of Natural Religion on the Happiness of Mankind* (1822) quoted by Willey, p. 135.

7. 2d ed.; London, 1832, p. 63.

8. Francis Warre Cornish, *The English Church in the Nineteenth Century* (London: Macmillan, 1910), I, 109.

9. L. E. Elliott-Binns, *Religion in the Victorian Era*, p. 72.

10. Cornish, I, 171.

11. Elliott-Binns, p. 73; Cornish, I, 317-18.

12. S. C. Carpenter, *Church and People, 1789-1889*, pp. 50-51.

13. Cornish, I, 142-44.

14. Carpenter, p. 54.

15. The phrase is the title of John Keble's Assize Sermon of 1833 which Newman regarded as marking the birthday of the Oxford Movement (*Apologia Pro Vita Sua*, ed. A. Dwight Culler, p. 54).

16. *British Critic*, XIV (1833), 87-88; XVI (1834), 250-54, 489; XXIII (1838), 391; XXIX (1841), 5-30 cited by McGee, p. 51.

17. Newman's phrase is from *Lectures on Difficulties of Anglicans*, I, 102 quoted by Brilioth, pp. 180-83.

18. Alec Vidler, " The Tractarian Movement, Church Re-

vival and Reform," *The Ideas and Beliefs of the Victorians* (London: Sylvan Press, 1950), p. 115; cf. Brilioth, p. 14; McGee, p. 301.

19. See Brilioth, Chapter XII, " The Fundamental Forms of Tractarian Piety."

20. A. M. Fairbairn, *The Place of Christ in Modern Theology* (London and New York: Scribner's, 1894), p. 178.

21. Cornish, I, 80, 110; Dicey, p. 337.

22. McGee, pp. 192-93, 301.

23. See the correspondence between Newman and Whately in *Apologia*, pp. 351-58. Newman expressed his deep regret that the admired teacher of his college days had lent support to a measure which, as he said, diminished the Church in Ireland by providing for " the extinction (without ecclesiastical sanction) of half her Candlesticks . . ." (p. 352).

24. Brilioth, p. 84; Vernon F. Storr, *The Development of English Theology in the Nineteenth Century, 1800-1860*, pp. 97-98.

25. Carpenter, p. 98.

26. *Life of Blomfield*, quoted by Carpenter, p. 101.

27. MWA, pp. 214-26.

28. Cornish, II, 327-34. The right of sale of advowsons was recognized.

29. For Arnold's statement of the doctrines generally agreed on, see my discussion of *Principles of Church Reform* (1833) below.

30. Carpenter, pp. 58-59.

31. Cornish, II, 315.

32. *Tom Brown's Schooldays*, p. xv.

33. Carpenter, p. 278.

34. A. P. Stanley, *Life and Correspondence of Thomas Arnold*, II, 191, 393 (hereafter cited as *Life*).

35. L (January, 1834), 560.

36. John Henry Newman, *Letters and Correspondence during his life in the English Church*, ed. Anne Mozley (London: Longmans, 1891), pp. 374-75.

37. *Sermons*, III, 386; Arnold Whitridge, *Dr. Arnold of Rugby*, p. 230.

38. Whitridge, p. 162.

39. *Life*, I, 14; Reginald J. Campbell, *Thomas Arnold*, pp. 159-60.

40. Henry P. Liddon, *Life of Edward Bouverie Pusey*, I, 282, 409-12 (hereafter cited as *Life of Pusey*); cf. Waldo Hilary Dunn, *James Anthony Froude, 1818-1856* (London: Oxford University Press, 1961), I, 85.

41. *Life*, II, 6, 106, 295; Newman, *Letters*, I, 180, 220; II, 47, 440-43; *Apologia*, pp. 52, 273; Randall Davidson and William Benham, *Life of Archibald Campbell Tait* (London: Macmillan, 1891), I, 86 (hereafter cited as *Life of Tait*).

42. *Life of Pusey*, I, 271.

43. *Sermons*, III, 372. Elsewhere he stated his belief that the idea of a priesthood originated in error and was perpetuated in error (*Life*, II, 243).

44. *Life*, I, 387; cf. A. Dwight Culler, *The Imperial Intellect* (New Haven: Yale University Press, 1955), p. 103.

45. Henrietta Hampden (ed.), *Memorials of Renn Dickson Hampden*, p. 37.

46. As Arnold later pointed out, this course of action was said to have the approval of the Duke of Wellington, the Chancellor of the University (Whitridge, p. 219).

47. Storr, p. 103. The incident is discussed in many biographies of the period, e.g., *Life*, II, 7, 8; *Life of Pusey*, I, 359-90; *Life of Stanley*, I, 154-64.

48. Whitridge, p. 216. The article is reprinted as Appendix I.

49. *Literary Remains*, III, 386 quoted by CLH, p. i.

50. CLH, p. ix; cf. Storr, p. 259: ". . . if there was ever a case of history being interpreted in the interests of a particular theory, Tractarianism supplies it."

51. *Life*, I, 337, 339-40; cf. *British Critic*, XIV (April, 1833), 410; *Quarterly Review*, L (January, 1834), 560; James Mozley, *Essays Historical and Theological*, II, 46; *Edinburgh Review*, LXXXI (April, 1845), 535-53.

52. M. J. Jackson and J. Rogan (eds.), *Principles of Church Reform*, pp. 70-71, 81.

53. W. H. G. Armytage, "Matthew Arnold and W. E. Gladstone: Some New Letters," *University of Toronto Quarterly*, XVIII (April, 1949), 222.

54. Unpublished letter from Matthew Arnold to his mother (13 February 1869) in possession of Mr. Arnold Whitridge; cf. *Works of Matthew Arnold*, ed. George Russell, XIV, 188 (hereafter cited as *Works*).

55. William Harbutt Dawson, *Matthew Arnold and His Relation to the Thought of Our Time* (New York: G. P. Putnam's Sons, 1904), p. 281.

56. *Works*, IX, 356, 365, 378.

57. C. R. Sanders, *Coleridge and the Broad Church Movement*, pp. 7-13; Fairbairn, pp. 176-79; W. J. Coneybeare, "Church Parties," *Edinburgh Review*, XCVIII (October, 1853), 273-342. Had the term been in use in the 1820's, it would doubtless have been applied to the Oriel Noetics who had similar views.

58. Frances J. Woodward, *The Doctor's Disciples*, pp. 47, 61-62.

59. *Edinburgh Review* (January, 1873) quoted by Woodward, p. 65.

60. *Essays Chiefly on Questions of Church and State from 1850 to 1870* (London: John Murray, 1884), p. vii. Had they known about it, Stanley's opponents would have made good polemic use of a dream which he reported to friends while he was Dean of Westminster. Stanley dreamed that he had been elected Pope (*The George Eliot Letters*, ed. Gordon S. Haight [New Haven: Yale University Press, 1955], VII, 9).

61. *Life of Stanley*, I, 225-29; cf. Woodward, pp. 36-37; Whitridge, pp. 52-53; Wymer, pp. 52, 88.

62. *Life of Stanley*, II, 119-20; cf. *Life*, II, 180.

63. *Life of Tait*, I, 277-80, 287-302, 308; *Life of Stanley*, II, 37; *Memoirs of Temple*, II, 617-19. Tait's own moderate liberalism in Biblical inquiry can be seen in his *Dangers and*

Safeguards of Modern Theology (London: John Murray, 1861). See especially the essay, "Suggestions Offered to the Theological Student, Under the Present Difficulties" (1846).

64. W. S. Knickerbocker, *Creative Oxford*, p. 84.

65. *Life of Tait*, II, Chapters 24-26.

66. Cornish, II, 347; Percy V. Norwood, "A Victorian Primate," *Church History*, XIV (1945), 4-5.

67. *Life of Tait*, I, 193. To Lord Shaftesbury (writing in 1856) Tait was " by very much the best " of the " dangerous Arnoldian school."

68. Speech at Rugby (February, 1897) quoted by Whitridge, p. xv; cf. Temple's farewell speech of 1869 quoted by Charles H. Dant, *Archbishop Temple* (New York: Scribner's, 1903), p. 60.

69. *Memoirs of Archbishop Temple by Seven Friends*, ed. E. G. Sandford, I, 357, 424 ff., 566, 578-79.

70. *Memoirs of Temple*, I, 558-59, 577-79; cf. *Sermons*, III, 276, 279.

71. *Memoirs of Temple*, II, 294-302; cf. II, 52, 127, 150-51.

CHAPTER FOUR

1. A. W. Benn, *The History of English Rationalism*, I, 295.

2. A. V. Dicey, *Lectures on the Relation between Law and Public Opinion in England during the Nineteenth Century*, p. 147.

3. Dicey, p. xxix.

4. *Miscellaneous Works of Lord Macaulay*, ed. Lady Trevelyan (Philadelphia: University Library Asssociation, n.d.), IV, 353-58.

5. Yngve Brilioth, *The Anglican Revival*, p. 84.

6. C. E. Osborne, *Christian Ideas in Political History* (London: John Murray, 1929), p. 172.

7. George Macaulay Trevelyan, *British History in the Nineteenth Century and After* (London: Longmans, Green, 1937), pp. 144-48.

8. Bernard N. Schilling, "The Condition of England," *Human Dignity and the Great Victorians* (New York: Columbia University Press, 1946), *passim.*

9. Schilling, p. 35.

10. Schilling, p. 36; G. M. Trevelyan, p. 143.

11. G. D. H. Cole and Raymond Postgate, *The Common People, 1746-1938* (London: Methuen, 1938), pp. 188-89; G. M. Young, *Victorian England: Portrait of an Age*, p. 21.

12. Charles E. Raven, *Christian Socialism, 1848-54* (London: Macmillan, 1920), pp. 8-9.

13. G. M. Trevelyan, pp. 148-49, 250.

14. L. E. Elliott-Binns, *Religion in the Victorian Era*, p. 22.

15. *Reminiscences* (London and New York: Everyman's Library, 1932), p. 355 quoted by Walter E. Houghton, *The Victorian Frame of Mind, 1830-1870* (New Haven: Yale University Press, 1957), p. 55.

16. Cole and Postgate, pp. 234-36.

17. G. M. Trevelyan, p. 252; Cole and Postgate, pp. 267-85, 313-20.

18. *Utilitarianism, Liberty, and Representative Government,* ed. A. D. Lindsay (New York and London: Everyman's Library, 1950), p. 148 quoted by Houghton, p. 163.

19. E. L. Woodward, *The Age of Reform, 1815-1870* (Oxford: Clarendon Press, 1938), p. 121.

20. G. M. Trevelyan, p. 186.

21. Basil Willey, *Nineteenth Century Studies*, p. 54.

22. E. L. Woodward, pp. 213-29; G. M. Trevelyan, p. 297; Arnold Whitridge, *Dr. Arnold of Rugby*, p. 191.

23. E. L. Woodward, p. 370; G. M. Trevelyan, p. 259.

24. E. L. Woodward, pp. 226, 351.

25. J. A. R. Marriott, *England Since Waterloo*, in *A History of England*, ed. Charles Oman (London: Methuen, 1913), VII, 158-59.

26. W. Davidson and Alfred Cobban, "The Idea of Empire," *Ideas and Beliefs of the Victorians* (London: Sylvan Press, 1950), pp. 320-33, *passim*; cf. Jack Simmons, "The Proconsuls," in the same work, pp. 410-16, *passim.*

27. Sir Joshua Fitch, *Thomas and Matthew Arnold and Their Influence on English Education*, pp. 124-25.

28. Whitridge, p. 196.

29. R. L. Archer, *Secondary Education in the Nineteenth Century* (Cambridge: Cambridge University Press, 1928), pp. 100-102.

30. Fitch, pp. 126-27.

31. Francis Warre Cornish, *The English Church in the Nineteenth Century*, I, 200.

32. Whitridge, pp. xlix-l.

33. Archer, p. 87.

34. On four occasions between 1827 and 1841 he began formal treatments of the subject (A. P. Stanley, *Life and Correspondence of Thomas Arnold*, I, 224 [hereafter cited as *Life*]).

35. *Politics*, III, v., 11, trans. H. Rackham (London: Heinemann, 1932), p. 215; cf. MWA, p. 435; *Life*, I, 52; Brilioth, p. 3; LMH, pp. 67-68.

36. *Life*, II, 191; MW, p. 506.

37. Cyril K. Gloyn, *The Church in the Social Order*, p. 87.

38. ER (18 June 1831), p. 97.

39. *Life*, I, 284; Fitch, p. 129.

40. *Life*, II, 11-12, 89-90; *Fitch*, p. 133.

41. *The National Church and the Social Order* (Church Information Office, 1956), p. 87 quoted by M. J. Jackson and J. Rogan (eds.), *Principles of Church Reform*, p. 6.

42. Unpublished letters in possession of Mr. Arnold Whitridge from Matthew Arnold to his mother (21 October 1863) and from Jane Arnold to Thomas Arnold, Jr. (23 November 1849). *Works of Matthew Arnold*, ed. George Russell, XIII, 143, 299; XIV, 157. Cf. W. H. G. Armytage, " Matthew Arnold and W. E. Gladstone: Some New Letters," *University of Toronto Quarterly*, XVIII (April, 1949), 222; and " Matthew Arnold and Richard Cobden: Some Recently Discovered Letters," *Review of English Studies*, XXV (July, 1949), 252.

43. W. H. Dawson, *Matthew Arnold and His Relation to the Thought of Our Time*, pp. 402-403.

44. J. Dover Wilson, "Matthew Arnold and the Educationists," *Social and Political Ideas of Some Representative Thinkers of the Victorian Age*, ed. F. J. C. Hearnshaw (London: Harrup, 1933), p. 190.

45. W. F. Connell, *The Educational Thought and Influence of Matthew Arnold*, pp. 253-56.

46. Connell, pp. 266-67.

47. Edward C. Mack and W. H. G. Armytage, *Thomas Hughes* (London: Ernest Benn, 1952), p. 35.

48. Mack and Armytage, pp. 43, 270.

49. *Foundations: a Study in the Ethics and Economics of the Cooperative Movement*, ed. Thomas Hughes and E. V. Neale, revised A. Stoddart and W. Clayton (Manchester: The Cooperative Union Ltd., 1916), p. 25. From Preface to the first edition by Hughes.

50. Raven, p. 131; Maurice B. Reckitt, *Maurice to Temple: a Century of Social Movement in the Church of England* (London: Faber and Faber, 1947), p. 58.

51. *Politics for the People*, quoted by Raven, pp. 111-12.

52. *Alton Locke, Tailor and Poet* (London: Macmillan, 1905), p. vii.

53. S. C. Carpenter, *Church and People, 1789-1889*, pp. 321-22.

54. *Tom Brown's Schooldays*. Preface to the edition of 1858, p. xv.

55. *Foundations*, p. 5.

56. Raven, pp. 375, 377.

57. Frances J. Woodward, *The Doctor's Disciples*, p. 31.

58. F. J. Woodward, pp. 24-25, 31-32; *Letters of Matthew Arnold to Arthur Hugh Clough*, ed. Howard Foster Lowry, p. 6.

59. James I. Osborne, *Arthur Hugh Clough*, pp. 15, 21-22; E. C. Mack, *Public Schools and British Opinion, 1780-1860*, pp. 314-15; F. J. Woodward, pp. 130 ff.

60. Samuel Waddington, *Arthur Hugh Clough* (London: Bell, 1883), p. 41.

61. Unpublished letter from Matthew Arnold to his mother (6 December 1865) in possession of Mr. Arnold Whitridge.

62. J. I. Osborne, pp. 22, 64; F. J. Woodward, *passim; Correspondence of Arthur Hugh Clough*, ed. F. L. Mulhauser (2 vols.; Oxford: Clarendon Press, 1957), I, 24.

63. *Letters of Arnold to Clough*, pp. 15-19.

64. F. J. Woodward, p. 175; Mack, p. 314.

65. *Correspondence of Clough*, I, 48.

66. J. I. Osborne, p. 43.

67. *Prose Remains* (London: Macmillan, 1888), I, 92 quoted by F. J. Woodward, p. 146.

68. F. J. Woodward, p. 151.

69. *Prose Remains*, p. 411.

70. F. J. Woodward, p. 173.

71. Cf. CLH, p. 353; *Sermons*, III, 362-63.

72. F. J. Woodward, pp. 80, 90, 105, 107, 112, 115-23, *et passim*.

73. Unpublished letter, J. D. Gellibrand to Gell (2 October 1883) quoted by F. J. Woodward, pp. 125-26.

74. Fitch, p. 153; cf. Mrs. Humphrey Ward, *A Writer's Recollections* (2 vols.; New York: Harper and Brothers, 1918), I, 47; Norman Wymer, *Dr. Arnold of Rugby*, pp. 198-99.

75. Cornish, II, 278.

76. *DNB*, I, 591; F. J. Woodward, pp. 181-92, 202.

77. *Prospective Review*, X (1854) quoted by F. J. Woodward, pp. 180, 204.

78. Unpublished letter from Jane Arnold to Thomas Arnold, Jr. (23 November 1849) in possession of Mr. Arnold Whitridge. The letter contains a summary of an earlier letter from Matthew to his sister.

79. F. J. Woodward, pp. 215-16.

80. F. J. Woodward, p. 180.

81. F. J. Woodward, pp. 218-22.

82. F. J. Woodward, p. 212.

Selected Bibliography

(See the Table of Abbreviations for
the editions of Dr. Arnold's works used.)

Bamford, T. W. *Thomas Arnold*. London: Cresset Press, 1960.

Barksdale, Richard K. "Thomas Arnold as Historian." Unpublished Ph.D. dissertation, Harvard University, 1951.

Bradby, G. F. *The Brontes and Other Essays*. London: Oxford University Press, 1932.

Briggs, Asa. *Victorian People*. London: Odhams, 1954.

Campbell, Reginald J. *Thomas Arnold*. London: Macmillan, 1927.

Christensen, Merton A. "Thomas Arnold's Debt to German Theologians," *Modern Philology*, LV (August, 1957), 14-20.

"Dr. Arnold after Fifty Years," *Spectator*, LXVIII (18 June 1892), 840-41.

Escott, T. H. S. "The Arnolds: a Study in Heredity," *Fortnightly Review*, New Series, LXXXIX (April, 1911), 662-80.

Fitch, Sir Joshua. *Thomas and Matthew Arnold and Their Influence on English Education*. New York: Charles Scribner's Sons, 1899.

Forbes, Duncan. *The Liberal Anglican Idea of History*. Cambridge: Cambridge University Press, 1952.

Gloyn, Cyril K. *The Church in the Social Order*. Forest Grove, Ore.: News-Times Publishing Co., 1942.

Jackson, M. J. and Rogan, J. (eds.). Arnold, *Principles of Church Reform*. London: Society for Promoting Christian Knowledge, 1962.

———. " Thomas Arnold," *Church Quarterly Review*, CLXII (June, 1961), 200-209.

Knickerbocker, W. S. *Creative Oxford*. Syracuse, N. Y.: Syracuse University Press, 1925.

———. " Matthew Arnold at Oxford: the Natural History of a Father and Son," *Sewanee Review*, XXXV (October, 1927), 399-418.

Mack, Edward C. *Public Schools and British Opinion, 1780-1860*. London: Methuen, 1938.

Maitland, E. "Life and Writings of Dr. Arnold," *North British Review*, II (February, 1845), 403-43.

Martineau, James. *Essays, Reviews and Addresses: Personal: Political*, I. London: Longmans, Green, 1901.

Mozley, James B. *Essays Historical and Theological*. 2 vols. London: Rivingtons, 1878.

Murry, John Middleton. *The Price of Leadership*. New York: Harper and Brothers, 1939.

Raven, Charles E. " Prophets: I Thomas Arnold," *Pillars of the English Church*, ed. Anthony C. Deane. London: Mowbray, 1934.

Sanders, Charles Richard. *Coleridge and the Broad Church Movement*. Durham, N. C.: Duke University Press, 1942.

Selwyn, E. G. " Dr. Arnold as a Winchester Boy," *Theology*, XXIV (June, 1932), 301-11.

Stanley, Arthur Penrhyn. *The Life and Correspondence of Thomas Arnold, D.D.* 2 vols. 4th ed. London: B. Fellowes, 1845.

———. *Life of Thomas Arnold*. Teachers' ed. with a preface by Sir Joshua Fitch. London: John Murray, 1901.

Strachey, Lytton. *Eminent Victorians*. New York: Harcourt, Brace, 1918.

Tuckwell, W. *Pre-Tractarian Oxford*. London: Smith, Elder, 1909.

Waller, John O. " The Arnolds and Particular Truth," *Notes and Queries*, New Series, VI (May, 1959), 163-64.

——. " Matthew and Thomas Arnold: Soteriology," *Anglican Theological Review*, XLIV (January, 1962), 57-70.

[Ward, W. G.] "Arnold's Sermons," *British Critic*, LX (October, 1841), 298-364.

Whitridge, Arnold. *Dr. Arnold of Rugby*. New York: Henry Holt, 1928.

Willey, Basil. *Nineteenth Century Studies*. London: Chatto and Windus, 1955.

Woodward, Frances J. *The Doctor's Disciples*. London: Oxford University Press, 1954.

Wymer, Norman. *Dr. Arnold of Rugby*. London: Robert Hale, 1953.

Index

Act of Supremacy, 174
Allan Bank, 42
Alton Locke, 211
Analogy of Religion, 32-34
Apologia Pro Vita Sua, 24, 85 n.
apostolic succession, 117, 136
Aristotle, 30-31, 32, 91, 171-72
Arnold, Mrs. Mary Penrose, 11, 217
Arnold, Matthew, 18, 21, 107-08, 111, 157, 166, 222; on Clough, 214; on Davison, 36; on Lake Poets, 40; on Stanley, 103-04, 151; on Temple, 108, 109 n.; Thomas Arnold's influence on, 21, 95-102, 147-51, 205-10
Arnold, Thomas: address to Mechanics' Institute, 204; author's conclusions on, 20-21; on Bible, 19-21, 55, 67-68, 75-83, 97-98; on British social conditions, 177-86; and Broad Church, 146, 151-55; and Bunsen, 62-66; and Christian Reform Party, 207; and Christian Socialists, 210-12; on church government, 129-33, 191; on church reform, 19, 27, 64, 121-46; on colonization, 193-98,
216-18; on dangers to Church, 113, 125, 127-28; on dissenters, 127-30, 132-34, 147-49, 152, 155-56; early religious doubts of, 31, 78; education of: at Corpus Christi, 11, 28-35; Oriel Fellowship, 11, 35-40; studies with Buckland and Cooke, 29; at Warminster Grammar School, 11, 26; at Winchester, 11, 25-28; and Hampden, 139-42; historical researches of, 25, 52-62, 75, 96; and J. T. Coleridge, 28, 31, 46, 48; and J. H. Newman, 19, 67, 85, 136-38, 142, 144; and Keble, 28; and later Biblical commentators, 18, 21, 95-111; and London University, 203-04; and middle-class education, 171, 198-206, 209-10; on need for Established Church, 122, 126-28; on need for factual, nonpartisan approach to social questions, 180-83, 187-88, 190-93, 205, 207-08; and Niebuhr, 54-55, 60, 62-63, 75; opposition to Tractarianism, 56, 136-46; on Oxford Movement, 56-57, 121, 135-38, 143-

46; on social mission of
Church, 148; theory of Christian State of, 31, 63, 172-77,
206, 213; theory of progress
of states of, 58-59; theory of
progressive revelation of, 87-
92, 103-04, 107; and Wordsworth, 42-46; *see also* Arnold,
Matthew; Arnold, W. D.;
Clough, A. H.; Coleridge, S.
T.; Forster, W.; Gell, J. P.;
Hughes, T.; Jowett, B.; Stanley, A. P.; Tait, Archibald;
Temple, F.
Arnold, Thomas, Jr., 38, 62-63,
219 n.
Arnold, William Delafield, 21,
216; father's influence on, 219-
22
Arnold's *Miscellaneous Works*,
13, 14, 213
Augsburg Confession of Prussian Protestantism, 64

Balliol, 105, 107, 155, 213
Bampton Lectures, 110-11, 139,
140
Bartley, William Warren, III,
19 n.
Benefices Act of 1898, 122
Bentham, Jeremy, 113-14, 159
Blomfield, Charles James, 119,
120
Brathay, 42
British Critic, The, 117, 139
Broad Church movement, 120;
liberalism of, 146-57
Brougham, Lord, 113, 163, 168-
69, 202
Buckland, William, 29, 71
Bunsen, C. C. J., 25, 53, 97;
Arnold's friendship with, 62-
66

Burke, Edmund, 171-72 n.
Butler, Bishop Joseph, 32-34

Cambridge University, 115, 169
Carlile, Richard, 167, 187
Carlyle, Thomas, 153, 164, 190 n.
Catholic Emancipation Bill of
1829, 135-36
Catholic Relief Act, 136
Cautions for the Times, 39, 120
Chartism, 164-65, 189, 195
*Christian Duty of Conceding
the Roman Catholic Claims,
The,* 12, 121, 135, 171
*Christian Life, Its Course, Its
Hindrances, and Its Helps
(Sermons,* IV), 13, 14, 75, 84,
121, 143
*Christian Life, Its Hopes, Its
Fears, and Its Close (Sermons,*
V), 13, 14
Christian Socialist, The, 212
Christian Socialist Movement,
210-12, 215, 222
church and state, relations be-
tween, 28, 38, 49, 159-60, 172-
75, 206-09, 213
Church of England, dangers to
in 19th Century, 113-21
Church Rates, 115, 127
Clergy Discipline Act (1892),
132, 156
Clerical   Subscription   Act
(1865), 130, 153
Clough, Arthur Hugh, 21, 107,
210, 212; Arnold's influence
on, 213-16
Cobbett, William, 166-67, 181,
188
Cobden, Richard, 206
Colenso, Bishop of Natal, 104
Coleridge, S. T., 36, 40, 41, 73,

84, 97, 126, 151, 171-72; Arnold's relations with, 46-52

Coleridge, John Taylor, 11, 28, 29, 31, 41

Confessions of an Inquiring Spirit, 47

Constitution of Church and State, 171

Convention of Cintra, 44

Cooke, George Leigh, 29

Co-operative Movement, 212

Copleston, Edward, 29-31, 35-36

Corn Law, 28, 192

Corpus Christi College, 11, 28, 41, 46, 136; curriculum, 29-31

Critical Essay on the Gospel of St. Luke, 65, 73

Culture and Anarchy, 148, 206, 207

Darwin's *Origin of Species*, 71

Davison, John, 35, 36-39

Discourses in America, 206

dissent and dissenters, 115-16, 130, 132-33, 139, 143, 147, 148-49, 152, 154-55, 156

"Dr. Stanley's Lectures on the Jewish Church," 24

Ecclesiastical Commission, 117, 119, 120

Edinburgh Review, 114, 140, 151

Eichhorn, Johann Gottfried, 69-70, 75

"The Education of the Middle Classes," 209

Elementary Education Act of 1870, 218-19

"The Effects of Distant Colonization on the Parent State," 14, 193

Eliot, George, 70

Enabling Act (1919), 147

Englishman's Register, 14, 44, 74, 77, 121, 178-79, 195

Essay on Population, 162-63

"Essay on the Right Interpretation and Understanding of the Scriptures," 67, 74, 77, 95, 104

Essays and Reviews, 63, 73, 105, 106, 108, 109 n., 110

Essays Chiefly on Questions of Church and State from 1850 to 1870, 213

Essays in Criticism, 148

Essays on Some of the Difficulties in the Writings of St. Paul, 39

Established Church Act of 1836, 119

Ethics and Politics, 91

Evidences of Christianity, 31

Extraordinary Black Book, The, 114

Fitch, Sir Joshua, 218

Forster, W. E., 21, 216, 222; Arnold's influence on, 218-19

Fox How, 42, 137

Fragment on the Church, 14, 121

Fragments on Church and State, 170-71

Franklin, Sir John, 216, 217

Fraser's Magazine, 221

French Eton, A, 206

Froude, Hurrell, 66

"Function of Criticism at the Present Time, The," 206, 208

Gabell, Henry Dison, 28

Gell, J. P., 21, 222; Arnold's influence on, 216-18

German scholars and 19th century crisis of belief, 68-70, 74

Gladstone, 115, 148, 153, 159, 206

"Gladstone on Church and State," 159-60

God and the Bible, 95, 98, 100, 101

Goddard, William Stanley, 26, 28

Grote, George, 113, 114, 159

Hampden, Renn Dickson, 35, 36, 139; Arnold's defense of, 140-42

Hare, Julius Charles, 53, 73-74

Hawkins, Edward, 35, 36, 198

Hegel, 105; Hegel's *Logic*, 107

Henley, Lord, 118, 126

Hertford Reformer, 121, 175, 192

History of the Later Roman Commonwealth, 13, 14, 53

History of Latin Christianity, 74

History of Rome, 13, 14, 53, 55, 96

Hooker, Richard, 31, 32, 171, 172

Howley, Archbishop, 125

Hughes, Thomas, 21, 86, 172, 222; Arnold's influence on, 210-12

Hume, Joseph, 113

Idea of a University, The, 34

Inquiry into the Origin of Sacrifice, 37

Introductory Lectures on Modern History, 13, 14, 53, 96

"Irish Catholicism and British Liberalism," 208

Irish Church Bill of 1833, 116-17

Irish Essays and Others, 148, 206

Jowett, Benjamin, 21, 95, 97, 109 n., 111; Arnold's influence on, 105-07; comments on Stanley, 213

Keble, John, 11, 28, 29, 117, 135, 136, 137, 138

Kingsley, Charles, 162, 211

Lake Poets and Arnold, 25, 40-52, 62, 68

Last Essays on Church and Religion, 95, 101-02

Leben Jesu, 65, 70

Lectures on the History of the Jewish Church, 103

Lessing, G. E., 48, 69, 108 n.

Letters on the Church by an Episcopalian, 122, 160

"Letters on the Education of the Middle Classes," 45

Library of Useful Knowledge, 168

Literature and Dogma, 95, 98-99, 100, 101

London University, 169, 219; Arnold and, 203-04

Lyell, Sir Charles, 71-72

Lyrical Ballads, 41

Macaulay, Thomas B., 53, 113, 159-60

Malthus, T. R., 162

Malthusian theory, 163, 183

Memorandum on the Admission of the Bible as a Class Book into Government Schools, 221-22

Mill, James, 113, 159, 168

Mill, John Stuart, 41, 113, 166

Milman, Henry Hart, 73, 74, 76

Miscellaneous Works, 58, 213

Mixed Essays, 148, 206

National Association for the Protection of Labor, 165
National Church, 116, 129, 132, 136, 138, 148-49, 152, 199
Neale, E. V., 212
Newman, John Henry, 34, 36, 37, 38, 64, 142; censure of Tract 90 by Tait, 154; defines liberalism, 85 n.; doubts Arnold's Christianity, 19, 24, 67; influenced by Whately, 160; and Oxford Movement, 117-18, 135-39, 144-45
Nicomachean Ethics, 31
Niebuhr, Barthold, 53-55, 58, 60, 62, 63, 75
Nightingale, Florence, 214, 215
Noetics, Oriel, 11, 35-37, 40, 120, 139
Northern Star, 167

Oakfield; or Fellowship in the East, 220
" Observations on Religious Dissent," 139
O'Connor, Feargus, 165, 167
Of the Laws of Ecclesiastical Polity, 31-32, 171
" On the Divisions of Knowledge," 171
" On Letters of an Episcopalian," 121
On the Peculiarities of Christianity, 39
Oriel College, 11, 29, 199; Arnold as fellow of, 35-38
Owen, Robert, 187
Owenites, 189
Oxford, 11, 25, 53, 71, 80, 104, 105, 107, 118, 137, 141, 169; Arnold's studies at, 28-34; Arnold as fellow of, 35-40; and dissenters, 115, 139; Stanley's career at, 102; William Arnold at, 220
Oxford and Cambridge University Acts of 1854-56, 115
" The Oxford Malignants and Dr. Hampden," 12, 121, 140
Oxford Movement, 28, 36, 117; Arnold and, 56-57, 121, 135-38, 143-46; Tait's opposition to, 153-54

Paley, William, 31, 163
Palmerston, Lord, 167, 196-97
Peel, Sir Robert, 113
Penny Magazine, The, 168-69, 202-03
Pentateuch and Book of Joshua Critically Examined, The, 104
Pluralities Act Amendment Act, 156
Politics, 30, 31, 171
Politics for the People, 212
Political Register, 167
Poor Laws, 163-64, 182, 185-86
population growth and church reform, 119
Principi di Scienza Nuova, 61
Principles of Church Reform, 12 121, 127, 146, 170
Principles of Political Economy and Taxation, 162
Providential Societies Act, 212
Public Worship Regulation Act, 154
Pusey, E. B., 69, 135-37, 139, 142

Quarterly Review, 53, 54, 134

rationalism and religion, 70, 72-73, 75

Reasons for Contentment Addressed to the Labouring Public, 163

Reform Bill, 42, 116, 125, 164, 170, 178, 188-89, 200-02

Renan, Ernest, 97

Ricardo, David, 162

Robinson, Henry Crabb, 69

Roman Catholic Relief Act, 116

Romilly, Sir Samuel, 113

Römische Geschichte, 53-54; *see* Niebuhr, Barthold

Rugby, 17, 20, 62, 77, 102, 107, 108, 110, 154, 179, 195, 205 n., 220; Clough at, 214; Temple headmaster of, 155; Thomas Hughes at, 210; William Arnold and, 219-21

"Rugby Chapel," 13, 210

Russell, Lord John, 168

Rydal, 42, 46

Sandon, Lord, 132 n.

Schleiermacher, Friedrich, 65, 73, 75

science and religion, 29, 70-72

science and theology 70-72

Sermons, I, 12, 15

Sermons, II, 12, 15, 24, 171

Sermons, III, 12, 15, 75, 121, 171

Sermons, IV, *see Christian Life, Its Course, Its Hindrances, and Its Helps*

Sermons, V, *see Christian Life, Its Hopes, Its Fears and Its Close*

Sermons and Essays on the Apostolical Age, 103

Sermons Chiefly on the Interpretation of Scripture (Sermons, VI), 13, 14, 74

Sermons on Prophecy, 49, 74, 83

Sheffield *Courant*, 121, 126, 179, 189; Arnold's letter to, 200

Smith, Adam, 162

"The Social Condition of the Operative Classes," 208

"The Social Progress of States," 58. 171

"Speenhamland Act," 163-64

St. Paul and Protestantism, 95, 101, 149

Stanley, Arthur Penrhyn, 21, 25, 96, 97, 107, 108, 111, 154, 157, 178; Arnold's influence on, 102-05, 147, 151-53, 212-13; and Christian Socialist movement, 210; on Clough, 214; writes commentary on Corinthians, 106

state and church, relations between, *see* church and state

Statesman's Manual, 49

Strachey, Lytton, 17

Strauss, D. F., 65, 70

Table Talk, 46

Tait, Archibald, 21, 147, 151, 156; Arnold's influence on, 153-55, 157

Taunton Commission, 209

Temple, Frederick, 21, 95, 151; Arnold's influence on, 105, 107-11, 147, 155-57

Test Act of 1828, 116

Thirlwall, Connop, 53, 73

Thirty-Nine Articles of Religion, 31, 115, 130, 139, 142, 150, 152

Thucydides, 12, 27, 30, 53, 60, 91, 96, 107, 171; Arnold and, 57-58

Tom Brown's Schooldays, 210

Tractarianism, 35, 37-39, 53, 56-

57, 117-18, 120, 130-31, 135-39, 140, 142-45, 151, 154

Tracts for the Times, 117, 136, 143

Trade Unionism, 164-67

Tucker, John, 76, 83

Two Sermons on Interpretation of Prophecy, 13, 37

Unitarians, 129-30, 139, 151

University Test Act of 1871, 115-16, 156

Useful Knowledge Society, 163, 202

Utilitarians, 64, 113-14, 116, 118, 128, 159-60

Vico, Giovanni, 58, 60-61

Ward, John, 178

Ward, William George, 214

Warminster Grammar School, 11, 26

" Wages Fund " theory, 163

Wealth of Nations, 162

Westminster Review, 113

Westmoreland, 41

Whately, Richard, 11, 35, 36, 38-40, 119-20, 122, 127, 160

Wilberforce, Bishop, 105

Willey, Basil, 19 n.

Wilmot, Sir Eardley, 217

Winchester, 11, 26-28; Bishop of, 125

Wolfenbüttel Fragments, 69, 108-09 n.

Wordsworth, William, 40-46